TURNING TO TRADITION

TURNING
TO TRADITION

Converts and the Making
of an American Orthodox Church

D. OLIVER HERBEL

OXFORD
UNIVERSITY PRESS

OXFORD
UNIVERSITY PRESS

Oxford University Press is a department of the University of Oxford.
It furthers the University's objective of excellence in research, scholarship,
and education by publishing worldwide.

Oxford   New York
Auckland   Cape Town   Dar es Salaam   Hong Kong   Karachi
Kuala Lumpur   Madrid   Melbourne   Mexico City   Nairobi
New Delhi   Shanghai   Taipei   Toronto

With offices in
Argentina   Austria   Brazil   Chile   Czech Republic   France   Greece
Guatemala   Hungary   Italy   Japan   Poland   Portugal   Singapore
South Korea   Switzerland   Thailand   Turkey   Ukraine   Vietnam

Oxford is a registered trade mark of Oxford University Press
in the UK and certain other countries.

Published in the United States of America by
Oxford University Press
198 Madison Avenue, New York, NY 10016

Library of Congress Cataloging-in-Publication Data
Herbel, Oliver.
Turning to tradition : converts and the making of an American Orthodox
church / D. Oliver Herbel.
p.   cm.
Includes bibliographical references.
ISBN 978-0-19-932495-8 (cloth : alk. paper) 1. Orthodox Eastern
converts—United States—Biography. I. Title.
BX739.A1H47 2013
281.9092'273—dc23
2013023100
9780199324958

1   3   5   7   9   8   6   4   2

Printed in the United States of America on acid-free paper

CONTENTS

ACKNOWLEDGMENTS

Throughout the course of researching and writing, I have had the support and assistance of many people. My family has remained important throughout the entirety of this project. I am indebted to the emotional and financial support of my wife Lorie. It not easy to be married to an independent scholar. Lorie's sacrifices are greatly appreciated and without them, this work would not have been possible. I am also thankful for our three children: Micah, Macrina, and Anastasia ("Tasha"). They have encouraged me and kept me focused on things that really matter.

Support from many within the academy has also been vital. Funding from a Calihan Research Fellowship from the Acton Institute enabled me to pursue some of my research on St. Alexis Toth, as well as Fr. Nathaniel Irvine, who is mentioned in the conclusion. David Murphy and Evgueni Kadossov have each read different portions of my translation work for the chapter on St. Alexis Toth, though any errors remain entirely my own. Michael McClymond, who directed my dissertation (from which this book developed), and Fr. John Erickson, professor emeritus of church history at St. Vladimir's Orthodox Theological Seminary, have been sincerely supportive and helpful in ways too numerous to mention. I must also thank good friends Scott Kenworthy for his ongoing support and encouragement and Brandon Gallaher not only for encouragement but also the willingness to read pre-submission drafts, offering highly useful feedback along the way.

I am also thankful for all the various ways that others have helped contribute to the scholarship within this work. Matthew Namee, who blogs about Orthodox Christianity in America, called my attention to pertinent newspaper articles and ship lists concerning Fr. Raphael Morgan as well as an open letter Morgan had published. Fr. Anastasius C. Bandy, a local Orthodox Church historian of the Philadelphia area also helped point me in some directions during the earlier phases of my research into Morgan. Sadly, Fr. Anastasius died in February, 2012. May his memory be eternal! I would certainly be remiss were I to omit the hospitality of two people mentioned in this book, Fr. Moses Berry and Frederica Matthewes-Green. Fr. Moses Berry offered wonderful hospitality in addition to personal interviews, and Frederica Matthewes-Green kindly provided not only some letters from her personal files at home, but also encouragement on this project itself. Others, such as Fr. James Bernstein, Fr. Mel Gimmaka, and Ron Zell were kind enough to discuss the life of the Evangelical Orthodox Church and its conversion over the phone while Dr. Carla Thompson engaged in an exchange of email correspondence, as did Fr. Ted Wojcik. Fr. Thomas Hopko was kind enough not only to discuss his work with the Evangelical Orthodox Church but also provided important documentation. I am also indebted to those who were willing to provide me with additional primary sources for the chapters discussing the former members of the Evangelical Orthodox Church but who must yet remain anonymous due to the nature of some of the issues discussed.

Many within the Orthodox Church have also been supportive along the way. The prayers of the parishioners at both Nativity of the Virgin Mary Orthodox Church in Madison, Illinois, and Holy Resurrection Orthodox Church in Fargo, North Dakota, have been greatly appreciated. Were it not for the collective efforts of everyone and many others whom I have neglected to mention, I would not have completed this endeavor.

TURNING TO TRADITION

INTRODUCTION

IN 1870, NICHOLAS BJERRING, A Danish immigrant to America, who had already converted to Roman Catholicism in Europe, decided to become an Eastern Orthodox Christian.[1] His conversion was met with much fanfare. One reason for the attention was Bjerring's open letter to Pope Pius IX, in which Bjerring claimed he once understood the Church of Rome to be the institution graced with the vocation of fulfilling social ministries, such as education. At one time, Bjerring believed that the Roman Catholic Church existed as "the only Catholic and Apostolic Church," but his mind had changed. He viewed the Roman Catholic Church's response to modernism as defensive and was concerned that the Church had distanced itself from social issues and concerns of the day. At the same time he was reaching these conclusions, he had personally experienced the failure of his own attempt to establish a minor seminary in Baltimore. This led him to write to Pius IX:

> St. Paul, the great convert of Damascus, said in his Epistle to the Galatians: "Though an angel from heaven preach any other gospel unto you than that which we have preached unto you, let him be accursed." I do not go as far as is permitted by St. Paul. I do not anathematize you, Holy Father, but I pray God to bring back your truly angelical soul to the truths of the gospel.[2]

Bjerring journeyed on to St. Petersburg later that year, where he was brought into the Orthodox Church, was ordained, and earned a doctorate from the St. Petersburg Academy. Upon his return to New York, Bjerring served a small chapel that sought to present Orthodoxy to America, especially to the Protestant Episcopal Church members in America because of the generally friendly relationship between the Russian Orthodox Church and the Anglican Communion. Bjerring published sermons and gave lectures on a regular basis and his career embraced the Social Gospel Movement in America at the time. He later became a Presbyterian pastor when the Russian Orthodox Church decided to save money and close the small chapel. Shortly before his death in 1900, he returned to the Roman Catholic Church, ironically noting that the papacy was best suited to address various social concerns.

Although Bjerring did not remain Orthodox, many converts to Orthodoxy have retained their newfound faith. Furthermore, many have engaged the American society around them, as Bjerring had. A few intra-Christian converts to Orthodoxy have acted as exemplars, leading and inspiring whole groups of people to follow them into the Orthodox Church. Their journeys touched on concerns shared by many non-Orthodox Christians in America and served as inspirational examples to thousands of fellow converts who followed them into the Orthodox Church. These converts serve as the focus of my study here. Specifically, I shall examine Alexis Toth (1853–1909), Raphael Morgan (ca. 1869–1916), Moses Berry (1951–present), Peter Gillquist (1938–2012), and the converts who have followed after them.

As leaders of movements of people, their conversions have been seen as iconic and theologically normative in America. This monograph shows that what has occurred

in these intra-Christian American conversions to Orthodoxy can be best understood as a turn to tradition, one that
occurred through a unique kind of restorationism, an Eastern
Christian ecclesiastical restorationism.[3] Their cases show
that non-Orthodox Christians are using the very American
context of religious choosing and religious novelty-creation
to make what might seem a very un-American choice in
favor of an unbroken tradition, which they find in Orthodox
Christianity, in a very American way.

Furthermore, this turn toward tradition has inspired a
direct engagement of the American context on the part of the
Orthodox, challenging the standard sociological narrative of
the ghettoization and defensiveness of Orthodox Christianity.
Through intra-Christian converts to Orthodoxy, this engagement is circular: the Orthodox have engaged potential converts, potential converts have become Orthodox, and these
new Orthodox converts have both evangelized and directly
engaged American societal, religious, and political questions.

In many respects, the idea that such a traditional church
in America would attract outsiders seems counterintuitive.
In Western culture in general, "intellectual discourse . . .
remains on a movement forward."[4] What is more, "it is rare
to encounter persons who pride themselves on the espousal
of a tradition, call it that, and regard it as a good thing."[5] For
some, there is even the fear that they might be "encumbered
by something alien."[6] Paradoxically, what one encounters in
the West, then, is a tradition of change, or an anti-traditional
tradition, as found in the scientist, whose duty it is to find a
flaw in the tradition that has gone before.[7] The point is not
that an exemplar of the anti-traditional tradition will reject
any and all aspects of what went before, but rather that he or
she may select some individual part of the preceding tradition

in order to enact something entirely new or at odds with the tradition itself.[8] American religion is also characterized by an anti-traditional tradition. As a phenomenon within American religion, it is denoted by a long tradition of mavericks who engage in religious choosing and novelty-creation by selecting and emphasizing a part of the religious tradition they inherited in order to create something new. The result over the last two centuries has been that the American religious scene has become ever more diversified and complex.[9] Indeed, here one ought to think of the many restorationist movements dedicated to restoring, or re-embodying, the early Christian Church.[10]

Yet, as a sign that such diversification itself has become a tradition, one might note that the architectural structures of worship buildings for Mormons, Jehovah's Witnesses, Christian Scientists, and Mennonites are very similar, and recent church structures across denominations have tended to resemble secular schools and office buildings.[11] This architectural similarity supports the observation that even those who could be perceived as religious outsiders have, in some way, lived out this tradition of change by utilizing individualistic self-sufficiency and creativity to demonstrate their Americanness.[12] This use of architecture has often accompanied a rhetoric intending to demonstrate a patriotic Americanness. The paradox here is that in American religious history, groups that could be considered outside the American Protestant mainstream have often devoted energy to showing just how American they were. The anti-tradition tradition has also found a religious expression in American millennialism.[13] This particular tradition of change derived from a Protestant effort to reach back and reclaim the Book of Revelation.[14] The reclamation of Revelation was progressive, linking America with the millennial Kingdom of God.[15] Such notions developed out of (1) the view of the Reformation as spiritual progress, and (2) the need for a country to further protect the people of God who have sought to overthrow the tyranny of the ages. This view of American history runs deep through the country's history and can be traced from the colonial era to the present day.[16] For example, the belief that America is the biblical "city on a hill" has existed for over three hundred years, from John Winthrop's sermon in 1630 to Ronald Reagan's speech in 1980.[17] The anti-traditional tradition remains thoroughly American.

In the converts studied here, their conversions demonstrated their Americanness in two different (though overlapping) ways: as a response to oppression and as an ironic species of the anti-traditional tradition. For Toth, the turn to tradition was a theological response to an ecclesiastical problem, the perceived and experienced Roman Catholic prejudices and abuses toward Eastern Catholics. His conversion was enacted as a reclamation of the faith of his ancestors, exemplified in an Eastern Christian praxis and dogmatic purity. As America could be the city on a hill, the Russian Orthodox Church was called to unite all the Slavs under the banner of Orthodoxy. For Morgan, the turn to tradition proved to be a means of addressing the struggles of African Americans within American churches at the time (especially the Protestant Episcopal Church). In the examples of Morgan, Berry, and Gillquist, the turn to tradition actually becomes an ironic species of the anti-traditional tradition. Though intended as a break from the anti-traditional tradition, by utilizing restorationism, the turn to tradition becomes an expression of religious identity creation in a very novel way. The conclusion (Eastern Orthodoxy as *the* Christian Tradition over and against a diversified, fragmented American Christian landscape) may at first appear rather un-American, since it is not the creation of a new subset of Christianity, much less a new religion, but the road to that conclusion is, ironically, precisely an expression of the anti-traditional tradition. Furthermore, inasmuch as these converts are seen as exemplars for other converts, these conversion patterns themselves establish a tradition, one more tradition built out of the anti-traditional tradition.

In a country defined by a tradition of anti-tradition, Orthodox Christianity may be one of the starkest examples of traditional Christianity, but it consistently draws new American converts. All of the converts studied here are exemplars of this phenomenon because they have been followed and/or imitated by many other Orthodox converts. Although both the questions asked and the concerns raised varied from convert to convert, there were a few shared general concerns that, when taken together, suggest that intra-Christian conversions to Orthodoxy in America occur in such a way that the Orthodox Church is understood to be *the* "Christian Tradition" itself and not merely one tradition among many. This view developed when each convert prioritized a period in church history as the standard and sought its continuous institutional existence on the basis of doctrinal and spiritual characteristics important to the convert, which he or she found within the Church of the previous period. Tradition, then, has been understood as the ongoing life of the Church, of a structured community, or institution, down through history in full continuity with the early Church. Tradition, therefore, is an ecclesiological reality.

Incidentally, understanding these conversions as ecclesiological conversions arguably means reassessing Lewis

R. Rambo's influential view of the assigned role for theology in the religious conversion process, which is "the creation of norms for what is expected in the conversion process and the shaping of expectations and experiences of converts."[18] Although each convert studied here began with restorationism, theology did much more than provide behavioral norms for these four representative converts. Theological reflections led to conclusions that propelled the converts not only to look to what they took to be a historical standard in the history of Christianity, but then also to seek that church in her current existence, and eventually to enter the Orthodox Church. Contrary to Lewis's view, only later did the converts accept certain theological norms in the sense of patterns for behavior during the conversion itself. In fact, many of these converts would not have previously considered what they had to go through (such as extensive catechesis and a sacramental chrismation to complete their baptism) if theological arguments had not already changed their views. For example, the converts following Gillquist into the Orthodox Church were brought in by chrismation, an anointing that is seen as the completion of baptism, as the bestowing of the gifts of the Holy Spirit in a fuller way. Yet, the Orthodox theological norms that justify this approach would not appear normative or acceptable to evangelical Christians unless they had already worked through prior theological arguments.

That said, in the cases of three of the four converts studied here, one could argue their conversions actually pioneered theological norms for intra-Christian conversions to Orthodoxy, becoming a tradition of conversion. As will be seen below, Raphael Morgan's efforts led only to a small fraternity of African Americans interested in Orthodoxy, and though he inspired the later work of Patriarch

McGuire and the African Orthodox Church, which later led to thousands of conversions to Orthodoxy in Africa, he did not inspire a large number of conversions during his ministry in America. The exemplary status of the other three converts (Toth, Berry, and Gillquist), however, have led not just to groups of people following them with interest, but to groups of people who converted for reasons that patterned themselves after the conversions of those three converts. The point here is not that other converts copied the conversions of Toth, Berry, and Gillquist exactly, but that the pattern of conversion, the kind of conversion that these men exemplified, resonated deeply with others who undertook similar conversion journeys. Those following Toth used the American freedom found in the anti-traditional tradition to follow his conversion to the Orthodox tradition as a return to the safe haven of the faith of their ancestors. Those looking to Berry and Gillquist have expressed an ironic twist on the anti-tradition tradition by breaking from the anti-traditional tradition itself.

THE ANTI-TRADITION TRADITION AND CONVERSIONS TO ORTHODOXY

Indeed, the numbers of converts who have followed in the footsteps of people such as Berry and Gillquist suggest this tradition of conversion is worthy of investigation. The percentage of growth of Orthodox Christianity in America was higher than any other major classification of Christianity mentioned by the *Encyclopedia Britannica* in 1995.[19] Despite the prevalence of anti-traditional approaches, including restorationism, within American Christianity, Orthodox

Christianity continues to show signs that some Americans are taking the time to trouble themselves with Orthodoxy.[20]

Admittedly, it is difficult to establish whether such growth creates a net gain. The 2008 US Religious Landscape Survey suggested that if there is growth, it is statistically insignificant. According to the survey, the number of people claiming they were Orthodox in childhood stands at .6 percent of the American population, while the current number of Americans claiming to be Orthodox is also .6 percent.[21] Nor can one gain clarity from the 2008 American Religious Identification Survey because it included the Orthodox together with the mainline Protestant bodies, populations that are much larger, thus obscuring Orthodox details.[22]

Despite the question of whether the attraction to Orthodox Christianity has created a net gain, the US Religious Landscape Survey showed that nearly one quarter (23 percent) of the American Orthodox population had previously not been Orthodox. The phenomenon of turning to the Orthodox tradition as a means of responding to the novelty-creation inherent in the presence of the anti-traditional tradition in the American Christian scene has clearly benefitted the Orthodox Churches in America numerically. Moreover, a number of these converts are having a significant effect upon the Orthodox. Currently, 12 percent of the clergy in the Greek Orthodox Archdiocese of North America and 59 percent of the clergy in the Orthodox Church in America are converts.[23] Moreover, converts constitute 29 percent of the laity in the Greek Orthodox Archdiocese and 51 percent of the laity in the Orthodox Church in America.[24]

Amy Slagle has insightfully and convincingly argued that, ironically, it is the American "spiritual marketplace" that has enabled many converts to Orthodoxy to utilize the individualistic self-sufficiency and creativity so common in America in order to become Orthodox.[25] For the converts she studied in her ethnographic work, Orthodoxy became seen as a steady, stable response "forged in narrative opposition to a variety of cultural 'isms.' "[26] Yet in her study, she also noted that although the American context remains important, such conversions can neither be reduced to that context nor simply expressed as a reaction to that context. The converts she interviewed were often drawn by theological reasons and were especially influenced by the early Christian period and the idea of tradition.[27] The importance of theological reasons to an attraction to Orthodoxy is precisely the focus of my investigation here—the theological influences and decisions at play, how the converts' turn to tradition is both typical and atypical of the American religion scene, and how this theological outlook has inspired direct engagement with American society.

EXEMPLARY CONVERTS

As noted above, this work uses the theological concerns of exemplary intra-Christian converts to Orthodoxy in order to demonstrate how through this turn to tradition converts to Orthodoxy are making what may seem to be a very un-American conclusion (the Eastern Orthodox tradition) in a very American way (by means of restorationism). Each of these men saw Orthodox Christianity as being *the* tradition of Christianity, and each inspired and led groups of converts and/or prospective converts. I examine the reasons for each representative convert's conversion, using both their own given reasons and their additional writings and surrounding context. In the cases of Berry and Gillquist, other prominent Orthodox converts who followed their lead are brought into the discussion in order to provide an overview of their influence on such converts and on the groups themselves. Each of these four converts had a unique background and influenced different groups.

Toth (1853–1909), covered in Chapter 1, was born in Slovakia and arrived in the United States in 1889 in order to serve the growing Carpatho-Rusyn immigrant population. After a falling out with Bishop Ireland later that same year, Toth and his Minneapolis parish sought assistance from Bishop Vladimir, the Russian Orthodox bishop in San Francisco, and entered into the Russian Orthodox Church in 1892. Upon his reception into the Russian Orthodox Church, Toth began a mission of evangelization. He traveled to many Carpatho-Rusyn and Galician Eastern Catholic parishes, leading to the conversions of several thousand Eastern Catholics to Orthodox Christianity. His missionary zeal even affected communities in his homeland. Throughout the course of his life, he held rigidly to the conviction that as Eastern Christians, he and his fellow Carpatho-Rusyns should be able to live according to the Eastern Christian tradition of his ancestors, a freedom he found only in the Russian Orthodox Church. Theologically, Toth looked to the Eastern Orthodox Church, prior to the movements among the Slavs for union with Rome. His primary point of reference was the Orthodox Catholic Church prior to the ninth century. For his missionary endeavors, the Orthodox Church in America canonized Toth on May 24, 1994.

Morgan (ca. 1869–1916), the subject of Chapter 2, was a contemporary of Toth's, but moved in different Orthodox circles. He was a Jamaican, served briefly as a missionary in

Africa and a deacon in Delaware in the Protestant Episcopal Church. In each case, his ministry was to Africans or African Americans. When, after a spiritual journey, he became Orthodox, he maintained that emphasis, being appointed an apostolic-vicar to America by the Patriarch of Constantinople with the express purpose of evangelizing fellow African Americans. Although he established a religious fraternity in Philadelphia, his true religious effects may be found in his connection to the African Orthodox Church. Morgan inspired George Alexander McGuire, who formed the independent African Orthodox Church in 1921; a large portion of its African contingency later entered into the Orthodox Church through the Greek Orthodox Church in Alexandria Egypt.

Chapter 3 assesses Berry (1951–present), who has also led African Americans, but has been more successful in directly influencing converts to Orthodoxy. Berry upheld an emphasis on otherworldly Christianity and ancient African Christianity as well as a desire to lift up African American suffering, prayers, and worship to God and sought racial healing. This approach to Christianity led him to believe that African American concerns were best addressed in the Orthodox Churches, whose faith he has continued to believe resonates with African American spirituality. His convictions and experience inspired him to found the Brotherhood of St. Moses the Black, a pan-Orthodox community dedicated to reaching out to African Americans in North America with the purpose of informing them of their spiritual roots and the Orthodox Church.

Gillquist (1938–2012), the focus of Chapter 4, was a contemporary of Berry, but has been influential primarily on white Evangelicals. Gillquist helped form what became the Evangelical Orthodox Church, a sectarian group that combined a zeal for evangelizing nonbelievers with a desire for continuity with the apostolic faith. In fact, the Evangelical Orthodox Church established itself precisely as a restoration of the New Testament Church, which they believed the Orthodox Churches also represented. Thus, they believed they were one of the Orthodox Churches, albeit a restored, superior expression thereof. Because of that belief, the Evangelical Orthodox Church engaged in several dialogues with actual Orthodox Churches, which led them to converting to Orthodoxy. Upon becoming Orthodox, Gillquist not only understood himself to be entering fully into that apostolic faith he so desired, but redirected his evangelical intensity, becoming the director of missions for the Antiochian Orthodox Christian Archdiocese of North America.[28] He also authored works intended to further this cause and has served as a guest speaker in numerous settings. His evangelism came to include not only the message of Jesus Christ, but a message of where to find the Body of Christ—in the Orthodox Church. Gillquist saw it as part of his calling (and indeed the calling for all the former members of the Evangelical Orthodox Church) to bring Orthodoxy to America.

For the former members of the Evangelical Orthodox Church (EOC), however, their journey included several post-conversion events that serve to highlight the extent to which they were a restorationist movement but also uncover an ongoing deconversion from that restorationism. These events are discussed in Chapter 5. One of the paradoxical components to conversions to Orthodoxy that Gillquist and the EOC raise is just how it is Protestants could come to accept a church with chanting, incense, the invocation of saints, and other things generally considered anathema. As we shall see, restorationism had to be connected to Eastern Orthodoxy specifically in order for this to work (at least in their cases). This deconversion was needed because the EOC converts were, in some ways, just as ignorant of Orthodoxy in America as a lived tradition as the larger American public.

ORTHODOX CHRISTIANITY IN AMERICA AND THE STANDARD SOCIOLOGICAL NARRATIVE

It is not difficult to demonstrate that Orthodoxy is a relatively unknown form of American Christianity. One conclusion drawn from the religion results from the General Social Survey, 1973–1996, conducted by the National Opinion Research Center at the University of Chicago, was that "Orthodox Christianity is also invisible despite its relative prevalence."[29] A significant factor is that the survey includes the categories Protestant, Catholic, Jewish, None, Other, Don't Know, and No Answer, which results in Orthodox Christians comprising about 19 percent of the "Other" category.[30] Furthermore, "despite the attention directed to such groups, wiccans, pagans, and other neo-pagan expressions comprise only 2% of the 'other' category in the 1989–1996 period, and are virtually invisible before then."[31]

Often, the Orthodox themselves are blamed for their relative obscurity on the American religious scene. Peter Berger, noting that the United States is a pluralistic society, claimed that the Orthodox witness has been "defensive" and "negative," demonstrating that there is a Christianity other than Protestantism or Roman Catholicism.[32] Having mentioned that Orthodox Christianity is similar in size to Judaism but not nearly as effective in influencing American culture, Berger called upon the Orthodox to "engage American pluralism" with "aggressive self-assertion."[33] A key component to this, Berger believed, could be the fact that Orthodox Christianity had a trend of conversions to Orthodoxy, something Judaism did not have to nearly the same degree. Berger believed this ought to provide the context for Orthodox changing from a defensive posture to an aggressive posture.

Nor is Berger alone. Elizabeth H. Prodromou has noted a distinction between Orthodox Christianity's "potential versus its performance in engaging in the theoretical and the practical enterprise of paradigm building with regard to defining limits for religion in the American public sphere."[34] She has specifically noted that by the time the Protestant Christian paradigm had created the Judeo-Christian construct during World War II, Orthodox Christians had reached "more than negligible numbers," but that none of this produced "a meaningful engagement of Orthodox Christianity with the theoretical and practical formulation of the Judeo-Christian construct" a construct intended to show that America was inclusive of all faiths.[35] In fact, Prodromou went so far as to claim that excepting the clergy-theologians John Meyendorff, Alexander Schmemann, and Georges Florovsky, Orthodox engagement "was absent."[36] Alexei D. Krindatch, in his demographic survey of American Orthodoxy, and Victor Roudometof and Alexander Agadjanian shared this assessment of American Orthodoxy, the latter claiming Orthodoxy has not been "self-adjusting."[37]

Certainly, there is some legitimacy to the blame-the-Orthodox prognosis. Initially, when Orthodox immigrants arrived in America, they sought to reconstruct their particular cultural expressions of Orthodox Christianity. In these cases, the local parish became the place where one could worship as one had previously and could gather with others who shared the same language and cultural assumptions. One movement in this regard was the Greek American Progressive Association (GAPA), which promoted the preservation of Greek language, customs, and traditions, including Orthodoxy.[38] Similarly, various lay societies, such as Slavic brotherhoods and Greek lay organizations, acted as fraternal societies for early Orthodox Christian immigrants.[39] Having their historical roots in Europe, the brotherhoods affected Orthodox immigrant life at the local level by raising parish funds, providing financial assistance, and searching for clergy. Such societies were important to the new immigrants, who were often subject to abuse and hostilities, especially in situations where labor issues came to the fore.[40] Although the days of prominent lay societies have passed, Orthodox Christianity in America has continued to exist in administratively separate jurisdictions resulting from Orthodoxy's earlier American history.

True as this "defensive" posture may be, I have already noted Slagle's cogent argument that American Orthodoxy actually exists squarely within the American "marketplace" of religions. In a similar vein, the stories explored here likewise question the accuracy of reducing Orthodoxy to a defensive posture. Indeed, within theses conversion movements, one finds that the conversions themselves demonstrate an active engagement of America on the part of the Orthodox, even if often through the efforts of lead converts. That is to say, large groups convert to Orthodoxy and become Orthodox through an ecclesiological conversion, a turn to tradition. This turning to tradition occurs in a very American way, in the context of religious novelty and the spiritual marketplace, but provides a very un-American answer—a tradition, rather than a novelty, continuing the anti-tradition tradition. For some, this turn to tradition has been a response to experienced and perceived oppression while to others, especially the more recent converts, it has acted as an ironic subspecies of the anti-tradition tradition: a turn to "tradition" itself becomes not just an intended break from the anti-tradition tradition but also an intended expression of a more legitimate religious identity. This very dynamic, however, continues the process, whereby these same converts directly engage the American context, perpetuating additional intra-Christian conversions to Orthodoxy. In so doing, they promote the turn to tradition as a tradition expressing that very American anti-tradition tradition.

AN OVERVIEW OF ORTHODOX CHRISTIANITY AS CONTEXT

Given both Orthodoxy's relative inconspicuousness and its importance as the bearer of *the* Christian Tradition to intra-Christian converts to the Orthodox Church, it may be useful to provide a brief synopsis of Orthodox Christianity and what Orthodox Christians mean by "tradition." In its details, tradition is a multivalent reality for modern Orthodox theologians, though a general pattern may be seen, which functions as a usable definition.

John McGuckin, in a work concerning Orthodoxy as "living tradition," highlighted the Orthodox Church's "fidelity to the continuing guidance of the Holy Spirit," claiming this could be seen through "the manner in which it [the Orthodox Church] joins in the divine process of sanctifying and healing the tormented world of its day."[41] He made his case by taking a historical examination, in which he sought to account for various facets of tradition, as seen through the works of early Church Fathers and then important modern Orthodox theologians. For example, he highlighted whether tradition was used as a verb or noun, whether it referred to an oral or written tradition, and so forth. This inner ability to sanctify and heal led many modern Orthodox theologians to make a distinction between outer manifestations and the inner tradition, or between "traditions" and "Tradition."[42] One of the issues raised by modern Orthodox thinkers, and often discussed within the Tradition/traditions framework, has been how to respond to the Bible/Tradition dichotomy that arose from the Reformation. This is often addressed directly by speaking of Orthodox tradition as an inner life of the Church, as a guidance of the Holy Spirit for the proclamation of the Gospel.[43] In addition to the Bible/tradition question, tradition is connected to the liturgical life of the Orthodox Church. Here, again, one sees a Tradition/traditions type of distinction, wherein the liturgy has an "essence," as a "living tradition," but also has sources that act as a deposit, as well as particular practices.[44]

Although one could easily enough write a monograph on what tradition (that essential "Tradition") means for Orthodox Christianity, at the risk of oversimplification one may note that modern Orthodox theologians emphasize tradition as "living" and ongoing in some sort of way. This living reality has an internal core, or essence ("Tradition"), which is surrounded by practices, teachings, and opinions that might change ("traditions") and has sources to which one might appeal. It was this dynamic conception of tradition that confronted the converts and caused some tension from an anti-traditional, restorationist perspective, especially in the case of Gillquist and his fellow Evangelical converts.

This understanding of tradition (a "lived" Tradition core surrounded by traditions) can be useful in outlining a brief introduction to the Orthodox Church itself. The Orthodox Church is (numerically) the second-largest Christian church in the world, after the Roman Catholic Church. Though the numbers are difficult to ascertain accurately, the world-wide Orthodox Christian population numbers somewhere around 200 million.[45] If one includes the Oriental Orthodox Churches, the numbers increase to about 350 million.[46] These 200 million Orthodox believers comprise a global communion of churches spread across the world, though concentrated in Eastern Europe, Northern Asia (in areas of the former Soviet Union), and the Middle East. Indeed, the following countries are predominantly Orthodox: Russia, Ukraine, Serbia, Romania, Bulgaria, Georgia, Greece, and Cyprus. Significant Orthodox populations reside in Palestine, the other various countries that once made up the Soviet Union, the Czech Republic, Slovakia, Albania, Japan, and Finland. Perhaps unexpectedly, a number of Orthodox believers (around 1.5 million) reside in the United States, and in the late twentieth century, growth has been seen in Africa. Significant Oriental Orthodox populations may be found the Middle East, India, Armenia, Egypt, and Ethiopia, with a steadily increasing presence in North America as well.

The Orthodox Church traces its spiritual heritage, its "Tradition," down through the centuries, through the modern, Byzantine, and early Christian periods to the apostles and their successors. In so doing, it upholds tradition not only as a noun, but also as a verb, as something that is continually "handed on" through prayer, worship, study, and love—though on well too many occasions the Church has failed to live up to its own standards. For Orthodox Christians, then, the historical date of origin would be the Annunciation, when the Archangel Gabriel proclaimed to Mary that the Holy Spirit would come upon her and she would bear Jesus, the Son of the Most High, to which Mary wholeheartedly assented.[47] It is here that Orthodox Christians see an image of the Church (in Mary).

As a community, the Orthodox Church looks to the Seven Ecumenical Councils, gatherings of bishops that produced dogmatic statements and canon law important to the Orthodox Church to this day. In fact, it was a division at the fourth of such councils (in Chalcedon in 451) that led to the distinction between what we now call the Orthodox Church and the Oriental Orthodox Churches. The Oriental Orthodox Churches disagreed with the council's findings, though headway has been made in the mid to late twentieth century. An earlier group of (largely Syrian and Persian) Christians had left the larger Christian community at the prior council in Ephesus in 431. Today, that church is known as the Assyrian Church of the East and comprises a little under 200,000 members, mostly concentrated in Syria, Iran, and Iraq. Orthodox praxis and ethos includes not only a determination to hold to apostolic dogma as expressed in those seven councils, but also a focus on correct worship, a commitment to asceticism, an emphasis on the mystical aspects of faith, and flexibility on teachings and opinions within the confines of the dogmas of the Church.

Orthodox ecclesiology (governing structure) is hierarchical and male-dominated, as only men may be ordained as priests and bishops, but the Orthodox Church does not answer to a single bishop as Roman Catholics relate to the

Pope, the bishop of Rome. The Orthodox Church maintains a collegial governing structure. This recalls Acts 15, where the apostles, the leaders of the Church, gathered to discuss and decide upon the tensions between Jewish Christians and Gentile Christian converts.

Within the history of Orthodoxy, this ecclesiology has undergone its own journey (its own changing "traditions"). Following the transfer of the Roman government from Rome to Constantinople (under Constantine the Great), the bishop of Constantinople took on a prestige not held before. In the early Byzantine Empire, the bishops of five major sees (Jerusalem, Antioch, Alexandria, Constantinople, and Rome) became known as "patriarchs" and oversaw vast territories and important ecclesiastical decisions. The bishop of Rome (now called the Pope) was treated as the "first among equals," with important prerogatives such as often serving as a final court of appeals and holding the right to give the final arguments before a decision was made at an Ecumenical Council. In the West, the prerogatives of the Roman patriarch became increasingly defined by tensions with secular rulers such as the Merovingians and Carolingians. At the same time, linguistic differences (between the Greek East and Latin West) grew increasingly problematic. Cultural differences also began to show and in the ninth century a theological controversy over whether the *filioque* (translated as "and the Son") should describe the Holy Spirit's "procession" from God the Father brought all of these factors together. The disputes were settled with a council in 879–880, which included papal legates, and declared that no additions should be made to the creed and that Rome and Constantinople needed to recognize one another's governing decisions. Although the controversy did not lead to a permanent split between the two halves of the Christian Church, it prefigured the eventual split that would occur in the eleventh century, in which the issues became raised again and a crusade (which ended up targeting Eastern Christians as well as Muslims and Jews) solidified a split that produced the separate Roman Catholic and Eastern Orthodox Churches as we know them today. To this day, the Roman Catholic Church does not recognize what the Orthodox Church sees as the full import of the 879–880 council (both in terms of the Trinitarian theology expressed in the creed and in terms of church governance). The Roman Catholic Church continues to include the *filioque* in the Nicene Creed and has developed a monarchical form of ecclesiology centered upon the bishop (Pope) of Rome.

Through the Eastern Church's own unique and complex ecclesiological history, the collegial approach to church governance has developed into a system of "patriarchs," bishops who oversee large, self-governing (autonomous), and self-led (autocephalous) churches. Because of Rome's separation, the seat of honor as "first among equals" now resides with the Ecumenical Patriarch in Constantinople. Within this system, metropolitans and archbishops, bishops of large territorial areas, oversee large archdioceses or even self-governing churches. For example, the Russian Orthodox Church maintains a patriarch in Moscow and is, thus, both self-governing and self-led. On the other hand, the Orthodox Church in Finland is an autonomous (self-governing) church, whose archbishop is appointed by the patriarch of Constantinople/Istanbul. For this reason, scholars and Orthodox Christians themselves will sometimes refer to the Orthodox Church as "the Orthodox Churches," a practice I will continue here. At other times, I may follow colloquial conventions and simply use the word Orthodox in place of Orthodox Christians.

In America, immigration fostered an interrelation between ethnicity and Orthodox Church jurisdiction. Because
the Orthodox Churches developed governing structures
along certain national lines, immigrants looked to their
homelands for clergy and ecclesiastical support. While the
Russian Orthodox Church had a mission in North America beginning in the last decade of the eighteenth century,
it was initially concentrated in Alaska, with only a nominal
presence in the lower 48 states at the end of the nineteenth
century. The other immigrating groups of Orthodox, with
only a few exceptions, neither formally joined the Russian
mission nor understood themselves to be part of such a mission. Even when immigrating groups did join the Russian
Orthodox mission, they did not do so *en masse*, but in clus-
ters. This led to a situation where many Orthodox Christians
looked to the churches of their homelands for guidance.
Thus, the Russians were initially part of the Russian Orthodox Church, while the Greeks, with a few exceptions, looked
to Constantinople, then to the synod of Greece, and then to
Constantinople yet again. Eventually, each national Orthodox Church had a governing structure in place for its respec-
tive immigrants in America.

This assortment of Orthodox governing structures in
America has served as the bearer of tradition for the intra-
Christian converts studied here. It might seem that having
diverse administrative bodies would preclude seeing Orthodox Christianity as having a unified tradition (that essential
"Tradition"), but Orthodoxy's emphasis upon dogma and
worship has created a vision of a spiritually united faith in
continuity with the Byzantine church of the Seven Ecumenical Councils and the early Church prior to that. The chapters
that follow present just how four exemplary intra-Christian

American converts to Orthodoxy have seen these Orthodox Churches as the bearers of *the* Christian Tradition. For them, conversion has been a turn to tradition situated in the American anti-traditional tradition. In each case, the reader will find that a rather un-American decision (turning to tradition) has occurred in a very American manner. For the earlier two converts (Toth and Morgan), this meant turning to tradition served to help solve the problem of suffering under oppressive power structures (ecclesiastical and racial). For all of the converts, however, the turn to tradition occurred through the doorway of restorationism, with Morgan, Berry, and Gillquist each first joining a restorationist before then entering the Orthodox Church.

ST. ALEXIS TOTH, LEADER

OF EASTERN CATHOLIC CONVERTS

WHEN EAST MEETS WEST

On December 18, 1889, Fr. Alexis Georgevich Toth, an Eastern Catholic priest from the Subcarpathian region of the Austro-Hungarian Empire, arrived in Minneapolis and presented himself to his bishop, John Ireland. After venerating (kissing) the bishop's hand, per Eastern Rite, Slavic custom, rather than genuflecting, Toth handed his papers to Ireland.

> I remember that no sooner did he read that I was a 'Uniate' than his hands began to shake.[1] It took him fifteen minutes to read to the end, after which he asked abruptly (we spoke in Latin):
> "Have you a wife?"
> "No."
> "But you had one?"
> "Yes, I am a widower."
> At this he threw the paper on the table and loudly exclaimed, "I have already written to Rome protesting against this kind of priest being sent to me!"
> "What kind of priest do you mean?"
> "Your kind."

"I am a Catholic priest of the Greek Rite, I am a Uniate.
I was ordained by a lawful Catholic bishop."

"I do not consider either you or this bishop of yours Catholic.
Besides, I do not need any Uniate priests here. A Polish priest
in Minneapolis is sufficient. The Greek Catholics can also have
him for their priest."

"But he belongs to the Latin Rite. Our people do not
understand him. They will hardly go to him. That is why they
built a church of their own."

"I gave them no permission to build, and I shall grant you
no permission to work there."

The Archbishop lost his temper, I lost mine just as much.
One word brought another, so that the thing had gone so far
that our conversation is not worth putting on record.[2]

This exchange would inspire Toth to undergo a conversion
he had already been considering and lead to the conversion
of tens of thousands of Carpatho-Rusyns, a people native to
the Subcarpathian region.[3] As this chapter will show, Toth
(and the Carpatho-Rusyns who followed him) responded to
their situation of perceived and experienced difficulties at
the hands of the Roman Catholic Church by turning to the
Orthodox tradition of their ancestors. In so doing, Toth encouraged his fellow Carpatho-Rusyns to look to Russia and
to unite under the Russian Orthodox Church.

For Toth, as well as for large numbers of Carpatho-Rusyn
converts who followed him, America provided the opportunity to turn to tradition not merely as a means to escape
Roman Catholic prejudices, though as shall be seen below,
that was an important dimension, but as a way in which to
return to the Eastern Orthodox Christianity of their ancestors. Toth perceived Orthodox Christianity to be true, apostolic Christianity, and for him, this was a highly important

point, even while defining (and presenting) the Orthodox tradition as being an integral part of Carpatho-Rusyn ethnic heritage. He believed the Eastern Orthodox Church of his forefathers, not the Eastern Catholic Church (Eastern Christians under the Roman Catholic Church), was the legitimate church of his people. Furthermore, his understanding of church history included the belief that Western Christianity had deviated from true Christianity in the ninth century. He also saw that the Roman Catholic Church was often heavily biased against Eastern Christian practices, even when Eastern Christians submitted to Roman Catholic authority. Toth, therefore, saw Eastern Orthodoxy as the true Christian tradition and the solution to the religious difficulties faced by the Carpatho-Rusyn people.

America provided Toth with a context in which he was able to act on his beliefs and feelings in new ways. In America, he would encounter a country that had forged a tradition of anti-tradition known as *restorationism*. This created a context that provided the flexibility necessary for the beginnings of what became known as the "Toth Movement," a movement based on an appeal to the Orthodox origins of the Carpatho-Rusyns' Christianity. In fact, it is precisely through his apologetical writings that one can ascertain just how important that earlier Orthodox tradition was for Toth.

For his evangelization efforts and pastoral work on behalf of his fellow Carpatho-Rusyn immigrants, Toth would later be canonized as a saint by the Orthodox Church in America.[4] The Orthodox Church in America itself is an autocephalous Orthodox Church whose make-up consists of a significant number of parishes that can trace their history back to Toth's own personal efforts.[5] For example, one can look to Minneapolis (1891), Mayfield (Pennsylvania, 1902),

Wilkes-Barre (1892), Streator (Illinois, 1898), Bridgeport (Connecticut, 1894), Joliet (Illinois, 1907), and the Pennsylvanian towns of: North Pittsburgh (1891), Osceola Mills (1893), Philipsburg (1894), Catasauqua (1891), Lopez (1907), and Edwardsville (1910).[6] In fact, Toth helped form seventeen Orthodox parishes in Pennsylvania alone.[7] Although Toth was not the first Carpatho-Rusyn in the West to consider Orthodoxy, it was his activities that led to the Toth Movement, the conversion of tens of thousands of Carpatho-Rusyns to Orthodox Christianity.[8] This movement occurred by way of newly converted Orthodox Carpatho-Rusyns who returned to their homeland and so successfully encouraged their fellow countrymen to convert to Orthodox Christianity that the number of Orthodox adherents went from about 440 in 1900 to over 118,000 by 1930.[9] The Toth Movement proved to be most effective after Toth's own lifetime and set the stage for further Roman Catholic–Orthodox tensions in a region that had experienced continual Latin Rite–Eastern Rite struggles since the ninth century. The strife would continue throughout the twentieth century.[10]

During Toth's own lifetime, the Carpatho-Rusyn immigrants would be forced to discern between a Roman Catholic Latin Rite clergy who held negative views of the new Eastern Catholic immigrants on the one hand, and Russian Orthodox clergy who had a love-hate relationship with their newfound brothers in Christ on the other. Often, the Carpatho-Rusyns would vacillate between the two, with some returning to Eastern Catholicism even after they had formally converted to Orthodox Christianity. This was certainly the case for the Carpatho-Rusyn clergy in America during Toth's time. As shall be seen below, several factors were involved in this vacillation, including the fact that the

Carpatho-Rusyn parishes were lay-dominated entities. Other likely factors included the relatively poor pay of the clergy themselves and tensions with the Russian Orthodox clergy. The Americanist controversy also affected the outcome inasmuch as it helped shape the views of the Latin hierarchy, including Archbishop John Ireland, in North America.[11]

A QUICK PRIMER ON CHRISTIANITY IN THE SUBCARPATHIAN REGION

As important as the American setting would become, Toth's promotion of the Eastern Christian tradition had a well established history of its own in his homeland. These West–East struggles in the Subcarpathian region prior to Alexis Toth, as well as those struggles he himself experienced and knew, greatly shaped his viewpoint. The tensions between Eastern Christians and Western Christians in Subcarpathia, combined with intra-Western religious tensions (between Protestants and Catholics), had led to the eventual Union of Užhorod. No documentation exists, but it seems that on April 24, 1646, 63 priests made a profession of faith before the Roman Catholic bishop of Eger.[12] Efforts to Magyarize the Carpatho-Rusyns, that is, to assimilate them to the Hungarian nationality, language, and culture, began in the late eighteenth century. When the 1867 *Ausgleich* (compromise) established a dual monarchy for the Austro-Hungarian Empire, however, the Hungarians enacted a policy of forced Magyarization that was much more intense than what had been established previously.[13] Protestants and Orthodox created autonomous groups immediately, which were recognized by the government, but the Hungarian government refused to grant autonomy to the Carpatho-Rusyn Eastern Catholics.[14] Those involved in the forced Magyarization sought to rewrite the actual history of the Carpatho-Rusyns, so as to eliminate the Carpatho-Rusyns' own national and religious identity and subsume them under the Magyars, or Hungarians themselves.[15] To this end, the Hungarians sealed Carpatho-Rusyn archives and established a Latinization religious policy, whereby the Carpatho-Rusyns were to adopt an increasing amount of Latin and Western Rite practices in addition to suggesting, in some cases, that Hungarian could replace the Carptho-Rusyns' Slavonic liturgical language.[16]

The ethno-religious element, that of overlapping national and religious concerns, greatly shaped the Carpatho-Rusyn context prior to and during Toth's ministry. Toth found himself living within a context that included Russophilism, Ukrainophilism, and Rusynophilism.[17] Both the 1848 pan-Slavic conference held in Prague and the advance of the Russian army into Ukraine and the Subcarpathian region when it put down the Kossuth rebellion inspired Carpatho-Rusyn Russophilism.[18]

An additional complicating factor was the conflict between the episcopal sees of Užhorod and Prešov. The establishment of the eparchy of Prešov created two eparchies for the Carpatho-Rusyns.[19] This was done in order to divide the Carpatho-Rusyns against themselves and allow for a more pro-Hungarian approach to church life.[20] Although Toth had been a student at Užhorod before teaching at Prešov, he seems to have aligned himself more closely with the thinking at Prešov.[21] The priests from Užhorod were more pro-Hungarian than those from Prešov, which can be seen from the fact that in America, the clergy from Prešov were far more likely to react against Latin practices and become Orthodox.[22]

The Hungarian divide and conquer tactic exacerbated the plight of the Carpatho-Rusyns and this exacerbated tension was about to explode on the American scene.

TOTH'S ARRIVAL IN AMERICA AND HIS TURN TO (THE ORTHODOX) TRADITION

When Alexis Toth arrived in America, he was part of a larger movement that was already underway. During the period of 1880–1908, around 200,000 Carpatho-Rusyns emigrated to America.[23] These immigrants were in need of pastoral oversight, which was to be assigned from Subcarpathia, transplanting the Eastern Catholic-Roman Catholic tensions onto American soil Indeed, as described in the encounter with Archbishop Ireland, Toth was about to encounter a situation that would strike him as being too much to bear from Roman Catholic hierarchy.

In 1885, Metropolitan Sylvestr Sembratovych assigned Fr. Ivan Volans'kyĭ (1857–1926) to the Eastern Catholic parish in Shenandoah, Pennsylvania.[24] Volans'kyĭ not only helped organize the Shenandoah parish, but also parishes in other areas of Pennsylvania and the East Coast as well as Denver and Minneapolis (Toth's future parish).[25] Volans'kyĭ 's interaction with Catholic hierarchs in America foreshadowed what Toth was about to experience. In Minneapolis, Archbishop Ireland refused to let Volans'kyĭ serve liturgy in any of the Western Rite parishes.[26] In Philadelphia, Archbishop John Ryan refused to meet with him, forcing Volans'kyĭ to write both to Sembratovych and the Roman Congregation for the Propagation of the Faith.[27] Volans'kyĭ later returned to Galicia, was sent to Brazil as a missionary, and ended his career in Galicia.

It should be pointed out that bishops were not the only ones who held such views. For example, Fr. Albert A. Lings, Archbishop Corrigan's dean in New York, expressed relief in 1892 that the wife of Fr. Eugene Szatala, a Carpatho-Rusyn Eastern Rite Priest, remained in Europe.[28] An 1898 trip to L'viv would force Lings to admit later that married priests could be effective.[29] Although Lings should be commended for changing his mind on the effectiveness of married priests (at least in the European context), his is but a more tolerant example of the sort of prejudice the Eastern Catholics encountered from both bishops and priests of the Latin rite.[30]

In response to the arrival of the Carpatho-Rusyns (and their priests, notably Volans'kyĭ and later Toth), Ireland began working on a "solution" to the "problem" of the Eastern Catholic Immigrants.[31] When Toth returned to his parishioners shaken, upset, and distraught, Ireland told the local Polish priest to denounce Toth from the pulpit, instructing the laity not to accept any ministrations from Toth.[32] This decree was later published in Roman Catholic parishes throughout the Minneapolis area.[33] About six months after the confrontation with Toth, in May of 1890, Ireland raised the issue of "priests of the Greek rite" before the annual meeting of bishops in Boston.[34] He believed strongly in a change of rite, claiming that changing from Eastern Rite to Western Rite would assist in breaking down ethnic ghettos and further the "Americanization" of the new immigrants.[35]

Ireland had the explicit support of the other American Catholic bishops in this regard as well as Rome's.[36] For example, Bishop Richard Phelan of Pittsburgh claimed, "a married priest could neither be a good priest, nor a good Catholic."[37]

One might be tempted to think it was only those who could be termed "Americanists" who supported this view, but even those who were not "Americanists" opposed the immigration of Eastern Rite clergy and snubbed the Eastern Rite practices.[38]

Toth responded to his situation by eventually turning to his Eastern Christian tradition, a move not wholly unlike American Protestant restorationism, but though he claimed he had long considered becoming Orthodox, he did not immediately make this turn toward Orthodox Christianity.[39] First, he tried to operate from the platform of his Eastern Christian tradition within the larger Catholic Church. Toth wrote to his bishop (Ivan Valyï) three times but claimed a "Reverend Dzubay" asked him to write a fourth letter detailing the difficulties, which could then be forwarded to Rome (though the letter proved to be "too harsh" to be sent).[40] After the letter exchange, Toth called and chaired a meeting of Carpatho-Rusyn clergy in America.[41] The clergy met on October 29, 1890. The group attending the clergy meeting was small, with eight of the ten priests in America attending.[42]

At this meeting, the Carpatho-Rusyn priests adopted nine proposals: (1) to petition for a bishop over the Eastern Rite Roman Catholics (2) that the Eastern Rite be maintained (3) bishops in Europe should send only married priests (4) parish property should be appropriately deeded, i.e., not left solely in the hands of a small group of the laity (5) Church organizations are not to accept non-Catholics and officers must be installed in a church building (6) parish boundaries must be flexible, so that people have the freedom of attending the parish they helped build (7) the local priest is the one who should head parish finances and property (8) those assigned the duty of collecting pledges must be honorable men and their collection books must contain an introduction by a pastor (9) each parish should have an annual meeting.[43]

One can extrapolate two factors that will become important to Toth's later success from the nine proposals. First, there was a clear desire to promote and maintain their traditional Eastern Christian heritage to the fullest extent, even going so far as to bypass Western Rite clergy within the American dioceses that already existed. Second, the parishes were largely controlled by lay members, often a small group of lay members.[44] The first three proposals speak directly to the Carpatho-Rusyns' difficulty with maintaining their religious tradition. In proposal two, demanding that the Eastern Rite be allowed, they wrote of the "intolerance and total ignorance" of the American Catholic clergy and claimed such "negative influence can only harm our Greek Catholic tradition and draw our faithful into the Latin rite."[45] The final six proposals addressed the situations caused when a parish was deeded to a member, or handful of members, of a given congregation without including the governing oversight of the local priest and his bishop.[46]

Following the meeting, Toth sent a summary to Bishop Valyi. In this report, Toth wrote, "The first alarming piece of news came form [sic] Philadelphia, where suspicious-looking individuals were said to be trying to lure Hungarian Greek Catholics to the side of the schism."[47] That is to say, the seeds of discontent had been sown and looking to Orthodox Christianity was something Carpatho-Rusyn immigrants had begun to consider. Toth was not alone, not even the "first," but as we shall see, he became a catalyst who established a tradition-focused pattern.[48] Having already claimed in the aforementioned December 16, 1889, letter that some Carpatho-Rusyns were in the habit of taking a two to three day journey one way to Alaska for a major feast where they attended an Orthodox parish, he claimed that unless Catholic clergy in America changed their position, "one portion of the faithful will turn against religion, another portion will join the [Orthodox] and still another portion will become Roman Catholic."[49] Toth's concerns expressed not only the reality for many a Carpatho-Rusyn immigrant, but for his own parishioners and himself as well.

America provided them precisely the opportunity they needed to follow through on asserting their commitment to their Eastern Christian tradition. Two different versions of how Toth and the Minneapolis parish contacted the Russian Orthodox bishop, Vladimir, exist, though they are not necessarily mutually exclusive. One version places the impetus in the hands of one John Mlinar and some fellow lay members. According to John Mlinar himself, after traveling to San Francisco with the intention of collecting funds for the parish, he secretly met with some fellow lay people, who then went to Toth, asking for Toth's endorsement of their decision to become Orthodox.[50]

Toth's account describes the meeting as occurring upon his decision to gather together his parishioners in order to inform them that given the circumstances, it would probably be best if he left. They responded by reminding him that the situation would be no different for the next priest and that they ought to go to "the Russian Orthodox bishop."[51] Since neither Toth nor his parishioners knew where Bishop Vladimir resided, Toth wrote to the Russian Consulate and learned the whereabouts on December 18, 1890.[52] The parish then sent John Mlinar to San Francisco, during which time (and after some difficulties communicating linguistically), Mlinar wrote to Toth wondering what Church it was to which they belonged since he only knew himself to be "Orthodox."[53] This point from Mlinar is an important one, for even though they had been under the papacy in Rome since 1646, the Carpatho-Rusyns had continued to call themselves Orthodox (*pravoslavnii*).

The meeting was a success in that Mlinar and Bishop Vladimir were able to further the petition of the Minneapolis congregation. Igumen George Chudnovski, rector of the cathedral (and whose own native dialect allowed him to understand Mlinar reasonably well) wrote to Toth, explaining the status of the Russian Orthodox Church in America and informing Toth, "your business has been forwarded to St. Petersburg. Write also to the remaining churches that they may follow your blessed path."[54] In February of that year, Toth traveled to San Francisco and on March 25, Bishop Vladimir visited Minneapolis and received Toth and the parish into the Russian Orthodox Church.[55] When news reached Prešov, Bishop Valyï requested that Toth accept another parish in America as a temporary assignment before returning to Europe, a futile request since Toth no longer understood himself to be under Valyï's jurisdiction.[56]

Toth quickly earned the love and respect of Bishop Vladimir and by September of 1891, Vladimir asked if Toth would be willing to serve both Minneapolis and Chicago and praised Toth's evangelization efforts toward Carpatho-Rusyns in Pennsylvania, exclaiming, "May the Lord help you win Pennsylvania over to the truth. Do not be dejected. Be patient, and may the Lord bless and help you."[57] In July of 1892, the Holy Synod officially recognized the reception of Toth into the Orthodox Church by Vladimir and the Russian Mission, though by that time, a new bishop, Nicholas, had been assigned to America.[58]

Toth had started his ecclesiastical career in tension-filled Subcarpathia and ended it by adhering to Orthodox Christianity in America. In so doing, he was on the forefront of a mass Carpatho-Rusyn movement from Eastern Catholicism to Russian Orthodoxy. The Eastern Christian tradition was, for him, paramount and the American context allowed him to pursue it more fully than he had been able previously. Initially, holding fast to his Eastern Christian roots meant writing to his bishop back home and meeting with fellow Eastern Catholic clergy, but that proved to be but a short-lived initial step. For both Toth and his parishioners came to believe that the only way to maintain their Eastern Christian tradition was to turn to the Orthodox tradition, to restore Orthodoxy as the Carpatho-Rusyn faith. For Toth, this turn, or conversion, had a serious religious grounding. To understand how he perceived his conversion to Orthodoxy to be a return to the tradition of his Orthodox ancestors, however, one has to engage his apologetics, both in evangelistic efforts and his writings because it is there that one finds his motivations and beliefs expressed and witnesses what drew others to follow him.

TOTH TAKES THE OFFENSIVE IN THE NAME OF TRADITION

In November of 1892, Toth's efforts with people residing in Pennsylvania bore fruit and he was contacted by the Eastern Catholic parish in Wilkes-Barre, asking him to become their pastor.[59] Initially, Toth thought it could be a joke, but after being assured otherwise, he made the trip in order to inform them about Orthodoxy.[60] Toth served the liturgy and explained to them what would be necessary should they become Orthodox, including differences in teachings and practices as well as the fact that they would have to submit to Bishop Nicholas, which included deeding the property to him and the Russian Mission.[61] Toth spoke at length and then left the people alone in order that they might decide whether the teachings and practicalities of such a conversion were acceptable. They agreed and sent a petition to Bishop Nicholas.[62] Bishop Nicholas responded by way of telegram, accepting the parish and assigning Toth as their rector.

Toth's methods in Wilkes-Barre would not prove unique. In his personal encounters with groups seeking to convert and form an Orthodox parish, Toth responded in a manner that demonstrated an awareness and concern for who the Carpatho-Rusyns actually were. In each case, Toth held meetings with the entire group of interested people and proceeded carefully to inform them of the doctrinal and jurisdictional aspects of converting to the Russian Orthodox Church. Toth kept to this approach even when it seemed that a less structured approach might work (at least temporarily). One example occurred in Mahoney, Pennsylvania:

> I found there only seven people. After one and one-half hours of waiting, finally the rest came. . . . To my question, what motives brought them the wish to reunite with the Holy Orthodox faith, after a long silence one of them finally said in the Slovak language, "We don't have any more patience with the premacy [sic] of Mr. Smith [the local lay-leader] and we cannot pay so much to the priest and to have so many collections, and in the church treasury there is nothing" . . . To that I told them it is not the interest of the Holy Orthodox Church and faith to make now [sic] disagreements and unrest in a Uniate parish,

and because of that, if you think that the goal of Orthodoxy is to liberate you from the "rule" of Smith and others, you are mistaken. You are mistaken also that in the Orthodox Church it is not necessary to pay the priest and deacon. . . . I started to give them a dogmatic and historical explanation of Orthodoxy and Unia. I did it for more than an hour. They listened with attention and when I finished, the brother of the president came and he began to talk. He was very drunk. . . . I saw that there the matter was not about the soul, not about the church, nor about the faith, but only about private interests. I told them simply that an Orthodox can be only that one who has a real love of God, the church of our forefathers, and of the Russian nationality, that the Holy Orthodox Church does not want to use the means used by the Uniates and their ksendzes [priests], that the Orthodox Church is going in a simple way, does not twist, does not dodge, but teaches God's truth and honesty and I left them.[63]

Although nothing came of this meeting, Toth's description proves consistent with his aforementioned encounter with the parishioners in Wilkes-Barre as well as his description of meeting Carpatho-Rusyns in Scranton.[64] In each case, Toth was concerned for both proper and legitimate conversions. This may be seen in the way in which he described the Orthodox tradition to them, as "the church of our forefathers" and as something belonging to "Russian nationality." One may also see Toth's concerns for the people themselves, displaying an awareness of the sort of concerns and agendas and behavior his fellow Carpatho-Rusyns tended to have. This latter point of sensitivity for his fellow Carpatho-Rusyn will prove important but is by no means secondary to Toth's emphasis on the need to look to the Orthodox tradition for an answer to their plight.

According to Toth, Carpatho-Rusyns converting to Orthodox Christianity were turning to the tradition of the true, historical church of Christianity and the faith of their fathers. Toth made this clear from the very beginning of *Where to Seek the Truth?*, a self-published treatise that went through several editions but was first written in 1893. The treatise itself begins with sixteen opening questions that are followed by short answers. The first question asks who established the Christian faith, the answer being Jesus the Christ, the Son of God. The next ten questions, however, which seek to define where the Christian church began, where the Ecumenical Councils assembled, and where the greatest fathers lived all have answers that begin with a reference to "the East." So, for example, questions eight and nine read as:

> 8. Where did the greatest holy fathers of Christ's church live?
>
> In the East—such fathers as St. Basil the Great, St. John Chrysostom, St. Athanasius, St. Gregory, St. Nicholas the Wonderworker, and others.
>
> 9. From where did our ancestors, the Russians, accept Christianity?
>
> From the East—Constantinople.[65]

The point is clear. There is no mention of Augustine. The greatest fathers were in the East and it is this faith that their Slavic ancestors adopted. Although the omission of Augustine might make a contemporary Western reader wonder whether Toth himself actually believed this, it is important to remember that Augustine's stature in the East is but a glimmer of what it is in the West. It should hardly be surprising that Augustine did not make Toth's list of greatest saints.

The argument that Orthodoxy is the traditional faith of the Carpatho-Rusyns may be found in the second part of the pamphlet, titled under the heading "church," thus linking church, tradition, and ethnicity. Continuing the question-answer format, Toth wrote:

> 3. What do the words "schism" and "dissidence" mean?
> They mean "renegade." Such a faith or church, is one which has splintered off—separated itself from the ecumenical church in its observance of rites.
> 4. What does the word "heretical" mean?
> Heretical is a faith or church, which has not only reneged from the ecumenical church in observance of rites, but is teaching the opposite of the church's teachings, something false or invented which is not acceptable to God.
> 5. Can a person please God as a member of a schismatic or heretical faith?
> No, especially if he knows or hears that he belongs to a misguided faith.[66]

Toth, as a former professor of canon law and church history correctly distinguished between the notions of schism and heresy, though it is intriguing to see the manner in which he did this. A schism was caused when a group continued to teach correct doctrines, but on its own changed the forms of worship and discipline. A heresy occurred when a group not only changed the forms of worship and discipline but also began teaching doctrines contrary to those held by the historical, apostolic church. Interestingly, though, the results, for Toth, were the same. People in either situation have placed their salvation at serious risk, especially if a person learns that he or she is a member of a schismatic and/or heretical group.

Naturally, the question arises as to what churches are schismatic and heretical. Toth answered this in question fifteen:

> 15. When were these churches founded?
> (1) The Papist, or Roman-Catholic church was founded in the ninth century after Christ.
> (2) The Protestant (Lutheran, Calvinist, and others) were founded in the sixteenth century after Christ
> (3) The Uniate (Greek-Catholic or *kalakuts'* church) was founded in the seventeenth century after Christ.[67]

On the basis of the importance of both rite and doctrinal teaching, Toth claimed there were four types of Christianity. In this way, he set up Orthodoxy as *the* Christian tradition because the Orthodox Church had stood as the church while the other groups had left either by way of schism or by way of both schism and heresy.

Later, in section five (entitled "Unia"), Toth continued to argue that the Orthodox faith was the faith of the Carpatho-Rusyn ancestors prior to the 17th and 18th centuries.

> 1. What does the word "unia" mean?
> This is a Latin word (unio) that means union or joining, and the faith and church that keeps such union is called the Uniate faith and the Uniate Church. . . .
> 14. When did the Unia start in Hungary and why?
> It started in Hungary in 1649. The Orthodox people were persecuted there by the wild Hungarian-Papists, who persecuted them as did the Poles in Poland. . . . They were forced to denounce their grandfathers' Orthodox Church and not only their faith and church, but also their nationality.[68]

Clearly, Toth was playing on emotions, here, referencing "their grandfathers' Orthodox Church," but the point remained. Prior to the Union of Užhorod in 1646, there was no Unia and the Slavic people in the region were members of the Orthodox Church, the one true church that had maintained the faith of Christ.

The broad outlines of Toth's understanding of the history of Christianity may be seen from these last few quotes. Toth believed there was one church until the ninth century, when the East and West formally split.[69] The Eastern Churches held to the true faith and kept the faith of the Eastern fathers, making it the traditional Christian church. This same Eastern Orthodox Church Christianized his ancestors and the Slavic peoples beginning in the ninth century. The Western Church persecuted the Carpatho-Rusyns even after they formally accepted Roman Catholic oversight. On this point, he made no distinction between the local Hungarian Catholic Church and the Roman papacy. The one served the other.

Since Toth closely linked the true faith of his Rusyn ancestors with their Slavic heritage, denouncing their Orthodox Church went hand in hand with denouncing their "nationality" (narodno). "Each true Russian, even if he is not the Czar's citizen, every person who has even one drop of Slavic blood, has to pray for his health and for his royal house because the Russians and the Slavs have in the Russian Czar their only protector on this planet."[70] This and other very similar remarks, which permeated not only this treatise, but all of Toth's writings, simply verifies the final point he raised in the opening section of the pamphlet:

> What does the word "catholic" mean? This word is Greek and it means 'sobornyï.' This means that the Christian Faith must spread over all the world. . . . And why is the Orthodox faith also called 'Russian'? Because this faith is confessed by the most

glorious, greatest, and most religious people, the Russians. It is
missionized by the great, glorious, mighty Russia where more
than eighty million people are Orthodox.[71]

According to Toth, the Russian Orthodox Church has been
charged with evangelizing the world on behalf of the Orthodox faith. Toth's statements situate him squarely within a late
imperial (1855–1917) Russian Orthodox movement that had
encompassed Nicholas Bjerring, the first American convert
priest in the 1870s and early 1880s, "Orthodox patriotism."[72]

Although he was an Orthodox patriot and believed religion intertwined with the historic destiny of the Russian,
Slavic people, which included the Carpatho-Rusyns, one
should assume neither that this means Toth subsumed the
theological arguments under nationalistic arguments nor
that Toth promoted some sort of tribalism.[73] The guiding
factor was Orthodox Christianity. Its connection to Russia
and the Slavic peoples was that they were given a special
calling by God to spread and defend the Orthodox faith
throughout the world. Although Toth was clearly writing
to Carpatho-Rusyns whom he believed were part of the
larger Russian people, their guiding principle was to be
their faith.

These were two important arguments for Toth. Orthodoxy was the traditional faith of the Carpatho-Rusyns and
the Carpatho-Rusyns were part of the Russian people, whose
lives were furthered by the tsar and the Russian Orthodox
Church. These two contentions were brought to bear upon
a central point that Toth wished to emphasize—the Roman
Catholic Church had persecuted and continued to persecute
both the Orthodox and the Eastern Catholics. Specifically,
Toth listed four main abuses:

(a) Their [the Orthodox] holy, only-saving Christian faith and church were called 'peasant.'

(b) Their priests were called 'Jews' and under the leadership of Polish *ksendzes* or Jesuits. The priests were attacked, beaten, even dragged on the ground by their hair and beards.

(c) Corpses were thrown from their coffins. During funerals the dead and mourning parishioners were dragged to the marshes or to waste places. The priests and Orthodox believers were hit and many times people were even killed.

(d) The Orthodox churches, it is horrible to say, were turned over to the Jews to control. When an Orthodox priest needed to have a service, to baptize or wed or bury people he had first to pay money to receive the key and to be admitted to the church.[74]

One needs to be careful in assessing the list of abuses Toth provided. The Hungarians looked down upon the Carpatho-Rusyns and did consider them peasants (which they largely were, though in this case, it was clearly a pejorative term). The Hungarians were also clean-shaven and expected the Eastern Catholic clergy to be clean shaven as well, per the standard Western custom of the time. We also know that Hungarians (as well as Poles and Russians) would hire Jews and use Jews to further their own intra-Christian struggles.[75] One must be cautious, however, of giving too much weight to dead and mourning parishioners being dragged off and corpses stolen from their coffins. Orthodox have had their dead stolen from coffins, most recently by Presbyterians and Methodists in Alaska in the early twentieth century, but Toth was almost certainly referring to abuses attributed to Josaphat Kuntsevych.[76]

Kuntsevych joined the Catholic Church and eventually became the Eastern Catholic bishop of Polotsk. Toth compared him to the leaders of the Spanish Inquisition:

> The Spanish Inquisition was an ecclesiastical court, where Dominican monks judged everyone, using horrible tortures . . . The main villain inquisitors were Peter Arbuesis and Thomas Torquemada. These were shouted out as saints by the pope as also was the *kalakut* Josaphat Kuntzevich! God protect us from that type of saint. Whoever does not believe us should take the service book, the L'vov edition, and there in the *proskomide* can find that after Ss. Basil, John, Nicholas, and Athanasius, is also written, 'St. Holy Martyr Josaphat.'[77]

To this day in Poland and other areas of Eastern Europe, one may find pamphlets describing a host of abuses attributed to Kuntsevych, though many of the abuses themselves cannot be verified.[78] For Toth, church history all too readily bequeathed a history of abuses in the name of papal authority against those who did not accept Latinization. By including Kuntsevych in the proskomide prayers, the propagators of union with Rome displayed a triumphalism Toth found intolerable. The *proskomide* service is a service of preparation in which an Eastern Rite (whether Orthodox or Eastern Catholic) priest prepares the bread that is to be placed on the altar during the divine liturgy. This service occurs on a small table to the north of the altar (which is oriented east) from which the bread and wine is processed to the altar during the portion of the liturgy known as the Great Entrance. The priest performs this preparation service with prayers that include commemorating significant saints of the church. To include Kuntsevych would be to elevate his importance for Eastern Catholics and would make the implicit theological statement that his actions and uniatism are on par with the actions and doctrinal writings of St. Basil the Great. Nor did Toth present the persecution simply as Roman Catholic versus Orthodox. He noted the more recent Carpatho-Rusyn church history and reminded his readers that in Hungary, the Eastern Rite Roman Catholics themselves "are beaten and persecuted; their Uniate church and their church rite is displayed for mockery by the Latin rite."[79]

Toth's arguments must have resonated deeply with the common Carpatho-Rusyn peasant-immigrant, for whom he wrote. Toth's commitment to his parishioners and the common Carpatho-Rusyn is not difficult to demonstrate. His people were largely impoverished miners working dangerous jobs for very little pay.[80] Toth ministered to them regardless of the conditions and on at least one occasion had himself lowered into a mine in order to hear a dying miner's final confession.[81] His desire to address the average Carpatho-Rusyn immigrant can be found in both his publication efforts and in his personal interaction with immigrant groups seeking to establish an Orthodox parish.

With regard to his publications, Toth sought to present arguments in a manner that not only might appeal to the common Rusyn sentiments, but would be readily accessible. The important pamphlet, *Where to Seek the Truth?*, already analyzed, is probably the most obvious example, given that it went through many editions over the years and was distributed to large groups of people. Some of the changes to the editions are also notable. One of the prominent Russophile exponents during Toth's lifetime in Subcarpathia was Ievhennii Fentsyk (1844–1903), who published the journal *Listok*.[82] The journal included a supplement intended for the less educated simply entitled *Dadotok*. In the later 1907 edition of *Where to Seek the Truth?*, Toth likewise added two supplement sections (also entitled *Dadotok*), which addressed the sorts of concerns one might expect from a Carpatho-Rusyn peasant, such as why Eastern clergy had beards while the

Roman Catholic clergy were clean-shaven.[83] He also added a section that discussed the various types of crosses, including the Slavic three-barred cross.[84] For the average Carpatho-Rusyn, such things were the marks of the Eastern Orthodox tradition, of which they felt a part.

Toth also founded the paper *Svit* because he believed that the Russian Orthodox Mission needed a paper written for the average Carpatho-Rusyn immigrant, akin to the Eastern Catholic paper *Amerikanskiĭ Russkiĭ Viestnik*. He belabored this concern many times in his letters to Bishop Nicholas. For example, in the letter to Bishop Nicholas, wherein he argued that Bishop Nicholas should not have written the letter to *Svoboda* or *Amerikanskiĭ Russkiĭ Viestnik*, Toth claimed that having their own newspaper could serve as a means of responding to the Eastern Catholic voices.[85] At one point, by way of a passing remark, he even wrote, "I would have liked to enclose several more letters from people in which they are constantly asking about a newspaper."[86] In a later letter, Toth noted that the *Amerikanskiĭ Pravoslavnyĭ Viestnik* (the Russian Mission's paper, which was also known as the *Russian Orthodox American Messenger*) "would be a magazine in which only learned people would find pleasure, but our uneducated people will not understand anything and because of that—I am convinced—venia sit verb!—that the best would be not to get occupied with grandiloquent questions in the magazine, and with more easy questions for example with the intemperate behavior of the local Russian people."[87] In another letter still, he wrote, "Your Eminence! Our magazine somehow is writing only for educated persons. Wouldn't it be possible that in it would also be written something for the people?"[88]

Toth's concern for the average Carpatho-Rusyn was well founded. For as convincing as Toth's arguments on behalf of the Orthodox tradition were to thousands, many also waivered and sometimes reversed course on him. In fact, this happened within the Wilkes-Barre parish that had called him from Minneapolis. Despite Toth's care to ensure that all the parishioners knew what they were doing, the parish soon split, with some members claiming that Toth and a faction within the congregation stole the parish from the Eastern Catholics. A lawsuit ensued, which was not finally settled until the Pennsylvania Supreme Court ruled in favor of the Eastern Catholic party. The court did not reach this ruling because it thought that the property had not been deeded correctly to the Orthodox Church. Nor did the court think that the parishioners had not become Orthodox. Instead, it based itself on a case involving a Lutheran parish, wherein the court had decided the property should go to the group representing tenets of the original, founding members, and so ruled in favor of the party that could claim to be Eastern Catholic, the faith of the parish before it converted to Orthodoxy.[89] The length of the trial and the church-political machinations and expense it required exacted a toll on Toth.[90]

It is interesting to note that the court treated the parish as a Protestant institution rather than either Roman Catholic or Orthodox. At one point, the Supreme Court of Pennsylvania even claimed, "We think there is no evidence that would warrant us to placing this church under control of the Roman Catholic bishops."[91] This is a bold statement given that the ruling itself placed the parish under the control of "the Roman Catholic bishops." The court was either unable or unwilling to treat this situation other than how they would treat warring factions in a Protestant parish. Almost certainly, this is because the case went to court during a time of transition. The court in the Watson v. Jones case of 1871 had invoked the principle of church autonomy, which meant that in cases involving hierarchical structures, the court was to follow the decision of church hierarchy.[92] This was a change from the prior English-law approach, known as the Lord Eldon's Rule, which sought to determine the doctrinal position of the religious body in question and then rule in favor of the group that most closely held to correct doctrine.[93] As Toth's case demonstrates, it took time for the implications of Watson v. Jones to be fully appreciated and implemented within the American court system.[94] From the ruling of Watson v. Jones, Toth and his Orthodox parishioners should have won the case, since the parish had been properly deeded to the Orthodox hierarchy, but Lord Eldon's Rule influenced the court's thinking and so the court prioritized the founding, Eastern Catholic doctrinal position.

The Supreme Court did not even discount the general outline of events, as presented by Toth's party. This should dissuade us from making the sort of speculative judgment offered by Konstantin Simon, who insinuated that during the trial, Toth must have mitigated "the amount of persuasion and prompting, as well as the use of half-truths" he had supposedly used to convert the parish.[95] The court at the time certainly did not insinuate any such thing and even if one grants Simon's claim for sake of argument, an honest reading of the sources themselves makes it very difficult to understand why only one party in this suit could be blamed for such behavior. Neither side was pulling any punches. Furthermore, Toth's rendition, which the Supreme Court accepted as true, was in complete accordance with how he interacted with other parish groups seeking to enter Orthodoxy. Toth's approach was always to make an apology for the Orthodox tradition as the faith of the Carpatho-Rusyns' ancestors and the church to which they should return.

Toth's troubles during his tenure as an Orthodox priest were not limited to Eastern Catholic Carpatho-Rusyns. From the beginning of Bishop Nicholas' episcopal oversight, Toth also had to struggle against Russian Orthodox prejudices, all the while furthering the faith of the Russian Orthodox Church. In many ways, the source of this tension was Russian prejudice against Carpatho-Rusyn liturgical practices and culture. In parishes that converted, the Carpatho-Rusyn plainchant was replaced by the Russian liturgical, musical tradition. Even Toth had made passing remarks how he knew the parishioners in Bridgeport "would like their children to go to a Russian school and learn to sing, read, and write as their delegates heard and saw it during the conference at Wilkes-Barre."[96]

Toth himself personally suffered from the Russification efforts of the Russian Mission. In Minneapolis, an assistant was assigned to Toth in order that the parish would have the services of a priest when he needed to be absent to pursue evangelistic ventures among Eastern Catholic Carpatho-Rusyns.[97] For this purpose, Bishop Nicholas assigned Fr. Sebastian Dabovich. According to Toth, Dabovich immediately began instituting changes in order to adhere more strictly to Russian practice, changes Toth noted ought to have occurred slowly over time. Toth claimed Dabovich then proceeded to instigate ill-feelings toward Toth, only to pull back from the fray later and feign innocence.[98]

In addition, the Russian Mission's periodical, the *Russian Orthodox American Messenger*, included essays that contained negative assessments of Toth's Eastern Catholic background and of Eastern Catholics more generally, written by two prominent clergymen, Alexander Hotovitsky and Benedict Turkevich.[99] Hotovitsky criticized liturgical differences between the Carpatho-Rusyns and the Russians, argued against longer sermons (which at least one converted priest, Fr. Hrihoryĭ Hrushka, suggested fit the American context better), and even went so far as to claim that a newspaper recently started by Toth (*Svit*) had no right to exist. Turkevich, for his part, had a different view than Toth regarding the Carpatho-Rusyns' place in America. Although Toth argued that it was possible to be fully American and maintain one's culture and ethnicity, Turkevich believed the only nationality that mattered was that of the Russians and in an article in Toth's *Svit*, suggested that the Carpatho-Rusyns should not be going to America, but to Russia, their homeland.[100]

It must be noted, here, that the Turkevich-Toth tension is not one of whether the Carpatho-Rusyns were wanted in the Orthodox Church. Turkevich was not saying "get out of Orthodoxy." Rather, there was an intra-Russophile division at work. For Toth, looking to the Orthodox faith of Russia did not preclude embracing the American situation. Indeed, the American context allowed Carpatho-Rusyns to restore Orthodoxy as their faith. For Turkevich, the Russian Orthodox mission in America was primarily to Russians and a new, large group of peasant converts should further Russia's ambitions. At the time, one of Russia's major endeavors was the settling, or colonization, of Siberia.[101] When Turkevich suggested colonization in Siberia, he was simply making a suggestion that would have fit with Russia's goals and would not have seemed unduly out of place, however much it might have contrasted with Toth's own vision and pastoral sensibilities (not to mention those of the immigrant-converts themselves).

The difficulties existed not only with fellow Russian Orthodox priests, who disliked aspects of the Carpatho-Rusyns religious life, but also with Bishop Nicholas himself. On February 24, 1896, Bishop Nicholas accused Toth of producing "an unpleasant feeling of irritation and dissatisfaction against you in all those, who have to deal with you."[102] Toth even claimed that Fr. Ambrosiĭ Vretta, then the priest at St. Vladimir's Orthodox Church in Chicago, told Toth that Bishop Nicholas suspected Toth of being nothing more than a Jesuit who joined Orthodoxy in the hopes of attaining some material gain and Vretta was to watch Toth.[103] About a year and a half later, Toth would also write, "Your Eminence, in the same letter you deign to ask me, 'Why does nothing happen like that, where the priests are Moscovites? . . . Naturally, because they always act more legally.'"[104] Despite these ongoing tensions, Toth continued to act as an apologist for the Orthodox Church among his fellow Carpatho-Rusyn immigrants.

Although Toth endured these tensions, every single other Eastern Catholic priest who had joined Toth, including his own brother, Victor, later returned to the Eastern Catholic Church. Likely, their reasons included tiring of the lay-dominated parishes, the related issue of poor clergy compensation, and tensions with the Russian Orthodox clergy. For Alexander Dzubay, the tensions with the Russian Orthodox clergy certainly proved to be too much. Dzubay attended the clergy meeting on October 29, 1890, which Toth chaired, and later followed Toth into the Orthodox Church. Alexander Dzubay would even be consecrated the bishop of Pittsburgh in 1916, but in 1923, he returned to the Catholic

Church with the expectation of being made a bishop to serve Carpatho-Rusyn Eastern Catholics. His expectations remained unfulfilled and he died defrocked in a monastery rest home in 1933.[105]

In the case of Victor Toth, he left because he refused to change his alcoholic ways. Alexis Toth, who occasionally provided statements that demonstrate an aversion to hard liquor and heavy drinking, drew a hard line with his brother. On the one hand, Alexis Toth reacted negatively to the embarrassing write-up his brother received in the *Amerikanskii Pravoslavnyi Viestnik*, which described Victor Toth's necessary removal from priestly service.

> Why does the entire world have to know, that he is a drunk, it is sorrowful to admit, that we have people like him? . . . Meanwhile we have had even worse matters happen . . . their 'sicknesses' were also not described as tragically as my brother's was! . . . Fr. Hotovitsky [the editor] is a nice young man, but he does not have experience—not for a cent![106]

On the other hand, Alexis Toth refused to provide communion to his censured brother (apparently because Victor continued living a reprobate life even after being removed from ministry). However, Alexis Toth still loved his brother and paid his fare back to Europe. "To my great regret I have to admit that my brother has thrown himself in with Uniate priests; the real reason was that I myself refused to communicate with him. However, in the end, I had to send him back to Europe at my own cost."[107]

Despite all this, one must note that Toth's relations with Bishop Nicholas and his fellow Russian Orthodox priests were not characterized only by tensions, misunderstandings, and mistrust. Alexander Hotovitsky did concelebrate (serve in the same altar) with Toth at times and Bishop Nicholas once wrote to the *Amerikanskiĭ Russkiĭ Viestnik* (*American Russian Messenger*, an Eastern Catholic paper) defending the Russian Orthodox Mission and its work among Eastern Catholics.[108] Bishop Nicholas sought to refute the two-pronged attack of the Eastern Catholics at the time (that the Russian Orthodox Mission used "itinerant disciples" and offered promises of material improvement). At the outset, he claimed:

> The Orthodox Mission in America under my supervision has never employed, nor does it employ, unfair means for the conversion of Rusin Uniates—and never has dealings with 'itinerant disciples'—and never gives 'promises.' She accepted them into the bosom of the Orthodox Church since after repeated ordeals they were desiring to join the Orthodox Church—and only through persuasion, by a sincere offering of a confession of faith, did she join them to her Church.[109]

Toth responded to Nicholas with a mixed review, on the one hand cautioning that only "trouble" arises from engaging *Amerikanskiĭ Russkiĭ Viestnik* and/or *Svoboda* (*Freedom*), the two papers in which the letter appeared, while on the other hand noting that what Bishop Nicholas wrote was "the truth."[110] Two ways in which Toth believed Nicholas may have caused trouble was by bringing himself down to the level of those who were directly involved in the disputes and by encouraging Eastern Catholic Gallicians and Polish Roman Catholics to unite around a common enemy (Bishop Nicholas and the Orthodox). Toth claimed that the editor of *Amerikanskiĭ Russkiĭ Viestnik*, Zhatkovych, originally had decided not to publish it until he saw it in *Svoboda*, at which point he published it, adding some comments of his own in reponse. Whatever the personal suspicions and tensions between the two men, Bishop Nicholas proved capable of acknowledging Toth's importance with respect to the mission of the Russian Orthodox Church in America. In addition to this letter defending the mission (and, indirectly, Alexis Toth) Bishop Nicholas also awarded Toth for his efforts with a pectoral cross.[111]

Toth continued to receive the support of his bishops and fellow Russian Orthodox clergy throughout the remainder of his life, regardless of the tensions and cultural suspicions that existed. Bishop (Saint) Tikhon awarded him with various Russian imperial orders of distinction and a *palitsa*, or *epigonation*, and made him a mitred archpriest.[112] Bishop Platon (later Metropolitan Platon) also supported Toth by writing a eulogy.[113] Fr. (St.) Alexander Hotovitsky wrote a moving memorial for Toth, printed in the *Russian Orthodox American Messenger*.[114] The brother of Benedict Turkevich, Fr. Leonid Turkevich, a future Metropolitan, also wrote a tribute.[115] Toth's arguments on behalf of the Orthodox tradition among Carpatho-Rusyn immigrants were too effective to ignore.

CONCLUSION

Carpatho-Rusyn conversions to Orthodoxy Christianity did not end with Toth's efforts. The Roman Catholic Church would continue to struggle with the concern over Eastern Catholic immigrants in America even beyond Toth's lifetime. Valyï argued against Rome's ruling that married priests should not emigrate to America by claiming that until an apostolic vicariate was assigned (if not a bishop), the Carpatho-Rusyns should be subject to their bishops in Europe rather than the Latin Rite bishops in America. Following Toth's conversion and the beginnings of a movement toward Orthodoxy, Rev. Nicephorus Chanath worked as a liaison between the American Roman Catholic bishops and the Eastern Catholic clergy, though the bishops paid him relatively little attention. Back in Hungary, the bishop of Mukačevo (Firczák) considered the American situation as one "caught between the Scylla of poverty and the Charybdis of schism [Orthodoxy]."[116]

Eventually, the Right Reverend Andrew Hodobay was assigned as the Apostolic Visitor but after a few years (from 1902–1906) he was recalled due to in-fighting among the various Eastern Rite Catholic groups. In 1907, Rome consecrated Stephen Ortinsky to be an Eastern Catholic bishop in America but he was given no real jurisdiction, being nothing more than a vicar of Rome and an auxiliary to the American, Latin Rite bishops. He was given full jurisdiction in 1913, but died unexpectedly in 1916, before he could fully initiate needed changes and pastoral oversight. Upon his death, the Eastern Catholics in America split between a Carpatho-Rusyn camp and a Ukrainian camp. The Carpatho-Rusyns did receive Bishop Basil Takach in 1924, but Fr. Orestes Chornock led a group of Carpatho-Rusyns—much as Toth had earlier—to join the Orthodox Church. They chose to enter as an autonomous Church under the Ecumenical Patriarch due to concerns of Russification (e.g. establishing Russian language schools in Carpatho-Rusyn parishes, replacing Carpatho-Rusyn chant and liturgical practices with Russian ones, and telling the faithful they are really part of the Russian people).[117]

Nonetheless, Toth's own personal efforts effected the intra-Christian conversions of tens of thousands of his fellow Carpatho-Rusyns. Throughout his dedicated career of service to the Russian Orthodox Mission in America, Alexis Toth consistently argued that Orthodoxy was both the apostolic faith and the traditional religion of the Carpatho-Rusyn people. He joined this argument to the belief that the Carpatho-Rusyns were part of the Russian people, whose lives were furthered by the Tsar and the Russian Orthodox Church. In this way, Toth looked to restore the pre-*unia* Orthodox Church of the Carpatho-Rusyns. In many ways, the Carpatho-Rusyn resistance against Hungarian and Latin Catholics was a matter of preserving their culture and their Eastern Rite tradition. Here, the point expressed by Mlinar was important. The Carpatho-Rusyns knew themselves only as Orthodox, which enabled Toth to argue successfully that to be a Carpatho-Rusyn Eastern Christian meant they needed to turn to the Orthodox tradition of their ancestors.

Toth believed that the Orthodox faith was given to the Slavs and had her defenders in the Tsar and the Russian Orthodox Church. What needed to be done was not defend Eastern Catholic prerogatives, but to join the Russian Orthodox Church, where the Carpatho-Rusyns could see the Slavic Orthodox life continuing to exist. To further this end, Toth's tactics centered upon the Carpatho-Rusyn peasant immigrant rather than intellectuals, as evidenced by his responses to his Eastern Catholic critics, the manner in which he engaged prospective convert parishes, and his use and understanding of the role of church publications.

It could be tempting to claim Toth became Orthodox simply because he was a Russophile, but this would not do justice to the theological aspects of his conversion, aspects he himself highlighted as important. He could have lived as a pan-Slavist and remained an Eastern Catholic, but the ecclesiological imperative was too great. He believed Eastern Catholicism was a schism from the Orthodox Church and if the Carpatho-Rusyns returned to Orthodoxy, their conversion would end that schism. It was not enough simply to preserve their Eastern Rite. For Toth, there were four main groups: the Orthodox Church, the Eastern Catholics, the Roman Catholics, and the Protestants. Three of the four were in schism. Only the Orthodox Church preserved the Orthodox tradition fully intact.

The American context proved to be important for both Toth and the Carpatho-Rusyn conversions to that Orthodox tradition in two ways. First, from a Roman Catholic ecclesiastical perspective, the American situation was too reminiscent of the Old World situation. In Hungary, Magyarization had created a difficult situation for the Eastern Catholic Carpatho-Rusyns. In America, Toth and his fellow Carpatho-Rusyn immigrants encountered a combination of factors at play in the Roman Catholic Church that created a situation no less tolerable. On the one hand, Americanists like Ireland desired to create a Catholic Church that would be more accommodating to American society. It is not difficult to find motivations for this. A Protestant centric perspective affected public perceptions and even immigration laws.[118] Non-Western rites and languages and cultures were too un-American in character for many in the Catholic Church in America at that time. Additionally, Roman Catholic clergy in America did not wish to accept a married priesthood. Given that opposition to Eastern Catholics included even the bishops and priests who opposed Americanism, one should also allow for cultural and ethnic prejudice as a factor.

Second, the American context provided for the freedom necessary for Eastern Catholic immigrants to safely enter the Russian Orthodox Church as a way of preserving their Eastern Christian tradition. In America, church and state were much more independent than the situation within the Austro-Hungarian Empire. Moreover, as noted in the introduction, American Christianity has an anti-traditional tradition of restoration, of looking back to an idealized period of church history and attempting to restore that same church. Although Toth was not operating out of an American Protestant restorationist movement, he did utilize his religious freedom in America to prioritize the Eastern Christian church of the first nine centuries and argued that that was the same church that had Christianized the Slavs and therefore was the same church to which the Carpatho-Rusyns should return. While some Protestant restorationists might look to America as the biblical city on a hill, Toth looked to the Russian Orthodox Church as the entity that was to promote and defend all Slavs and, ultimately, all Orthodox Christians worldwide, thus becoming a beacon even to the non-Orthodox.

In this way, the Toth Movement anticipates the conversions that follow in the later chapters but with one key difference. The Toth Movement was addressing an Old World dilemma in a New World (American) context. The conversions of Morgan, Berry, Gillquist, and those who followed them, however, will directly enter into the American Christian restoration anti-traditional tradition itself as a way to reestablish their theological bearings and then formally turn to tradition itself.

FR. RAPHAEL MORGAN AND EARLY

AFRICAN AMERICAN ORTHODOXY

ON AUGUST 15/28, 1907, THE Feast of Dormition, a black Jamaican immigrant to the United States was ordained to the Orthodox priesthood in Constantinople.[1] This marked the culmination of a journey in search of the "true church." On that day, Robert Josias Morgan was ordained as Fr. Raphael and became the first man of African American descent born in the New World to be ordained in the Orthodox Church. One scholar found Morgan's story so incredible that he wrote, "the Morgan story is so utterly improbable that one tends to dismiss it as a hoax."[2] On the other hand, the journal *Epiphany* included a brief summary of Morgan's story in a special volume dedicated to "African-American Orthodoxy."[3] In the introduction, the editor noted that while sources for Morgan's story were not extensive, they were substantial enough to prove his story was no hoax. The editor went on to speculate about possible motives for Morgan's conversion and how Morgan may have understood his own conversion from the Protestant Episcopal Church to the Greek Orthodox Church.[4]

Morgan's ordination and subsequent ministry within the Orthodox Church was a considered response to the difficult situation black Americans faced, often being viewed as second class even within somewhat integrated churches, as was the case for his own Protestant Episcopal Church. One might expect that Morgan would have turned to one of the historically black churches in America, of which he had knowledge. One might alternatively think that if none of those were appropriate for him, he would seek to establish his own church. As this chapter shows, however, Morgan sought a different solution, one not grounded in the anti-traditional tradition but in the tradition of Orthodox Church, which he entered by the gate of restorationism.

Although he initially considered an independent church, in keeping with American restorationism, and hoped for a furthering of ecumenical relations between Anglicanism and Orthodoxy, Morgan soon decided against such a move. Rather than continue the tradition of breaking from one's previous tradition to join or start another sect in an attempt to restore the early Church, Morgan looked an outside tradition that could serve as a grounding, even critique, of that very anti-traditional tradition. The Orthodox tradition offered Morgan precisely that, for he saw it as a tradition that could stand on its own apart from the racial problems that beset Western Christianity. Indeed, he saw the Orthodox tradition as standing authoritatively *prior* to Western Christianity.

Morgan's religious journey is an American one, though it has roots in the Caribbean. Unfortunately, we can only but sketch Morgan's life prior to his arrival in America, though one early biography does seem based on correspondence with Morgan.[5] The date of his birth is not known, but sometime around 1869 seems likely.[6] Morgan was born in Chapelton, Clarendon, Jamaica, to Robert Josias and Mary

Ann (Johnson) Morgan, though his father died when Morgan was but six months old.[7] Although he had a dark skin tone (according to both photographs and source descriptions), he was actually of mixed racial heritage.[8] According to both biographies, Morgan traveled extensively. Eventually, he ended up at Freetown, Sierra Leone, where he became a school teacher and was appointed as a lay-reader under Samuel David Ferguson, the bishop of the Protestant Episcopal Church in Liberia.[9] He later went to England, where he possibly studied at King's College, University of London and Saint Aidan's Theological College, Birkenhead.[10]

MORGAN IN THE PROTESTANT EPISCOPAL CHURCH IN AMERICA

In 1895, he came to America and was ordained a deacon in the diocese of Delaware, by Bishop Leighton Coleman, a bishop known for opposing racism.[11] He was subsequently assigned to be honorary curate at St. Matthew's Protestant Episcopal Church in Wilmington, Delaware.[12] Gavin White noted that Morgan served St. Matthew's from 1896 to 1897, subsequently serving in Charleston, West Virginia from 1897 to 1901, in Richmond, Virginia, from 1901 to 1905, in Nashville, Tennessee in 1905, and finally in Philadelphia in 1906 at the Church of the Crucifixion.[13]

A close examination of his movements during this time demonstrates that Morgan moved within the same circle of black clergymen that included Rev. George Alexander McGuire (who would later go on to lead the African Orthodox Church, which shall be discussed further below). Morgan may have even known McGuire personally.[14] Their points of contact and overlap provide a strong circumstantial case in favor of this. McGuire had been Morgan's predecessor in Richmond, having served until November of 1900. They both served at the Church of the Crucifixion in Philadelphia. McGuire served there in the 1890s, under Rev. Henry L. Phillips while Morgan served the Church of the Crucifixion several years later in 1906.[15] From 1902–1905, McGuire served as rector at St. Thomas's Protestant Episcopal Church in Philadelphia.[16] A.C.V. Cartier, a personal friend of Morgan, served as rector of St. Thomas Protestant Episcopal Church after McGuire left. Morgan and McGuire also had an important mutual acquaintance in Rev. George F. Bragg. Bragg included Morgan in his work on African American church leaders. In a letter to the editor of the *Living Church*, Bragg both referred to himself as a "friend and admirer" of McGuire and raised Morgan as another example of an African American who left the Protestant Episcopal Church in search of Orthodox holy orders.[17] All of these men were serving within African American parishes of the Protestant Episcopal Church.

It was while moving within this very circle that Morgan would have first encountered the idea of turning to Orthodox Christianity. Serving within the Episcopal Church at the time was a difficult undertaking for African Americans inasmuch as ordination to the priesthood was often slow in coming and when it did, they were always under white bishops, even if such bishops were the likes of Leighton Coleman. In conjunction with the racist context in which he lived, however, Morgan also had some unanswered theological questions. He shared with one of his early biographers that he had doubts concerning his service to the Protestant Episcopal Church (indeed, to the larger Anglican Communion), but doubts that were not (interestingly) primarily racial, but theological:

> For many years he maintained serious doubts concerning the teachings of the whole Anglican Communion; the change that came over him resulted in more than three years of special study of Anglicanism; . . . It was his final conviction that the Holy Greek Church is the pillar and ground of truth.[18]

Much is truncated here, of course, and it is unknown whether that is due to Morgan, his biographer (Mather), or both. What can be known, however, is that these doubts were quite legitimate and carried more than just a racial component. Or, to put it another way, the racism he experienced was about to be addressed fundamentally as a *theological* problem.

Within his circle of black Episcopalian clergy an Eastern Christian answer came to the fore, being first made in 1898, when Rev. George F. Bragg argued that an Eastern Christian episcopal succession, as exemplified by one Joseph René Vilatte's non-Chalcedonian consecration, could well prove important to African American concerns.[19] Vilatte was one of many *Episcopi Vagantes*, or bishops-at-large, who have characterized a subset of American Christianity. The thinking at the time seemed to be that if African Americans themselves could obtain apostolic succession through the consecration by Vilatte, then perhaps an independent African American church with African American leadership could be established. Vilatte's case suggested to Bragg (and, as we shall, Morgan and McGuire as well) that there might be an opportunity to create a new religious identity that could be authentically African American and fully traditional.

On the face of it, this seems to be a remarkable suggestion, for Vilatte has the dubious distinction of being known
as "the direct or indirect progenitor of more than twenty
schismatic churches."[20] A Frenchman who immigrated to
Canada, Vilatte fell under the spell of Pastor Chiniquy, a
former Roman Catholic priest-turned-Protestant-minister
convinced Vilatte to journey to Green Bay, Wisconsin, to
minister to Belgian settlers "drifting from Romanism into
spiritism and infidelity."[21] Vilatte worked under the auspices of Bishop J. H. Hobart Brown, the Protestant Episcopal
bishop of Fond du Lac. Brown soon provided Vilatte with a
letter to Bishop Herzog in Berne for the purpose of acquiring
Old Catholic succession.[22] Vilatte believed that if he could be
ordained by an Old Catholic bishop, he could claim to have
apostolic succession. He was subsequently ordained to the
Old Catholic priesthood in Switzerland and returned to Wisconsin, serving as the head of a sort of Old Catholic mission
of the Protestant Episcopal Church.

Vilatte soon had a falling out with the next bishop of
Fond du Lac, Bishop Charles Chapman Grafton, for trying
to obtain episcopal consecration in the Old Catholic Church
and then in the Russian Orthodox Church through Bishop
Vladimir. In 1892, Vilatte was consecrated by a Portuguese
group in communion with the non-Chalcedonian patriarch
of Antioch, Peter III, though no certificate of ordination
exists.[23] Eventually, he would be driven out by his congregants in Wisconsin, travel throughout Europe, and return to
America again, all the while trying to join one church after another. He also attempted to found Old Catholic jurisdictions
in England and America. He finally died in a monastery in
France, a reconciled layman in the Roman Catholic Church,
but on the verge of yet another ecclesiological escapade.[24]

Although such a career might strike us as merely unstable, what Vilatte brought to the table, and what was attractive to Bragg, was the idea of an apostolic succession beyond the bounds of the local white American church. Bragg was not alone, for Morgan shared this very same outlook, at least for a time. By 1906, Morgan was visiting the Greek Orthodox Church in Philadelphia as a member of Vilatte's very own church, "the American Catholic Church, an offshoot of the Protestant Episcopal Church."[25] The American anti-traditional tradition was luring Morgan. Here was the opportunity to break from his current church and join a new, indeed, a radically independent one. Doing so would mean continuing the tradition of anti-tradition and that was a real possibility for Morgan at the time, for by accepting Vilatte's church, even if but nominally, Morgan had come to act upon what Bragg had merely been willing to suggest. Morgan, however, was still interested in Orthodoxy as a tradition, as something more than merely a certificate of "apostolic succession," which seemed to be Vilatte's only concern. Morgan needed to learn more of Orthodox Christianity itself, however, and to do this, he ventured a trip to Russia.

THE TRIP TO RUSSIA

In 1904, Robert Josias Morgan published an open letter in the *Russian Orthodox American Messenger* as "a legally consecrated cleric of the American Episcopal Church."[26] In this letter, Morgan thanked the Russian Orthodox people for their sincere hospitality during his month-long visit to examine the life of the Orthodox Church in Russia. As he put it:

I came to Russia in no way to represent anything, and I was
not sent by anybody. I came as a simple tourist, chiefly with the
object to see the churches and the monasteries of this country,
to enjoy the ritual and the service of the holy Orthodox
Church, about which I heard so much abroad.[27]

We know that Morgan's black Episcopalian circle of friends
already considered Orthodox Christianity as an option, but
why the Russian Orthodox Church specifically? Aside from
any possible knowledge of positive Anglican–Orthodox relations,[28] he may have had secondhand knowledge of the positive treatment of people of African descent in the Russian
Empire.

It may not be common knowledge today, but Russia
was, for those of African descent, "a land of opportunity
where they could not only survive, but could attain high
social position."[29] Although the Russian Empire contained
African settlements in the country of Georgia, the cases of
black servants and visitors proves most relevant to Morgan's own journey. It had been common practice for upper-
class Russians to give slaves their freedom once arriving in
Russia even before other countries had outlawed slavery.[30]
Given Morgan's travels and the African American presence
in the shipping industry at the time, it would not be at all
unusual for Morgan to have learned of Russia's hospitality toward blacks. Morgan was hardly alone in traveling
to Russia as one of African descent. What made his journey unique was not that he traveled to Russia nor that he
was treated hospitably and kindly, but that he undertook
the journey for the purposes of pursuing a religious quest.
He may have traveled as a "simple tourist" rather than
an official church diplomat, but his purpose was of great

importance to him, for not long after, he would become an Orthodox Christian.

According to Morgan, his initial concerns in 1904 centered upon the question of Anglican–Orthodox union, as seen in his message of thanks to the Russian Orthodox for their kindness and hospitality:

> I leave your country with a feeling of profound gratitude and take back to North America all the good impressions I received here. And when there I shall speak boldly and loudly about the brotherly feelings entertained here in the bosom of the holy Orthodox Church towards its Anglican sister of North America, and about the prayers which are offered here daily for the union of all Catholic Christendom. My constant humble prayer is for the union of all Churches, and especially for the union of the Anglican faith with the Orthodox Church of Russia. I solicited the Metropolitans and the Bishops to grant me their blessing in regard to this prayer and obtained it. Now I pray daily and eagerly for a better mutual understanding between the character and their union. . . . In conclusion I must say, that my stay in Russia did me personally much good: I feel now much firmer and stronger spiritually than I did before I came.[31]

It would seem that in 1904, he was hoping that Anglican–Orthodox union might offer some sort of a solution for the African Americans, though he did not specifically state how he thought that might work. Indeed, it is doubtful the readers of the *Russian American Messenger* would have even been able to appreciate his situation. It is also unclear exactly how the Russian trip fit into his doubts concerning the legitimacy of the Anglican Communion more generally, though he did call the Russian Orthodox Church the "Apostolic" church of Russia.[32]

Readers certainly could tell Morgan had found, in Orthodox Christianity, something he believed would benefit the Anglican Communion and the Protestant Episcopal Church in particular. He had discovered a spiritual depth that permeated his own being and one he had seen within the Russian people as a whole. Morgan claimed to feel spiritually "firmer and stronger" and wrote, "it would seem as if the Christian religion penetrated the whole life of the people."[33] What Morgan had not experienced in America, he had experienced in Russia—a church that truly loved him, a Jamaican immigrant to America of African descent. In the Protestant Episcopal Church in America, he was a second-class citizen who sought a better religious identity. On his trip, he was received by the Russians with "their gentleness, their politeness, their amiability, and kindness," a reception he linked directly to the Russian Orthodox faith.[34]

It is clear that when Morgan left Russia with his personal mission of spreading the good news of the love of Orthodoxy for Anglican Christians, he left with some knowledge of Orthodox Christianity and already demonstrated evidence of one who was likely soon to convert. Concerning a possible Anglican–Orthodox union, Morgan asked his reader to "solicit the prayers of the Saints" and the "intercession of the holy Mother of God" and went so far as to write, "Virgin Mary, pray for us!"[35] This does not sound like a typical Protestant. He also asked that God grant Emperor Nicholas II and his family "a long life, peace and prosperity."[36] This phrase comes from the beginning of intoning "God grant you many years," a traditional Orthodox hymn. Although one should not make too much of this, it suggests that Morgan had begun to develop an intimate knowledge of Orthodox traditions and worship.

CONVERSION AND THE ORDER
OF THE CROSS OF GOLGOTHA

Following his return from Russia, Morgan began developing a close relationship with the local Greek Orthodox clergy in Philadelphia. The priest mentioned in the 1906 newspaper article noted above was Rev. Theodore Prussianos, who was a missionary priest traveling from parish to parish. His tenure in Philadelphia was short-lived. The subsequent priest, Rev. Demetrios Petrides, developed a relationship with Morgan and went so far as to advocate on Morgan's behalf before the Ecumenical Patriarch in Constantinople. Morgan's approach to his situation had shifted. No longer was he presenting himself as one interested in unity between Anglicanism and Orthodoxy. He was looking to become Orthodox and, as we shall see, to bring Orthodox Christianity to those of African descent in America, be they from the Caribbean or America proper. The Orthodox tradition was about to provide him with the opportunity for religious identity creation par excellence. By looking to the Orthodox tradition, he was breaking out of the anti-traditional tradition exemplified in Vilatte's movement and finding a platform from which he could stand over and against the entirety of Western Christianity, whether the Anglo-Catholic tradition or the American anti-traditional tradition, which characterized the likes of both Vilatte and even black Protestant denominations.

In June 1907, the Holy Synod of Constantinople received a letter from Petrides recommending Morgan for ordination and the minutes of the July 1907 meeting contain a discussion of Morgan's case.[37] Documents pertaining to Morgan's ordination provide a general outline of the events.[38] In July, the synod approved Morgan's request to be baptized and subsequently ordained to the diaconate and priesthood.[39] Morgan's case caused a stir in the local Greek population, as over 3,000 people attended his baptism.[40] The synod provided for Morgan's travel, vestments, liturgical books, a cross, and also granted him the right to hear confessions.[41] Despite this, Morgan's request for an antimension (i.e., an altar cloth with a bishop's signature) and holy chrism, for annointing the newly baptized, were denied.[42] These were denied because the synod wished for Morgan to serve under Petrides until he was, in fact, ready to open and serve in a separate parish.

Although his request was denied, Morgan's request for these items suggests that Morgan had a larger goal for his own conversion. Becoming Orthodox was not merely a matter of a personal religious journey. His outlook was evangelistic. The goal was to take the Orthodox tradition, which was "apostolic" and yet neither a restorationism such as Vilatte's church,[43] nor even Western, nor chained down by a legacy of racial segregation, and bring it to blacks in North America.

In fact, an evangelistic fervor characterized his initial actions upon returning to Philadelphia. According to the minutes from February 1908, Morgan returned and baptized his wife and children, though Annunciation Greek Orthodox Church of Philadelphia contains no records of this.[44] Then, in November of 1908, Morgan recommended his old friend Rev. A. C. V. Cartier for ordination into the Orthodox Church, but the request seems to have produced no attempts to pursue Cartier as a candidate for the Orthodox priesthood.[45] Most likely, the request was misplaced or forgotten because it was made just when the jurisdiction of the Greeks in America had been transferred from Constantinople to the Church of Greece.

FR. RAPHAEL MORGAN | 73

For Morgan, there was clarity, and not just from the Orthodox side. For in that same year, the Protestant Episcopal Church announced that he was suspended as a deacon.[46] For Morgan, there would be no turning back as the break with his previous tradition was now clear and obvious to all. He had turned to tradition.

Unfortunately for Morgan and his family, his frequent ministry assignments and marital disputes took its toll, and in 1909 his wife, Charlotte, filed for divorce.[47] Yet, Morgan did not let this turn of events completely dissuade him. In 1911, he journeyed to Athens, almost certainly to be tonsured a monk. This is suggested by at least two things. First, the Ellis Island ship records list Morgan as single, which fits his divorced status as of 1909, but also displays the name "Father, Raphael," which was then corrected by someone to "Morgan, Raphael."[48] In addition, Mather, one of his early biographers (and again, who seems to have received his information by way of correspondence with Morgan) noted specifically that "the family name of Morgan has been dropped and should never be used in addressing him."[49] The only times Morgan traveled to Greece or Constantinople were at his ordination and his 1911 trip, and since he was still married when ordained, it seems quite likely he was tonsured on his 1911 trip.

Morgan now had more of the authority and freedom that he sought to spread his message of the importance of the Orthodox tradition both as a response to racial inequalities within Western Christianity, especially the Anglican Communion, and as the bearer of the apostolic faith. In 1913, he even returned to Jamaica in order to deliver lectures throughout the country, something he had done on at least two previous occasions prior to becoming Orthodox (once in 1901 and again in 1902).[50] From the newspaper accounts, it seems that Morgan used the lecture circuit to support himself while he investigated the possibility of establishing an Orthodox Church in Jamaica.[51]

After spending a little over a year in Jamaica, he returned to America, though an article claimed Morgan intended to return to Jamaica to "start mission work under his Faith."[52] Morgan had, by this time, been active among a group of Syrian Orthodox Christians in Jamaica. Morgan had even informed the *Gleaner* that he was in contact with "the Syrian Orthodox Bishop of Brooklyn," which would have been Bishop Raphael (Hawaweeny), who held the post from 1904 until his death in 1915.[53] Incidentally, at one point on his Jamaican mission, he was able to rekindle his Russian connection, concelebrating a divine liturgy on board the Russian Warship *Rossija*, together with the ship's chaplain, with the service "sung in Russian for the benefit . . . of the Russians and in English for the benefit of the Syrians."[54]

When Morgan returned to Philadelphia after lecturing and attempting to establish a more permanent mission in Jamaica, his efforts bore some fruit. In 1916, Morgan penned an open letter that directly demonstrate the extent of his efforts and provides us with an important look into how he saw the Orthodox tradition as responding to the racial concerns of his day. Morgan had chosen to argue against Marcus Garvey.[55] Garvey, who was himself from Jamaica, had founded the Universal Negro Improvement Association in 1914 in order to unite all Africans and those of African descent scattered throughout the world. He had arrived in America in March, 1916, in order to go on the lecture circuit and raise money.[56] Morgan wrote his open letter almost immediately. Allowing himself but a brief introduction,

Morgan launched into the central arguments. Thirteen other Jamaican-Americans co-signed Morgan's letter to Garvey.[57] Morgan himself signed as the head of the Order of the Cross of Golgotha, making it likely that the other thirteen Jamaicans were also members.

Two of Morgan's arguments stand out in particular. First, Morgan objected that Garvey "drew a deplorable picture of the prejudice of the Englishman in Jamaica against the blacks, portraying hypocrisy and deceit of his attitude towards blacks, and stated his preference for the prejudice of the American to that of the Englishman."[58] Morgan approached the problem of racial concerns primarily through an ecclesiastical lens. In American church life, Morgan had not found racial harmony, but rather the opportunity to forge and offer a new religious identity to African Americans, one grounded in the Orthodox tradition. Second, Morgan objected to Garvey's rejection of racially mixed marriages. Garvey had pressed for a pan-Africanism with an anti-white tenor, but Morgan did not view race relations in this manner and given his own racially mixed background, Morgan had to have been offended by the comments Garvey made concerning mixed heritage and mixed marriages.

Morgan was as committed to African American concerns as Garvey, but from a specifically religious context. He had placed his hope not in a return to Africa or pan-Africanism, but in Orthodox Christianity, a Christianity that not only ordained him to the priesthood but gave him the charge of reaching out to other African Americans. When he became Orthodox, he forged a new identity and did so with the intention of spreading the Orthodox faith amongst fellow African Americans, going so far as to recommend A. C. V Cartier as a candidate for the Orthodox priesthood.

There was no need to unite around Africa, for the answer was theological. The answer was a tradition that could be seen as untainted, as even prior, to the racially segregated Christianity of the West. For as Morgan told his biographer Mather, his initial doubts led him to pursue three years of historical and theological searching, from which he concluded that the "pillar and ground of truth" was the Orthodox Church.[59] That was not something American restorationism, with its independently formed churches, could normally bring, but American restorationism had, in fact, led Morgan to believe that a grounding in an ongoing tradition was precisely what was needed.

This would be the last time the public would hear from Morgan. The last year he appeared in the city directory of Philadelphia was 1916.[60] The 1921–1922 *Negro Year Book* contains a paragraph dedicated to Morgan, but it reads identically to the 1912 version and therefore does not necessarily indicate that Morgan was still alive. Morgan cannot be found in the U.S. census for 1920, so if he was still living in 1921–1922, he was most likely in Jamaica. Still, there is no further mention made of him in the Kingston *Gleaner*, suggesting that Morgan died in 1916–1917.

THE LEGACY OF THE ORTHODOX TRADITION AMONG AFRICAN AMERICANS

Morgan's immediate and direct efforts to bring the Orthodox tradition as a solution to black Christians in North America yielded little fruit other than baptizing his own family and establishing a small lay fraternity known as the Cross of

Golgotha (about which we know nothing other than that it consisted of a handful of Jamaican immigrants such as himself). Despite this, he had trail-blazed a path that was soon to become popular. In 1921, George Alexander McGuire established the African Orthodox Church, designating himself Patriarch Alexander when he was formally elected to lead the new religious body. Moreover, McGuire would establish the African Orthodox Church, through his consecration at the hands of the wandering bishop noted above, Joseph René Vilatte.

McGuire had initially been the chaplain for Garvey's Universal Negro Improvement Association (UNIA) before they had a falling out and McGuire pursued his ecclesiological endeavors independent of Garvey. McGuire patterned the services and church structure of the African Orthodox Church after that of the Anglican Church, but with a theological eye toward the historic Orthodox Church. For example, the African Orthodox Church did not include the *filioque* clause in the Nicene Creed.[61] Just as the African Methodist Episcopal Church and the African Methodist Episcopal Zion Church adapted the Methodist Church, so the African Orthodox Church adapted Anglicanism and Orthodoxy, creating what was to be a Western Rite Orthodoxy for people of African descent. McGuire sought to establish a church with an episcopal structure that would be headed by those of African descent and the African Orthodox Church even established a presence in Africa. For this work, McGuire consecrated Archbishop Daniel William Alexander. The African Orthodox Church grew quickly, establishing a seminary and a journal, *The Negro Churchman*. Although the African Orthodox Church had grown significantly during his lifetime, after McGuire's death in 1934, the church was unable to continue this momentum and today, the church exists as a small denomination with a presence in America and South Africa.[62]

It is McGuire's connection to Marcus Garvey's UNIA and the early years of the African Orthodox Church that has received the most scholarly attention. What Morgan's story helps highlight is the extent to which the African Orthodox Church was flanked by the Orthodox Churches themselves, being a factor when the African Orthodox Church began in 1921 and in 1946, when the Kenyan contingency of the African Orthodox Church formally entered the Greek Orthodox Church.

We have already seen that McGuire moved in the same social circles as the first known African American Orthodox priest, Fr. Raphael Morgan. Indeed, when one considers that McGuire was part of a circle that included George F. Bragg and A. C. V. Cartier, both of whom were also interested in Eastern Christian apostolic succession, McGuire proves to be not as unique as is sometimes thought, but rather perhaps just more successful in carrying out the endeavor. Indeed, accounting for this circle of African American members of the Protestant Episcopal Church in America in the late nineteenth and early twentieth centuries helps avoid the false dichotomy found in the secondary literature that seeks to determine whether the idea of the African Orthodox Church was Garvey's or McGuire's.[63] In reality, the answer is neither. The answer was a small group dynamic, suggested by George F. Bragg and first enacted by Raphael Morgan.[64]

The trailblazer who established the iconic path was not McGuire, as is commonly thought, but Raphael Morgan. Indeed, Morgan went farther than McGuire in one key respect. For McGuire, Eastern Christianity was merely a means to further the American anti-traditional tradition in a particular, African American restorationism. Thus, Eastern Christianity was merely a means to take from one's preceding tradition and establish a new denomination from that, thus perpetuating a tradition of change. When Morgan looked to Eastern Christianity, he may have initially also had eyes guided by a primitivistic pursuit but soon came to see the Orthodox Church as its own tradition. Morgan had considered Vilatte's church and moved on. McGuire thought another denomination was the answer.

One gets a sense for this even in September of 1921, when George Alexander McGuire was elected to head a group of independent black Episcopal parishes. McGuire took the title patriarch and a new name, Alexander, his middle name, being henceforth called Patriarch Alexander (similarly to how Morgan, in following Orthodox tradition, dropped his surname and went only by Fr. Raphael after his monastic tonsure). At McGuire's convention, there was a contingency from the Russian Orthodox Church, which had a well established presence in North America by 1921, thanks in large part to the conversions of Carpatho-Rusyn immigrants under Alexis Toth, as discussed in the last chapter, and new waves of immigrants and refugees. McGuire had even initially attempted to bring his African Orthodox Church into the Russian Orthodox Church. Ultimately, he did not do so, likely because he would have been placed under the leadership of non-Africans. McGuire wanted the African Orthodox Church to exist as an autonomous or autocephalous church. One of the representatives of the Russian Orthodox Church was one Fr. Anthony (Robert F. Hill) who, shortly after being given the assignment of attending the convention, affiliated himself with the African Orthodox

Church and later established an independent church in Harlem. Given that the African Orthodox Church allowed officiating roles exclusively to those of African descent, it would seem that Hill himself was an African American. Hill had been a clergyman at the Holy Transfiguration chapel, a chapel established by the efforts of Fr. Nathaniel (Ingram N. W.) Irvine and included other converts from the Protestant Episcopal Church.[65]

Better accounting for the African American circle that looked to the Orthodox tradition (and Raphael Morgan particularly) makes McGuire's own efforts feel less idiosyncratic (though also less original), but it is worth noting that the interest in the Orthodox tradition did not end there. Indeed, the African Orthodox Church itself eventually led thousands of Africans into the Greek Orthodox Church. The establishment of the African Orthodox Church in Africa occurred when Daniel William Alexander was elected bishop of a group of former members of the independent African Church in September 1924 in South Africa.[66] Alexander had learned of the African Orthodox Church through Garvey's UNIA journal, *Negro World*, and within days of becoming the head of a small church, he sent a petition to McGuire on behalf of himself and the four priests and congregations under his supervision.[67] McGuire responded warmly, and by October 1924, Alexander's church was functioning as a member of the African Orthodox Church. Alexander viewed the mission of the African Orthodox Church much in the same light as McGuire, omitting the *filioque* and noting, "the East and the West have met each other in the African Orthodox Church."[68] Alexander pressed to be recognized as a bishop and in 1927, he traveled to Boston, where McGuire, assisted by two of his bishops, consecrated Alexander.[69]

Alexander made his headquarters in Kimberley, South Africa, and began the task of evangelization.

Believing that within the African Orthodox Church, the East and West intersected, Alexander contacted Metropolitan Isidore, the Greek Orthodox bishop of Johannesburg:

> I herewith take this opportunity in writing to you, and to forward to your Grace the following questionnaire which we hope you will deign to answer, that they may be answered at our recent Synod which meets in December next . . . The African Orthodox Church having been organized particularly to reach the deepest parts of Africa and its people and implanting the true Orthodox Faith in them . . . that as much as we desire intercommunion we express the hope that the name African Orthodox be not interfered with, and its principles remain intact . . . that the control of the African Orthodox Church and its affairs shall always remain in the hands of an African Episcopate, except in complicated matters affecting the teaching and Faith of the Church, when the matter shall be referred to the Orthodox Communities for adjustment and advice. That since our people are not used to the Eastern habit of vesting and worshipping, the African Orthodox Church resolves to gradually introduce the Eastern Church Rituals.[70]

Alexander's attempt to facilitate intercommunion ultimately failed. We do not know how Metropolitan Isidore responded at that time, but the synod was held in December without any response from the patriarchate of Alexandria, something that disappointed Alexander and his synod.[71] A year later, in a letter concerning another matter, Metropolitan Isidore noted a defection from the African Orthodox Church that was in progress by stating, "I do not think you forget that your Christians in Uganda in Rhodesia and here applied to us to come in our church and become its members. And our church is oblige [sic] to examine their petitions, and accept them and establish greek orthodox mission."[72] The African Orthodox Church was about to lose a significant amount of its membership to the Greek Orthodox Church because of the instigation of Reuben Spartas.

Reuben Spartas established the African Orthodox Church in Uganda after a spiritual journey of his own. Born Reuben Sebbanja Ssedimba in a village near Kampala, Uganda, he later took the name Sparta, and then its masculine form, Spartas, due to his athletic prowess and being complimented by his primary school headmaster.[73] During his time at King's College in Budo, just outside of Kampala, Spartas reacted against the notion of "branch theory" and instead began "inquiring after the true old Church."[74] Initially, Spartas contacted Archbishop Daniel William Alexander and joined the African Orthodox Church.[75] In 1931, Alexander ordained Spartas to the priesthood and established the African Orthodox Church in Kenya.[76] It was not long, however, before Spartas and others looked to the Orthodox Church in Alexandria in spite of Alexander's desire to see intercommunion between the African Orthodox Church and the Orthodox Church of Alexandria.[77] Spartas had questioned the legitimacy of Alexander's episcopal succession.[78] Eventually, the African Orthodox Church of Kenya and many in Uganda would join the Orthodox Church through the patriarchate at Alexandria, though Spartas himself upheld a strong Ugandan nationalism and would later leave.[79] The Orthodox Church in Kenya grew rapidly until the 1950s, when it suffered through severe persecution at the hands of the British in Kenya in the 1950s.[80] Despite such struggles, the Orthodox Church of the Patriarch of Alexandria has rebuilt itself in Kenya and has approximately 280,000 members currently in

Africa.[81] The Greek Orthodox Church exists in Africa largely because of the African Orthodox Church and the undertakings of native Africans themselves.

CONCLUSION

Raphael Morgan's life and work provide us insight into just how multivalent the Orthodox tradition could become within the American context. Not only could the Orthodox tradition be the "true" tradition of one's ancestors, as in the case with the Carpatho-Rusyn converts beginning at the turn of the twentieth century, but so could the Orthodox tradition offer a tradition unencumbered by the heinous racial segregation of Western Christianity, as found in North America. Indeed, the Orthodox tradition, for Morgan, was *prior* to that racially segregated tradition, for Orthodoxy offered the "pillar and ground of truth." The American freedom for forging a religious identity spurred Morgan not to remain content to participate within the American anti-traditional tradition, as represented by Vilatte, nor to do so by creating his own church, but to turn to an established tradition completely outside of that model. Morgan turned to a tradition that could stand in critique of that very anti-traditional tradition model itself, for that model (at least to Morgan) remained largely bound to a highly segregated racist vision. Theologically, as well, the anti-traditional tradition did not seem to satisfy Morgan. Morgan utilized the American restorationist tradition to look to a church that was still in existence but with the ability to claim apostolic heritage.

His would not be the last attempt to bring the Orthodox tradition to African Americans, however. In the next chapter, we turn to a contemporary, Moses Berry, and his efforts to do just that through the Brotherhood of St. Moses the Black. As we shall see, Berry's efforts derive from a different context, answering different questions, but restorationism has a role to play in his conversion as well.

FR. MOSES BERRY AND THE ORDER

OF ST. MOSES THE BLACK

IN 1972, CARL BERRY TURNED 21 in a state penitentiary, serving time following a police raid in search of drugs. One night, not long into his sentence, the guards dragged out a man from a neighboring holding cell, wrapped a radio in a towel (in order to mask the nature and extent of the abuse) and beat the prisoner until he passed out. Every time the man passed out, one of the guards would urinate in his face to wake him and then they beat him again. Berry was so terrified that he went to the corner of his cell and offered a prayer up to God. According to Berry, it was possibly the most heartfelt prayer he has prayed before or since. He asked God for a miracle—anything—that could spare him a similar fate and pleaded to be let out somehow, in order to escape the beatings that would surely come sooner or later. The following morning, a guard came to his cell, told Berry to get out and dress, informing him that Berry was free to go. At first, Berry thought it was a trick, that he would be beaten and/or killed for supposedly trying to escape. As it turned out, the night before, around the time that Berry was praying, one of his arresting officers came forward and confessed to the illegality of the search of the residence in which Berry had been arrested. The evidence was illegally obtained and Berry was free to go.[1]

Upon his release, Berry would undergo a religious journey that eventually led to him being ordained in the Orthodox Church as Fr. Moses.[2] In this journey, Berry addressed racial concerns in a theological manner with a turn toward tradition, as Morgan had approximately 80 years prior. In Berry's case, however, there are a few unique differences. Berry's racial concerns, as we shall see, were neither about finding a church in which to serve as a black man nor about addressing different responses to the American and Caribbean racial inequalities. Oppression was not his overriding concern. Rather, multiracial and multi-ethnic representation and a desire for an "otherworldly" Christianity guided his journey.

As this chapter will show, Berry's emphasis on other-worldly Christianity was grounded in a restorationist vision, for he had come to believe that early Christian Egypt was important in this regard. He believed that one needed to return to a pre-racist Christianity, as exemplified in the early church's promotion of Egyptian monasticism. This restorationist vision became the means of turning to the Orthodox tradition, because Berry came to perceive the Orthodox Church to be the church that continued in full continuity with early Egyptian Christianity. As such, Eastern Orthodoxy was understood as *the* Christian tradition itself, thus being able to stand as a response over and against a denominationally and racially fragmented American Christianity, even if members of that very Orthodox Church sometimes exhibited the racial fragmentation of American society. Such a move is certainly an atypical choice in America, given the prevalence of an American anti-traditional tradition. Ironically, however, Berry's journey, like the others discussed in this book, may be seen as continuing an important element of that anti-traditional tradition for he was able to turn to an ongoing tradition only by first living the anti-traditional tradition, including restorationism.

THE FLOWER GARDEN AND OTHERWORLDLY CHRISTIANITY

When Berry was young, his mother told him that all of humanity are like flowers in God's garden.[3] This resulted in an ongoing search: "My question over the past years has been, why then haven't I heard about the brown, black, yellow, and red flowers that make up the Church?"[4] He felt uprooted, as though wherever he went, there were only certain types of flowers—in A.M.E. parishes or other black churches he would visit, it was one kind. In another parish, it might be a lot of white lilies, but nowhere had he found the garden of which his grandmother spoke. Berry admitted that his life had been rootless in other ways as well, but took a heightened religious form following his experience in prison.

Overwhelmed with the ordeal, Berry went to Hawaii to escape and reflect on what had happened. There, he came to appreciate the writings of George Washington Carver, connecting with Carver's emphasis on the presence of God in nature. Berry's prison experience had led him to believe that even though God transcended our world, he really could be anywhere, even a prison cell. Berry's experience of the natural beauty of Hawaii confirmed in him his desire to find the church that also worshipped and believed in a transcendent God who nonetheless permeates absolutely everything, lifting it up to himself in glory in a new, redemptive light.

At the same time that Berry was looking for a flower garden rather than a vase of one kind of flower, he was seeking an expression of "otherworldly Christianity." Berry first learned of "otherworldly Christian values" from his grandmother, Mamie, the daughter of the only black member of Missouri's Union Calvary Company D.[5] His other grandmother, Dorothy, taught him a similar perspective, informing him: "Don't forget that you are a minority in America, and this is not your world."[6] Berry has even gone so far as to blame many of the contemporary problems faced by African Americans on the failure to understand this. "We took our eye off the genuine prize, which is otherworldly Christianity, and we started focusing on what we could attain in this world. . . . They told our women that blondes have more fun, and lo and behold, the black woman dyed her hair. How absurd!"[7] This emphasis on otherworldliness was the theme of an article published only a year before, where he claimed, "The real 'spiritual trouble' began with social integration. I won't say that integration was the downfall of the black man in this country, but it did present a real problem. When we lived in a separate society it was very clear that we were "not of this world."[8] In his conference talk the following year, he reiterated this point.[9] Berry has also claimed that the "black church" had been redemptive, but ceased being so when it sold its soul to political causes that arose in the 1960s.[10]

FINDING THE OTHERWORLDLY FLOWER GARDEN

Initially, Berry joined the Holy Order of MANS (HOOM), a New Religious Movement with Christian, theological overtones, founded by Earl Blighton in the 1960s.[11] By the time Berry joined in the mid-1970s, HOOM had become more Christianized, but it still operated as an independent entity. At this stage in his journey, one clearly sees a typical American anti-tradition journey, whereby one does not follow an established tradition but joins a newly created entity in order to forge one's own religious identity. HOOM's Christianization was expressed precisely as a restorationist movement, as a reestablishment (reincarnation) of important apostolic figures, such as the biblical personalities of the 12 and Mary Magdalene.[12] Despite this, HOOM was not destined to remain merely one anti-tradition option among many, as evidenced by the increased attention to Christian teachings. Indeed, starting in the 1970s, HOOM would claim to continue a tradition of Christian teachings.

Berry became involved in HOOM and moved to Detroit in 1974 to study at HOOM's one-year institute known as Christ the Savior Seminary. Although not an accredited seminary or institution of higher learning, the informal school offered a year-long course of study that studied the early Church, the lives of Orthodox saints, and the Bible. He then spent the next several years moving around, which included serving a parish (Christian Community Parish in 1977) in Allston, a Boston suburb, and teaching youth in Harlem at a Protestant Episcopal Church in 1979.[13] He also served at a small teen shelter in Atlanta 1980 and then moved to St. Louis to pastor Christ the Good Shepherd, a parish that also subsequently became Orthodox and has now merged with St. Michael the Archangel Orthodox Church.[14] In all of this, Berry saw HOOM as offering an ecumenical, nondenominational means of re-engaging in the core values of the Christian tradition, including social outreach and education.

Soon thereafter, HOOM morphed into Christ the Savior Brotherhood by joining the St. Herman of Alaska

Brotherhood, co-founded by two monks of the Russian Orthodox Church Outside of Russia (ROCOR), Fr. (Abbot) Herman (Gleb Podmoshensky) and Fr. Seraphim (Eugene Rose).[15] Berry would go on to graduate from Christ the Savior Brotherhood's theological academy, known as the New Valaam Theological Academy (which offered a certificate following a four week summer course) in 1985.[16] Abbot Herman directed HOOM to a self-proclaimed bishop, one Metropolitan Pangratios Vrionis, who was actually a deposed Greek Orthodox priest (having been removed from his office due to pedophilia, for which he was convicted in a court of law). In 1988, shortly before Pascha, Pangratios baptized 750 members of HOOM into his "Orthodox" jurisdiction, resulting in the Christ the Savior Brotherhood.[17] Those 750 entrants were a culmination, not a beginning, as Berry had been ordained as a priest in Pangratios's jurisdiction in 1987.

For Berry, who prioritized an "otherworldly" Christian spirituality, HOOM and Christ the Savior Brotherhood were ideal, because mystery was emphasized and HOOM had structured lay communities across the country intended to be patterned after early Christian monastic communities. Podmoshensky himself advocated and highlighted a Christianity that was not chained to the world, but outside of it, even antagonistic to it, in his correspondence with Berry over the years. When Berry had been within Pangratios's church and a priest for but a year (in 1988), Podmoshensky wrote him a letter in which he spoke positively of the difficulties of living by physical work in a monastic setting on Spruce Island, Alaska.[18] A few years later, in 1993, Podmoshensky would go even farther, explicitly claiming, "persecution, rejection, unacceptance, no Christian love or understanding!! What else is new? . . . We must be persecuted by the world if you want to be accepted by Christ."[19] Berry's own spiritual father advocated for a kind of Orthodox Christianity that was at odds with the world around it.[20] Such an approach helped Berry see himself in line with the Christian tradition in a manner that could still be seen as otherworldly, inasmuch as it was in tension with the world around him.

As a member of Pangratios's self-styled Orthodox jurisdiction, Berry had taken on an Orthodox identity, but this was not an identity he initially desired, for he had been concerned that joining Pangratios's jurisdiction and accepting an Orthodox identity meant giving up on African American spirituality, especially with the two components he so desired to find (the flower garden metaphor fulfilled and an otherworldly Christian spirituality).[21] Yet, the experience of visiting a small Orthodox parish overwhelmed him and changed his mind.[22]

In the winter of 1984, while Herman Podmoshensky and the St. Herman Brotherhood were courting HOOM, Berry visited a small parish mission serving liturgy in a house. The liturgical language and praise pleasantly surprised him and the iconography, which included icons of St. Moses the Black and the Orthodox Chinese martyrs from the Boxer Rebellion, vividly expressed the catholicity of the Orthodox Church. Berry had found the garden for which he yearned in the midst of a liturgical context that included a reference point to early African Christianity and monasticism and which sought to lift the participant into heaven's very own worship itself. The striking, racially accurate iconography struck a cord with Berry, for as he would later claim: "If people don't have images of their racial group as being significant in the history of the Church, it is harder for them to strive within the Church for godliness."[23] More than that, he found iconography "otherworldly," in particular, the icon of St. Moses the Black, which left him "stunned by its terrible beauty and other-worldliness."[24]

Entering into Pangratios Vrionis's Archdiocese of Vasiloupolis (based in Queens, New York), Berry turned to the Orthodox Christian tradition, even if within a group the rest of the Orthodox world considered schismatic. He had found a representation of many races and ethnicities and a Christianity that was not entrapped by "the world," but expressed through art and music that evoked a feeling of transcendence within him. Moreover, he had entered a tradition, a tradition that preceded Anglocentric expressions of Christianity and so could be found through the restorationist tendencies first nurtured in HOOM. Berry claimed that the tradition of the evangelist Matthew's proselytizing in Africa, Athanasius the Great's consecration of Bishop Frumentius, and the presence of "countless Black saints and martyrs" all pointed to the importance of saints of African descent.[25] Berry learned of all of this after his encounter with the icon of St. Moses the Black. He had entered the American anti-traditional tradition by joining HOOM, a unique restorationist movement of the 1960s, and soon found himself pursuing the tradition of Orthodox Christianity.

NAVIGATING SCHISM AND EVANGELIZING AFRICAN AMERICANS

During his time within the Christ the Savior Brotherhood, Berry's activities increased significantly. One reason they did so had to do with his desire to bring Orthodox Christianity and African Americans together. For Berry, this was a very personal undertaking:

> The racism I found in the [Orthodox] Church was almost beyond my ability to endure. Once, I visited an Orthodox Church in St. Louis and asked if I could enter within to venerate the icons. I had heard that they had the most wonderful mosaics. I was told by the priest that I couldn't come into the church (although it was open). He went on to say that if I was interested in the Church, I would feel much more comfortable at the Coptic Church. This same priest, when asked by an interviewer on television why more people weren't joining the Orthodox Church, answered that the reason lay in obstructive immigration policies![26]

This event, which occurred a few years into his ministry while living in St. Louis, was especially hurtful to him because it related to the tension he felt between feeling he was Orthodox as a member of Christ the Savior Brotherhood and yet knowing he was not viewed as Orthodox by the actual Orthodox Churches themselves. His experience at this parish, of course, did nothing to encourage him to enter into one of the canonical jurisdictions, due to the racism he experienced.

Furthermore, as he looked at Orthodoxy in America, he also struggled to come to terms with the fact that Orthodoxy in North America consisted of so many different jurisdictions. Berry wrote, "There was divisiveness of an order that appalled me. Jurisdiction against jurisdiction, Old Calendar against New Calendar—some people saying even that the saints in Heaven prefer one over the other."[27] For Fr. Moses Berry, the Orthodox Church presented the same problems one could find anywhere—human sin—expressed in experiences of racism, administrative disunity, and legalistic debates. In response to this, Berry focused on what change he could effect and as he did this, he would eventually conclude that he needed to enter a canonical Orthodox Church.

In 1993, he helped guide a small Kansas City parish with an outreach ministry to racial minorities, "Reconciliation Ministries," into Pangratios Vrionis's jurisdiction.[28] That same year he also began holding annual conferences for the Brotherhood of St. Moses the Black.[29] A Lenten retreat in 1990 at St. Moses the Black Orthodox Church, also known as "St. Moses House," in Washington, D.C., provided Berry with the impetus for creating the Brotherhood of St. Moses the Black. This retreat was led by Elias Farajajé-Jones who was, at the time, an Orthodox priest of African American descent.[30] Farajajé-Jones encouraged Berry to pursue his idea of establishing the Brotherhood of St. Moses the Black, with regular, annual conferences to showcase "ancient Christianity and its deep African roots."[31]

The conferences were successful and in 1997, the Brotherhood of St. Moses the Black received funding for a book project, a publication of the essays from its fourth conference.[32] Berry himself contributed both an essay as well as the book's "final word."[33] As the book's subtitle indicated, the sole purpose of the essays was to connect ancient African Christianity with the African American experience. The emphasis on connecting African Christianity and African American experience has continued to resonate with the Brotherhood of St. Moses the Black. This is evidenced both in the annual conference presentations and in subsequent publications.[34]

For Berry, this has been vital because he linked "other-worldly Christian values" directly to the ancient Orthodox monastic tradition, especially in ancient Egypt and Africa. Commenting on the title of the book that published the conference's papers (*An Unbroken Circle*), Berry wrote, "Christ's Body, the Church, is also a circle. As this book has shown, not only are the people of Africa part of that circle, but they are a *key* part . . . By founding the monastic tradition, they preserved the otherworldliness of true Christianity."[35] Even Berry's solution to the problems faced by African American youth in contemporary culture may sound monastic to some: "Prayer and fasting are the only ways that we can begin to help our lost Black children of this day and age."[36]

Berry made this connection by linking the "old Black Church," especially as expressed during slavery in America, with the Christianity and monasticism of the early Christian period.[37] Slaves obtained a Christian faith from their white masters but their faith was in Christ himself and the older spirituals and hymnography were focused on salvation in the "world to come," not the world as it existed in their present moment. This vision has guided Berry to use the Brotherhood of St. Moses the Black to "root" and "nourish" African Americans "on the martyric experiences of their righteous Christian forefathers and foremothers, both in Africa and in America."[38] Doing this, Berry believed, meant being "at odds with the world," but being at odds meant not standing on one's own in one's own separate little group. Rather, "we cling to the Tradition of the Church as it has been preserved through the ages."[39] Berry sought not simply what could be labeled yet another expression of restorationism in the American anti-traditional tradition, but rather *the* Christian tradition, albeit one that preceded America itself and could connect African Americans today to their slave ancestors and even pre-slave African Christianity.

This emphasis upon tradition has continued to guide Berry. Not too many years after the publication of the 1997 conference papers, Christ the Savior Brotherhood began to learn, question, and wrestle with Pangratios Vrionis's pedophile criminal history. By 2000, the majority of them had entered canonical Orthodox jurisdictions, though some members considered themselves to have become Orthodox in 1988 after having joined Pangratios's self-styled jurisdiction, a jurisdiction recognized by no other Orthodox jurisdiction.[40] Berry claimed that had a canonical Orthodox jurisdiction approached Christ the Savior Brotherhood in the 1980s, they would have gone in that direction rather than accepting Pangratios Vrionis's self-created jurisdiction. When reflecting on the experience, he no longer saw himself as having truly entered Orthodoxy when joining Christ the Savior Brotherhood.[41] He remained "thankful" for what Podmoshensky had done but also felt "misled" by the man.

In November 2000, Berry was ordained to the Orthodox diaconate and priesthood since no Orthodox Christian Church could canonically accept Berry's ordination by a defrocked Greek Orthodox priest turned self-styled archbishop. This enabled Berry's parish, which he had founded in Ash Grove, Missouri, in 1998, to enter into the Orthodox Church in America's Diocese of the Midwest. Two years later, in 2002, he opened the Ozarks Afro-American Heritage Museum in Ash Grove, a project he had been planning since 1996. In 2006, his work also received some public encouragement from the hierarchy of the Orthodox Church in America.[42]

THE BROTHERHOOD OF ST. MOSES THE BLACK AND TRADITION

The Brotherhood of St. Moses the Black has attracted a small group of men and women for whom the connections between African American religious identity, slave identity, and early African Christianity are to be found in the Orthodox Christian tradition. Although attempting to examine each member would make this present work unwieldy, a quick look at two other prominent members of the order (Albert Raboteau and Carla N. Thomas) may help bear this out.

Albert Raboteau is a distinguished scholar of African American religion from Princeton who has published his own life's spiritual journey, wherein he connected the themes of joy and sorrow.[43] Raboteau recounted his Roman Catholic upbringing in the south as well as his professional and marital struggles. His professional work furthered his spiritual journey and prepared him for his encounter with Orthodox Christianity.

Like Berry, Raboteau connected African American spirituality to ancient African Christianity, though Raboteau emphasized otherworldly concerns as juxtapositions of joy and sadness. After researching historical African American slave sources, he concluded, "these voices were special; they resonated with the wisdom that comes from those who have endured suffering and triumphed over it. I was struck by the tenor of these voices, suffused with such sadness and yet juxtaposed with joy."[44] Raboteau was later moved by an exhibit of Russian icons. "It simply astonished me. I went back three times. One icon in particular attracted me with its spiritual power, an icon of the *Theotokos*[45] with sad loving eyes."[46] He soon met another man who had seen the exhibit. The individual turned out to be Orthodox and invited Raboteau to attend a divine liturgy: "My experience with the icons recurred. I was overwhelmed by the spiritual power of the Divine Liturgy . . . I was moved especially by the hymns. They had that same sadly joyful tone which I associated with down home and with slave spirituals."[47]

Although Raboteau did not become Orthodox through the work of the Brotherhood of St. Moses the Black, he has found a home there and it may be no accident that he shares a vision not so different from that of Fr. Moses Berry. Raboteau wrote in the afterword for the publication of the 1997 conference papers that he had found three "resonances, or points of convergence" between African American slave religion and Orthodox Christianity.[48] The first was historical, whereby ancient Christianity "is not, as many think, a European religion. Christian communities were well established in Africa by the third and fourth centuries."[49] Here, one sees the same effort Berry exhibited, to find the ancient Christian tradition that explicitly expressed itself on the African continent, among African people. The second was spiritual, whereby there were analogies between traditional African religions and Orthodox Christianity.[50] For example, he noted that there was not an antithetical relationship between soul and body, something African slaves had properly understood, and something expressed not simply in martyrdom, but also liturgically.[51] The third was "the experience of suffering."[52] Raboteau believed this "sadful joy" was expressed within the African American slave religion because the slaves lived a Christianity that was "in the world, but not of the world," as had early Christians, who were willing to undergo martyrdom.[53] These last two convergences bear a striking similarity to some of Berry's thought regarding the "otherworldliness" of true Orthodox Christianity.

Although Orthodox Christianity does often attract American men moreso than women,[54] and men feature prominently within the Brotherhood of St. Moses the Black, the Brotherhood of St. Moses the Black has appealed to African American women as well. Dr. Carla N. Thomas serves as the current vice president. One of Thomas's own cousins is Fr. Jerome Sanderson, a member of St. Moses the Black, and it was he who first introduced Dr. Thomas to Fr. Moses Berry.[55] Dr. Thomas not only found an African American community willing to offer her a sense of community and support, but she also found herself drawn to Mary, the Mother of God, something she claimed most Baptists (of which she was once a member) would consider "an advanced lesson." She was invited to attend the meetings of the Brotherhood of St. Moses the Black, found herself attracted to the community and the message, and soon became a member and vice president. Currently, she is a member of St. Luke Orthodox Mission in Anniston, Alabama, where she operates the Abba Moses Free Clinic, a clinic offering free services to the community in the morning following matins. Like Berry and Raboteau, Thomas believed the true African American spiritual heritage, or tradition, is one that is Orthodox. As a medical doctor, she found the unmercenary saints, those saints known for healing without any expectation of payment in return, to be consonant with the African American heritage exemplified by Martin Luther King, Jr.[56]

Raboteau and Thomas are not alone, as evidenced by other conference papers publicly available, thus showing that the Afrocentric, restorationist turn to tradition that Berry has made resonates with some fellow African Americans. For

Moses Berry, the need to maintain an otherworldly approach to Christianity and the desire to find a church that included a plurality of races and ethnicities led him to turn to a Christianity that existed before European and American Christians engaged in the Atlantic slave trade.

The resulting emphasis upon early Christianity and African monasticism might cause some readers to wonder whether this makes Fr. Moses Berry and the Brotherhood of St. Moses the Black more like Malcolm X than Martin Luther King, Jr., but with Orthodox Christianity as the terminus rather than Islam. Some scholars have looked at African American religious history as dominated by the trajectories of Martin Luther King, Jr., and Malcolm X. According to such an outline, King looked to what America could become while Malcolm X looked to what America had been and was during his own lifetime.[57] Furthermore, "Malcolm X based his view of America on the historical fact of slavery."[58] Slavery certainly was a lens used by Berry when discussing otherworldliness and is prominent in other voices (such as Raboteau's) within the Brotherhood of St. Moses the Black. Furthermore, Malcolm X's pilgrimage to Mecca, which amazed him with the interracial character of Islam parallels the Berry's experiences of Orthodox hymnography and iconography.

A careful assessment, however, demonstrates that Berry and the Brotherhood offer a different trajectory, one that is neither in the vein of Martin Luther King, Jr., nor in the vein of Malcolm X.[59] In contrast to Martin Luther King, Jr., the problem (according to Berry) was spiritual and ecclesiological and was so to such an extent that although he engaged in social ministry, he never felt a need to develop a social ethic. Berry even explicitly criticized such a move when he critiqued the black church for having sought after the wrong kingdom. Certainly, Berry's ministerial work, especially during his years in HOOM, and Thompson's free clinic are examples of social engagement, but social engagement does not equal placing one's hope in social advancement. Rather, such efforts are better understood here as examples of how an Orthodox Christian might strive to be in the world even while not being of the world. Therefore, Berry and others in the Brotherhood of St. Moses the Black do seem to lie within the general trend among some African American thinkers to find their true pre-slavery identity, but not in a manner that fits within Malcolm X's particular trajectory. It may be worth noting that Berry relates to Fr. Raphael Morgan in this regard as well, for the movement toward finding a true pre-slave identity had a strong presence in the early twentieth century, where it directly contradicted Garvey's enterprise.[60] Some turned to Judaism. Some turned to Islam. Some turned to the perceived universalism of Roman Catholicism. Morgan had turned to Orthodox Christianity and over half a century later, Berry and others in the Brotherhood of St. Moses the Black would follow suit, though in different ways.[61]

CONCLUSION

Examining Berry's religious journey and the outreach of the Brotherhood of St. Moses the Black, one concludes that the way to spiritual fulfillment for many African American converts to Orthodoxy is neither a black nationalism nor working exclusively for equality and higher social standing, but prayerfully praying and worshipping in the sadful joy of the Orthodox liturgical services. Berry sought out a Christianity that included engaged multiple races and ethnicities and was open to all. In this sense, one might argue, he sought catholicity. Yet he also sought an otherworldly Christianity, one that looked to God's transcendence as well as understanding that God could be present within one's own immediate suffering. Berry instinctively sought both catholicity and otherworldliness through a restorationist lens, looking to ancient African Christianity. Ultimately, Berry found this within the Orthodox Church, which he saw as the continuation of early Christianity, for which African Christianity played an integral role. This turn to tradition might appear to be a rather un-American maneuver, but ironically, Berry's journey explicitly utilized Christian restorationism, so common in America, to ground himself in Eastern Orthodox Christianity. This can be seen within the early portion of his journey, as he sought to find his way through HOOM, a restorationist New Religious Movement, built on the supposed reincarnation of biblical personalities, that was beginning to seek a more traditional Christian expression. Here, Berry utilized the anti-traditional approach to reset his bearings. By accepting the restorationist assumptions of HOOM, as well as its Eastern Christian preferences, Berry took two aspects of African American Christianity that went before him (African American slave identity and an awareness of early Christianity) and brought them together by emphasizing ancient African Christianity. Having done this, Berry was able to conclude that the Orthodox Churches were the continuation of that same ancient Christian church so shaped by its African experience.

THE CONVERSION

OF FR. PETER GILLQUIST

AND THE EOC TO THE

ORTHODOX CHURCH

FLYING TO BYZANTIUM

I was at home on the morning before the day of departure for Constantinople, helping feed our children breakfast. The phone rang. It was Bishop Maximos. His voice was that of a deeply disappointed man. "I don't know what has happened," he said, "but the Archbishop does not want me to go. I'm recommending that Father Gregory Wingenbach accompany you in my place." When Orthodox people joke about such sudden changes, they call it Byzantine Intrigue. This is when unexpected things happen at the highest levels of the Church, and nobody seems to know the reason why. It was all new to us. And the joke was not funny. . . . We have since been told that a few Greek Orthodox clergy along with a Greek government official were adamantly opposed to our going to Constantinople and to entering the Church. They reportedly felt we would somehow "water down" Orthodoxy in America to a pop version of the ancient faith and not be supportive of retaining a commitment to Hellenistic culture in the parishes. One report suggested we were out to "take over the church." . . . After the Liturgy [of the Ecumenical Patriarch Demetrios and his synod], we received the *antidoron*—the blessed bread [which is not to be confused with the Eucharistic bread]—from the Patriarch. Fr. Gregory quickly explained in Greek who we were. By now the Patriarch had already been fully informed about us. Though we knew that it was highly unlikely that our whole group could have the dialog with him that we had come for, we expected at least a brief courtesy visit. But no such visit materialized. Instead the Patriarch and his synod of Metropolitans exited the church, leaving us standing alone. . . . We gathered in the board room at the Seminary the morning after our arrival in Boston. I have never been more grateful in my life that a meeting was not preserved by tape recording. It was the closest we ever came to collectively turning our back from the Orthodox Church. But to forsake the Church, you must also forsake the faith, and we could not do that. We knew too much. Besides, there was no place else to go.[1]

During the 1970s and 1980s a group of evangelical pastors, many of whom had been associated with Campus Crusade for Christ, began questioning the legitimacy of parachurch ministries.[2] Their exploration led them to the doors of the Orthodox Churches, upon which they knocked until finally let in. Most of the other converts in this dissertation were welcomed in the Orthodox Church at the outset.

According to the standard published narrative, the former Campus Crusade group had to experience rejection at the highest level (the patriarch of Constantinople) in an offensive manner before hearing a welcoming voice from another corner of Orthodoxy. Peter Gillquist's book *Becoming Orthodox: A Journey to the Ancient Christian Faith* remains the primary and most popular published narrative through which one may assess both his own conversion and that of the majority of the denomination known as the Evangelical Orthodox Church (EOC). One can also find shorter complimentary essays written by other former EOC members and scattered across the Internet.[3] A closer look at additional sources, including many important unpublished sources, however, will show that such an assessment is a selectively presented perspective. The conversion involved a difficult shift from restorationism centered on the early church of the Christian East to the Orthodox tradition.[4] More precisely, American restorationism became the vehicle by which the former EOC members turned to the Eastern Orthodox tradition, a turn that was not nearly as easy and straightforward for them as their carefully crafted narratives attempt to portray.

The leader of this group of evangelicals was Peter Gillquist, who served as an archbishop of the EOC. His narration of the trip to Constantinople, undertaken by the leaders of the movement, encapsulates their journey. Their entry into the Orthodox Church took dedication and commitment to overcome not only concerns of some members of the Orthodox Church, including the Patriarch of Constantinople himself, but the reasons for those concerns—the EOC's own ecclesiastical habits and dysfunctions. Although some members of the EOC trickled into the Orthodox Churches earlier in the 1980s, in 1987, approximately 1,700 members of this same group of about 2,200 later joined the Antiochian Archdiocese of North America and formed the Antiochian Evangelical Orthodox Mission (AEOM). Of the remaining 500, many entered Orthodoxy in subsequent years. Today, the EOC continues to exist only as a very small denomination with approximately about one dozen churches and a monastery of two nuns.[5]

THE ESTABLISHMENT OF THE EOC AND THE ANTI-TRADITIONAL TRADITION

After spending the earlier part of the 1960s intrigued with what they were reading in the Book of Acts, some of the leaders in the Campus Crusade for Christ movement (including Peter Gillquist, Jon Braun, and Gordon Walker) used an annual meeting in the summer of 1966 to begin investigating the New Testament Church. By 1968, Gillquist was tiring of the parachurch movement and desired to find that New Testament Church: "Our impetus came from our dissatisfaction with being parachurch—a category we found neither in Scripture nor in church history. In evangelizing college campuses we saw a magnitude of initial response to Christ on the part of the students, but we did not see sustained results."[6] To put it another way, "the name of the game, we decided, was not parachurch but church."[7] Gillquist omitted another dimension, which was the combination of intra-evangelical disputes and a changing understanding of church authority (toward an increasingly authoritarian view) among those who would eventually come to form the core leadership of the EOC.[8] Nonetheless, Gillquist's dichotomy between church and parachurch was an operating distinction for him and one that was fully entrenched by 1979: "Just as it would be a bit aberrant for me to be a place-kicker or a tight end, yet refuse to be a part of a visible football team, so it is equally strange how we have been content to be teachers or evangelists outside the boundaries of the Church."[9] He also described such a situation as "a disconnected arm."[10] Gillquist had experienced the parachurch model as a schismatic enterprise rather than either a group of ministries united within a single church or a means of directing students to a particular church. In 1968, his tolerance with such a situation had reached its breaking point:

> It was February of 1968, and I was speaking on one of the satellite campuses of the University of Wisconsin, in La Crosse. Walking from the student union back to the dorm room where I was staying that evening, I sensed a specific nudge, a still small voice saying, "I want you to leave." When I reached the dorm, I telephoned Jon [Braun] at his home in California. "I'm through," I announced, not sure what else to say. There was a long silence on the other end. He finally said, "So am I." I mailed in my resignation letter later in the week. The exodus had begun.[11]

The following summer, Braun and Gillquist called together many fellow ex-leaders in the movement and began searching for the New Testament Church. Gillquist's description of this is shaped by biblical allusions. He considered their journey an "exodus," and wrote, "the Church was the answer, but not any church we had ever seen."[12] Their search continued over the span of several years and in 1973, at a publisher's convention in Dallas, a large group of people formed a network in order to find or re-establish the New Testament church. Although Gillquist claimed the group numbered 70, and no formal records were kept, a more likely number (one consistent with other sources) seems to be 55.[13] The number 70 does make a nice allusion to Luke 10:1–6, however, where Jesus called and sent 70 apostles.

Later that year, a group of men divided among themselves topics to be studied from the New Testament and early Christianity. Jack Sparks would investigate worship, Jon Braun would research church history, Dick Ballew would review doctrine, Gordon Walker determined to check whatever they found "against the Bible," Ken Berven and Ray Nethery volunteered to help with church history, and Gillquist was selected to be the overall administrator.[14] As Gillquist wrote about the meeting, "our motivation was to be the best Christian people we could be, to be a twentieth century expression of the first century Church. . . . We had agreed on the front end to *do* and *be* whatever we found that the New Testament Church did and was, as we followed her through history."[15] Their starting point was the American anti-traditional tradition of restorationism. They believed they could discover the New Testament Church and become that. By 1973, they had, however, begun to set aside a more Protestant notion of history, which emphasized discontinuity and the need to recover something supposedly lost, and in 1975 they formed the New Covenant Apostolic Order (NCAO), committed to finding the New Testament Church. They had accepted a more Orthodox or Roman Catholic view of church history, which emphasized historical continuity and a belief that any period called "dark ages" may not, in fact, have been devoid of the light of the church, the body of Christ. This could be seen in their willingness to trace the New Testament Church historically.

What they had not yet accepted, however, was the full implication of that: an Orthodox/Catholic view of apostolic succession. Instead, they retained a particular Protestant ecclesiology. This could be seen in the manner in which they developed their ecclesiology, or church governance, during the 1970s. The group attracted negative attention in the 1970s and 1980s because of this. One observer, relying upon interviews with defectors and published and unpublished brochures and papers, noted that although they claimed to accept "apostolic succession," they did not accept it as a historical, physical manifestation, but as a spiritual one, "in that those today who follow apostolic teaching and practices are the true successors."[16]

Tradition did not yet mean, for Gillquist and the NCAO, an ongoing, lived continuity, that "living tradition" one may find articulated by modern Orthodox theologians. Gillquist and the others had begun to realize that an ongoing continuity of some sort was important but they had not yet accepted that it must be found in a concrete, lived tradition. On the one hand, they understood themselves to be a part of the One, Holy, Catholic, and Apostolic Church, seeking out other parts of this church, but on the other, some still claimed to be "rebuilding the Church of the living God."[17] It would take time for the transition in their understanding of church history and ecclesiology to move beyond American Protestant restorationism.

In the summer of 1975, the group gathered together once again to report and reflect on their findings. Gillquist called the week "painful," and it seemed to have been so right from the start. He objected to the very first report on worship by Jack Sparks, who noted that the earliest sources pointed to a liturgical worship.[18] In fact, each report caused much consternation and discussion among the men. The church history report of Jon Braun noted the early presence of bishops.[19] Church history played an important role in their discernment, for the *filioque* dispute as well as concerns regarding the role of the papacy led the leaders of the group to view 1054, a date given as the formal separation of the Eastern and Western churches, as a fork in the road.

They chose to side with the church that conserved an unin-
terpolated creed and a conciliar episcopacy—the Orthodox
Church. Richard Ballew's doctrine report concentrated on
Christological issues.[20]

The group left their meeting committed to continuing on
their journey. Their findings caused problems among their
followers, however, as the men began to change their preaching, teaching, and worship to accord more closely with what
they had found. Gillquist noted, "people did leave us as we
began to preach and practice this real or sacramental view of
holy communion."[21] Nonetheless, they implemented a liturgical worship patterned after what they believed they found
in Justin Martyr, instituted a hierarchical governing structure, and on February 15, 1979, they changed their name to
the "Evangelical Orthodox Church" and formed the EOC as
a formal denomination.

One should be careful not to assume that the hierarchical structure and liturgical worship was consistent with
Orthodox Christianity. The manner in which they formed
the EOC demonstrated restorationism, even while seeing
the Orthodox Churches as somehow having continuity
with the early Christian Church. Rather than seek ordination from an already existing church body, the leaders of
the EOC formed a circle and laid hands on one another. In
other words, the same group of men who could acknowl-
edge a historical apostolic succession within the Orthodox
Churches believed that within their particular rite, they
had received "Charismatic Apostolic Succession" directly
from the Holy Spirit himself.[22] In both cases (ecclesiology
and liturgics) the NCAO-EOC took an approach that better
exemplifies American restorationism than the Orthodox
tradition.

LITURGICAL SYNCRETISM, AUTHORITARIANISM, AND RESTORATIONISM

Although intended to be patterned after early Christian worship and with an eye to the Orthodox Christian liturgical practices, the liturgical worship displayed some EOC-specific syncretistic aspects. The beginning portion of the anaphora (the section of the liturgy that includes the offering of bread and wine) began with a greeting and response not found in any Orthodox Church.[23] Likewise, communicants had their choice of "bread," which could include cornbread, muffins, bagels, or anything else that could be classified as a bread.[24] On at least one occasion, people who were late to the service because they were watching the children, were given bread from the kitchen even though the liturgy itself had been held in the living room with the breads in the living room (for the EOC operated out of small house churches).[25] More oddly, perhaps, was that the EOC gathering would then take their elements and disperse to their homes and commune there, rather than commune together as a larger group. This manner of receiving the Eucharist was not only a sectarian feature, but should also be labeled "anti-traditional." Traditional Eucharistic liturgies in liturgical churches (including Orthodox Churches) utilize the Eucharist as an expression of unity rather than a cause to disperse and commune in small groups. In this respect, the EOC was not so different from other restorationist groups in America. For example, Alexander Campbell, in his movement to find the New Testament Church likewise altered liturgical practices, even rearranging the furniture in the worship space.[26]

What set the EOC most strikingly apart from the Orthodox Churches in America, however, may well have been its ecclesiology, in which Gillquist himself played a central role.[27] At least two investigative studies critiqued EOC ecclesiology for being authoritarian. Bill Counts's pamphlet for the Spiritual Counterfeits Project at the time highlighted some cases of spiritual abuse, such as threatening to order a person joining the EOC to divorce a spouse who was not ready to do so.[28] The strong authoritarianism within one EOC community even led to a series of articles in the Gary, Indiana, *Post-Tribune* as an exposé. Robin Fornoff, a writer for the *Post-Tribune* of Gary, Indiana, wrote a series of articles on the EOC community in Gary, Indiana, which was headed by Fred Rogers at the time.[29] Although Rogers denied some of the accusations that led to Fornoff's report, Fornoff was able to establish the Church's heightened emphasis on "obedience," the regular use of disciplinary courts, and that church leaders believed God spoke to them often and about detailed aspects of parishioners' lives, such as whom people should marry, whether they ought to purchase a car, or even whether they should discontinue medications, even life-sustaining medications.[30] Even when the authority of the EOC leadership could not be exercised through spiritual courts and/or direct threats of shunning, manipulation was utilized, especially when dealing with those who were considering membership.[31]

Nor were EOC clergy immune to such mistreatments. Ron Zell served as the "deacon of music" for nine years for the church in Goleta, California, but was severely disciplined for requesting a vacation.[32] Zell requested a vacation from his priests in April. When his request was denied, he appealed to Ballew, who operated as a bishop. Ballew upheld

the priests' decisions and convened a spiritual court at which
Zell was told he was wrong to question priestly judgment.
According to Zell, he was even told that church leaders
could discipline his wife or children without his permission.
He was then "put out and cut off," or excommunicated, from
the EOC, and joined a Lutheran parish. He and his family
remained shunned from the group, losing all their EOC
friends. Another clergyman who left the EOC, Ray Netherly,
received a letter signed by other bishop-leaders, including
Gillquist himself, in which the leaders wrote that Netherly
had been "deceived" and they decreed a prophesy against
Netherly: "I am the Lord God . . . Cleanse the unrighteous-
ness from your midst. . . . . Do not make your relationship
idols. . . . Acting upon this word we are wielding our swords
in obedience to cut off that which is unclean in our midst."[33]
The voice of the EOC leaders had spoken. Therefore, God
had spoken. Therefore, Netherly was to be shunned. Jointly
signed letters were the rule of the denomination and was
justified, in the words of Jon Braun (who served as a bishop)
because "you fail in your duty as an elder if you fail to be a
'betrayer.'"[34]

According to Gillquist, the issue of authority was cast
in terms of biblical interpretation. Referring to 2 Peter 1:20,
which states that biblical interpretation is not to be a purely
private matter, he wrote:

> who is to determine what is orthodox? The answer is, the
> Church of Jesus Christ. . . . For there is one Church, and one
> faith and one Lord for all. To stand with a heterodox church
> which separates itself from the foundations of the One Holy
> Catholic Church, to stand in a faith outside the Apostolic Faith
> as determined by that Church, is to serve a Lord who is foreign
> to heaven itself.[35]

EOC authority was justified by an appeal to a particular kind of biblical understanding of authority. The EOC would eventually come to see this authority residing within the Orthodox tradition fully but during the 1970s and for much of the 1980s, the EOC itself believed this authority was given to its own leadership.

Although it could be debated whether one ought to consider the NCAO-EOC an authoritarian "cult,"[36] an overly sanitized narrative, which one encounters from Gillquist and the other former EOC members who have published their conversion narratives, certainly fails to discuss the group's clear sectarian and cultish tendencies. Indeed, such sanitized versions make it easy to miss just how representative the group was of America's anti-traditional tradition of Christian restorationism.[37] For it has been a characteristic of American Christian restorationism that "the sense of innocence and self-righteousness that almost inevitably results from identification with the primordium has led in turn to coercion and curtailment of freedom."[38] Often, this is actually expressed as an ironic feature of American religious life, inasmuch as many restorationist groups developed in order to find freedom for themselves.[39] As noted above, Gillquist had omitted other factors that led to the NCAO-EOC, which was intraevangelical disputes. Within the Campus Crusade for Christ in the 1960s, for instance, the EOC, especially Gillquist and Braun, had reacted against the "legalism" of Bill Bright.[40] In other words, when Gillquist told Braun in 1968 that he was "done," it was not only because of his distaste for "parachurch" ministries, but also because of Bright's more rigid approach to ministry. The NCAO-EOC, led by Gillquist, therefore, lies squarely within American Christian restorationism's tendency to produce authoritarian expressions, even while the

EOC was seeking freedom not merely from a strict leadership but also "parachurch" status itself.

At one point, in order to lay claim to being a legitimate church over and against a more sectarian existence, Gillquist had been instrumental in publishing a book by Jack Sparks through Thomas Nelson Press, in which Sparks labeled the Witness Lee and The Local Churches as a cult.[41] Thomas Nelson was quickly sued and had to retract the claim. According to testimony from the libel litigation, Gillquist had been instrumental in publishing the book.[42] Presenting others as "cults," Gillquist and Sparks and the NACO clearly did not see the NACO in the same way that others had viewed it.

Gillquist even explained the change in name from "New Covenant Apostolic Order" to "Evangelical Orthodox Church" precisely along the lines of a shift from parachurch ministries to the establishment of a new church:

> It may well be that denominations will continue on as sub-governments with the total government of the One Holy Church, confessing her common faith and worship. . . . it was the will of God for us to adopt as our name *The Evangelical Orthodox Church*, a denomination of the One Holy Catholic and Apostolic Church.[43]

Shifting from an order to a church proved consistent with the struggle Gillquist was having with the notion of parachurch. The importance of a church/parachurch distinction was such an important aspect of the EOC movement that the adoption of authoritarian hierarchy should be placed within the context of this very struggle.[44] What seems to have concerned Gillquist and his colleagues about the parachurch movement was that it was not ministerial arms within a unified church but, rather, independent entities unsupported by ecclesiastical oversight. Gillquist believed that hierarchical authority was an essential part of the Church.

One might wonder whether this concern for parachurch versus church isn't consistent with a trajectory of scholarly studies that have examined a trend toward more tradi- tional religiosity by many Americans, especially since the 1960s.[45] It has even been argued not only that conservative denominations were better at communicating what mat- tered religiously, but that the "demand" that conservative denominations placed on their adherents actually attracted members.[46] Not all have found this thesis convincing, how- ever, and have offered counter-examples and explanations.[47] My findings here likewise question the thesis. Although the development of the EOC itself might be seen as lending sup- port to that thesis, and one could argue that without such rigid conservativism, the former EOC members never would have become Orthodox, the full trajectory of the EOC- turned-Orthodox does not support it. The EOC's entrance into Orthodoxy actually required a journey of becoming less sectarian, authoritarian, and morally rigid. During much of its existence, though, the EOC remained in tension between the poles of sectarianism and Orthodoxy.

This tension between existing as an independent church and looking to the Eastern Christian tradition for its ground- ing could even be found within the public announcements of the establishment of the EOC. Gillquist could say, on the one hand, that one problem he had seen in the Campus Crusade ministry was that they and the students "weren't connected to the tradition of Christ," and define that according to the historical creeds,[48] while on the other hand claiming that the EOC's "dream" was "the restoration of the One Holy Catholic and Apostolic Church."[49] As this second claim suggests, however, the EOC's authoritarianism existed not for its own sake but in order to fulfill the moral component the group envisioned in the restoration of the traditional Church. For Gillquist and the EOC believed the universal church's calling was to create a "spiritual super race."[50] At this point, Gillquist was only willing to say that the Orthodox Church "had proximity to Christ . . . the Eastern church stayed closer to the truth than the Roman Church."[51] That EOC dream would change, but it would require time, further reflections, the indefinite tabling of their membership application to the National Association of Evangelicals, and dialogue with the Orthodox themselves, a dialogue that would include a dispute over whether and how EOC clergy should convert if they were not willing to wait for the group to be received *en masse*.

THE CASE OF FR. JAMES BERNSTEIN

One clergyman of the EOC who was ready and willing to make the shift into the Orthodox Church well before Gillquist was Arnold Berstein who, in 1981, wanted to leave to join the Orthodox Church in America as a layman.[52] The EOC was not yet prepared for such a maneuver, as Gillquist wanted the Orthodox Church in America (OCA) to accept the EOC clergy as OCA clergy, as though being transferred from one Orthodox jurisdiction to another. Jon Braun believed having EOC clergy leave to become laymen would hurt the EOC's standing. When it became clear to EOC leadership that they could not prevent Bernstein from leaving, Robert Guio, an EOC bishop, wrote to Bernstein, in which he enclosed a letter of apology that Bernstein was to sign and asked Bernstein to write the central leadership (Gillquist, Jon Braun, and Jack Sparks) an additional letter of apology.[53] The enclosed apology Bernstein was to sign included repenting for having met "secretly" with Fr. Michael Prokurat, an Orthodox priest. Although Bernstein had already informed Guio that Bernstein's entrance into Orthodoxy was to be seen as him "going ahead of you in order to prepare the way before you as your church moves towards entering the fullness of Orthodoxy," Bernstein was told by the OCA to hold off his own personal conversion.[54] For this reason, Bernstein's wife and children entered the Orthodox church first, on November 8, 1981. Bernstein also drafted a 13-page letter, which he shared with OCA Bishops Dmitri and Basil. In that letter, he critiqued two problems he saw within the EOC: its authoritarianism and its syncretism.[55] Against the former, he noted the case of the Donatists, rigorists who flourished as a separate church in North Africa in the fourth and fifth centuries and claimed that fear of punishment did not bring "lasting fruit." He saw the sacrament of confession, as practiced in Orthodoxy, as an antidote to the "excessive emphasis upon use of directive authority." Against syncretism, he claimed, "the road to true Catholicity does not lie in building bridges from the E.O.C. to other churches, rather it lies in having the E.O.C. cross the bridge that has already been built to Orthodoxy."

Despite the internal EOC tensions as well as the attempt by the OCA and EOC to retain a dialogue, Bernstein's 1982 conversion (after his wife and children) proved prescient for Gillquist and the rest of the EOC together with him. In *Becoming Orthodox*, Gillquist had noted how important the "New Testament church" was to him personally, and five years after entering the Orthodox Church, Gillquist wrote as much again when he retold his story in an article for *Christian Century*.[56] Yet a shift in the thinking of both Gillquist and the EOC leadership slowly occurred. When doing their earlier research in the 1970s, they had focused on the first 200 years of Christianity and, at times, incorporated sources from the first four centuries. They also developed the belief that the same church that existed as the Church in the New Testament must have continued down through history somehow and so they began to wrestle with the idea that perhaps it exists somewhere physically and not just spiritually. Restorationism was turning to lived tradition.

GILLQUIST AND THE EOC SEEK ENTRY INTO THE NAE AND THE ORTHODOX CHURCH

Around the same time that Bernstein left the EOC, Gillquist was connecting the New Testament Church to a concern for Christian unity in a new way. "Will we continue our march toward realtionship [sic] with the historic Church, or will we be content to simply be [sic] an isolated, sectarian schism from the One Holy Church?"[57] Gillquist was not alone, for others in the EOC felt similar pain at being in schism, or parachurch, as evidenced from another 1981 EOC article comparing the parachurch movement to a parasite.[58] This concern for being in the Church continued to guide Gillquist: "The choices for us are neither a Churchless Christ nor a Christless Church! Instead, we are called by God the Father, through the power of the Holy Spirit, to come to know and love the Lord Jesus Christ *in* His Church."[59]

In conformity with their desire to be officially part of the Orthodox Church, the leaders of the NCAO-turned-EOC developed relationships with the Orthodox Churches, beginning in 1977.[60] Initially, the group made contact with the OCA through Fr. Alexander Schmemann, an influential American Orthodox theologian who taught at St. Vladimir's Seminary from 1951 until his death in 1983, Bishop Dmitri, a long-time bishop of the diocese of the south, and Fr. Ted Wojcik.

While the EOC nurtured these relationships, the denomination also sought membership within the National Association of Evangelicals (NAE). In October 1984, Gillquist wrote to the administrative board of the NAE, asking that the EOC be admitted for membership. The executive committee discussed the situation, requested feedback from the board at large, and presented Gillquist with a request to respond to four concerns: (1) whether the EOC's beliefs in the Eucharist were close to transubstantiation, (2) the EOC's authoritarian "shepherding," (3) an emphasis on apostolic succession, and (4) whether the EOC was "in a state of flux both in doctrinal position and organization."[61] In addition to discussions within the executive committee, members of the board at large also expressed these concerns. These concerns formed the basis for the four points Gillquist was asked to address.[62]

Gillquist authored a response of just over four pages, which he sent to the NAE's executive director, Dr. Billy A. Melvin.[63] In essence, Gillquist responded by: (1) emphasizing a change of bread and wine "in mystery" rather than "a substantive or even chemical change"; (2) arguing that their authoritarianism is often "distorted," whereas they simply seek "a New Testament sense of righteousness"; (3) claiming that apostolic succession was "an undeniable fact of Church history," something into which the EOC believed it had entered through its commitment "to those forebearers of the faith;" and (4) explaining that the EOC developed a commitment to early Christianity and was fully committed to being accepted by the Orthodox Churches. This last point betrayed their American restorationism. As Gillquist had put it:

> we moved to a new love for the historic faith and to a sense of appreciation for the early Church . . . we gained a new understanding of the frustrations of so many of the Reformers, and what it was they were after . . . our days of pilgrimage are essentially over. From here, we desire to be received intact into the larger Orthodox Church.[64]

Gillquist and the EOC believed they had discovered what the historic, early Church taught, to such an extent, in fact, that they knew what the Protestant Reformers themselves had really been after. Although one might wonder how they could truly know that, such presumptuousness does indicate the extent to which they believed they had achieved a true restoration of the early church. Furthermore, it is expressly stated by Gillquist that by late 1984 there was no question at all about the future of the EOC—it was looking to enter into an Orthodox Church, a subtle but important shift from just a few years before, when it was seeking to be recognized as an already existing Orthodox Church. Nonetheless, Gillquist and the EOC hoped not to "sever" their evangelical "roots."[65] To put it another way, the EOC, though trying to find a way into the Orthodox Church, was hedging its bets. In April, Melvin wrote a letter to Gillquist informing the latter that, "After due consideration, a motion prevailed to table the matter."[66] The EOC's check for $150 was returned as well. Initially, Gillquist asked for a reason, but the response (in June) was merely to quote a portion of that previous meeting's minutes and to invite him and fellow EOC leaders to the NAE convention to be held in 1986 in order to begin developing a relationship. The NAE did not trust the EOC.

At the same time that the NAE rejected the EOC's membership application, the EOC was engaging in dialogue with the Greek Orthodox Archdiocese. By 1984, they had already begun discussing their situation with Bishop Maximos of Pittsburgh, the Greek Orthodox bishop of that city, who encouraged them to take their case to Constantinople. Their desire to enter Orthodoxy under the auspices of the patriarch of Constantinople occurred when they harmed their relationship with the OCA because of their willingness to accept a priest who had been disciplined by Bishop Dmitri. When Dmitri learned of this, he cut off the official dialogue, leaving only Frs. Alexander Schmemann and Ted Wojcik, members of the OCA committee in charge of dialogue with the EOC, willing to speak to the EOC.[67] In other words, the EOC continued to straddle both sides of the Protestant–Orthodox divide, accepting Orthodox clergy but still believing they could be accepted as a fully Orthodox group and integrated into the Orthodox Church. The trip to Constantinople, as recounted above, proved to be a disaster. Indeed, it would be difficult to find another contemporary example of the Orthodox Church displaying a less welcoming response to an interested group of Christians seeking to enter the Orthodox Church. As we have seen, though, Gillquist was told the Greeks did not trust the EOC to integrate properly and we also know the Greeks had learned of some of the authoritarianism within the EOC, a fact that seems to have affected the Greek response even though Bishop Maximos dialogued with the EOC after learning of this.[68] This left the EOC dejected. Gillquist used the word "despair."[69] Upon their return to America, the disappointed group met with Archbishop Iakavos at Holy Cross Seminary in Brookline, Massachusetts. The archbishop informed them there was no plan to bring them into the Greek Orthodox Church as a group.[70] The EOC had refused to let go of their restorationist ideals when dealing with the OCA, the NAE, and the Ecumenical Patriarch. Doing so had led to their humiliation in Constantinople. They were running out of options.

Despite their dejection, and likely out of desperation, they followed through with a previously scheduled meeting with Metropolitan Philip, the leader of the Antiochian Orthodox Christian Archdiocese of North America, which was under the Patriarch of Antioch, Patriarch Ignatius IV, whom they also met.[71] The meeting proved to be the beginning of a close relationship though contrary to Gillquist's published narrative, more work had yet to be done.

Gillquist wrote that Metropolitan Philip requested a report from them on how they would like to enter the Church, which they then wrote and gave to him.[72] In his efforts to overemphasize Philip's role in the EOC conversion, Gillquist omitted a key series of events, indeed perhaps *the* series of events that finally made their conversion possible, on a practical level.[73] Jon Braun had visited New York for a wedding in January of 1986 and stayed at St. Vladimir's Seminary, as the EOC leaders were wont to do when in the New York area. He asked Fr. Thomas Hopko, the seminary's dean at the time, to come out and spend several days with them in order to help them determine how to enter the Orthodox Church, which they were still wanting to do.[74] Hopko agreed on two conditions (that he first get Metropolitan Theodosius's blessing for such a trip and that after visiting with them, he write a memo for Bishop Maximos of Pittsburgh, Metropolitan Philip, and Metropolitan Theodosius).

From Friday, February 14, through Monday, February 17, 1986, Hopko visited them. Hopko described the visit as filled with intense conversations "from morning to morning" concerning many various theological, evangelistic, and ecclesiological issues.[75] One of the characteristics of the group at the time, Hopko noted, was that they still believed that they should enter as a group in order to serve as some sort of cohesive missionary arm of an Orthodox Church because they believed they could help carry "real Orthodoxy" to America. Despite the rejection in Constantinople, American restorationism was still a factor. This is not to say that Hopko questioned the doctrinal teachings of the EOC, for he explicitly stated that on the questions of the Trinity, the saints, sacraments, and so on, they were fine, but he did take pains to note that Orthodoxy is a "living Tradition," outside of which all else is an "abstraction."[76] Following their time together, Hopko wrote up a report, sent it to the EOC leaders for their feedback and approval, and then sent it on to the three bishops, recommending that the EOC be judged on its current existence rather than past behaviors.[77] Hopko's overall judgment was one of tempered enthusiasm, to the point where he suggested that perhaps the EOC would be in a position to create a new eight tone cycle for Orthodox hymnography, a cycle that would be more inviting to those accustomed to Western styles of music.[78] Of the three bishops, only one responded—Metropolitan Philip.

Philip invited Hopko out to the Antiochian Archdiocese's headquarters in New Jersey and had an intense meeting with Hopko concerning the memo. During this meeting, it became clear that Philip was going to accept the EOC into his church, but it also became clear that two points in the memo were objectionable to him. Two points in particular "enraged" Philip. The first was a proposal for a commission of EOC scholars and liturgical theologians to develop a common agreement for acceptable liturgical practice by the EOC.[79] The second was a proposal for the formation of a pan-Orthodox committee to develop a systematic method of receiving and ordaining the EOC clergy, so that even though one jurisdiction (here, the Antiochians) would be receiving the group, bishops from the Greek Orthodox Archdiocese and the OCA could be present as well.[80] To these, Philip informed Hopko (with a little shouting and fist thumping) that he (Philip) knew how to serve liturgically, so the EOC would learn to serve Antiochian style, and he knew how to receive people into the Orthodox Church and could do that just fine without any other bishop's help.[81]

In 1987, Metropolitan Philip brought the EOC into the Antiochian Orthodox Christian Archdiocese of North America. The former evangelicals received the designation Antiochian Evangelical Orthodox Mission (AEOM) with the calling of bringing Orthodox Christianity to larger segments of the American society. As such, the members of the AEOM were merged into the Antiochian Archdiocese, but allowed to maintain their publishing house (Conciliar Press) and a sense of identity and cooperation for the express purpose of converting non-Orthodox Americans to Orthodox Christianity.

Gillquist and the EOC had to let go of their restorationist notion that they truly were a "denomination within the one Holy Catholic and Apostolic Church," as their letterhead and various publicized statements claimed, but they had negotiated some level of acceptance and autonomy as a group. This created a syncretism of sorts and helped to sustain an anti-traditional mentality among some former EOC members. Metropolitan Philip of the Antiochian Orthodox Christian Archdiocese of North America (AOCANA) was ultimately willing to grant this arrangement, though it meant stepping outside the traditional practices of the Orthodox Churches, which simply would have integrated the EOC immediately into the normal diocesan structures. Furthermore, rather than holding many ordinations for the clergy of the EOC (who had to enter Orthodoxy as laymen), Metropolitan Philip performed a mass ordination. In short, the recommendations that Hopko had suggested were largely ignored by Metropolitan Philip.

As it turned out, the American anti-traditional tradition and the Orthodox tradition were on a collision course even on the issue of EOC ordinations. In October 1986, Metropolitan Philip wrote to Metropolitan Theodosius of the OCA, inviting him to send a representative to the mass ordination of many of the former EOC clergy.[82] As Philip put it, "a representative from the Orthodox Church in America will give the Evangelical Orthodox Church the feeling that they are belonging to the whole Church."[83] Theodosius responded by affirming that he would send Fr. Alexander Federoff as a representative but cautioning that "while the canons, I am told, do not forbid 'multiple' ordinations, the traditional practice of our Church prohibits them."[84] Philip took offense to the advice, writing, "no patriarch alone and no bishop alone can express the mind of the entire Church. Only an Ecumenical Council . . . please do not feel compelled to send any representative."[85] In April, Metropolitan Philip submitted a letter of resignation from the Board of Trustees of St. Vladimir's

Orthodox Theological Seminary.[86] Fr. John Meyendorff, the seminary's dean, had received a copy and the seminary faculty quickly met and petitioned Theodosius not to accept the resignation.[87] Philip had been sent a copy and responded to Meyendorff in which he claimed the advice from Theodosius "puzzled me beyond measure" and had been told the OCA synod had voted to allow each bishop to make up his own mind regarding the practice of multiple ordinations.[88]

At this point, Theodosius worked quickly to heal what could have become a de facto schism between the two jurisdictions. He sent copies of the correspondence to each of the bishops on the OCA's synod, informing them of the misunderstanding.[89] That very same day, Theodosius wrote two letters to Metropolitan Philip. In the first, he recounted Philip's sermon at the funeral of Fr. Alexander Schmemann, former dean and noted liturgical theologian of St. Vladimir's Seminary.[90] Theodosius remarked on how Philip had emphasized Schmemann's desire to see the seminary continue and asked Philip to withdraw his resignation. In the second, Theodosius clarified that OCA synodal discussions about multiple ordinations were never regarding whether such could be seen as "valid," but simply regarding the bishops' own practice and views and therefore there was no decision regarding whether to be in communion with the AOCANA.[91] He also reminded Philip that Federoff had been assigned as the representative and thanked Philip for the hospitality shown to Federoff at that time. After considering the situation during the month of May, Philip finally responded, withdrawing his resignation.[92]

With the reestablishment of relations between the OCA and the AOCANA, the EOC had entered into the Orthodox Church peacefully despite the ordination dispute. Gillquist and the EOC had been on a long journey, one that started by utilizing the American anti-traditional tradition of restorationism and ended by entering into the Orthodox Christian tradition. The manner in which this journey commenced, however, presents the Orthodox tradition as an ironic subset of American Christian restorationism even though the Orthodox Church itself would never make such a claim for its own tradition. Nonetheless, the Orthodox tradition became precisely such a subset, functionally, in that the EOC used the Eastern Orthodox Church as a rallying point for its own independence. Having tired of "parachurch," especially one under strict direction by Bill Bright (Campus Crusade for Christ) the group formed (ironically) an "excessively authoritarian"[93] independent denomination claiming to side with the Eastern Orthodox on questions of dogma. Through its restorationism, the EOC engaged in syncretism (in its liturgical practices and understanding of hierarchy) and claimed to be using sources such as Justin Martyr's description of the liturgy and Photios' arguments against the *filioque* to establish an Eastern Orthodox church independent of the other Orthodox Churches. The EOC's attempt to have its denomination recognized and its unwillingness to disband during the conversion process demonstrated just how difficult of a shift it was for Gillquist and the EOC to accept that they needed to do as Bernstein had done and admit they were an independent, non-Orthodox entity. Doing so meant both viewing themselves analogously to the parachurch standing they had in Campus Crusade ministry and the NCAO of the 1970s and accepting tradition as something embodied and not just spiritual. Although the narrative Gillquist constructed (along with other former EOC members) appears written to convince one that the EOC had simply been merely one evangelical denomination that came to realize the importance of tradition and started wondering where it could find the continuity of the New Testament Church, a more careful assessment reveals something different. The EOC had established itself independently, and self-consciously so, in conformity with American Christian restorationism, and attempted to use the Orthodox tradition itself in that process (by borrowing liturgical practices, certain dogmatic claims, and imitating the Orthodox hierarchical governing structure). The acceptance of the Orthodox tradition as an embodied tradition only came later after engaging that very Orthodox tradition—only after realizing that the Orthodox Churches did not view themselves through the same set of restorationist tinted glasses the EOC had been wearing.

THE DECONVERSION

OF THE EVANGELICAL

ORTHODOX CHURCH FROM THE

ANTI-TRADITIONAL TRADITION

THEIR CONVERSION TO ORTHODOXY DID not mean that Gillquist and the Evangelical Orthodox Church (EOC) rejected everything from their parachurch and EOC days. George Liacopulos noted that the evangelistic vision of the Antiochian Evangelical Orthodox Mission (AEOM) (the group formed from the EOC leaders' mass conversion) in the Antiochian Orthodox Church demonstrated that "a conscious decision has been made to reappropriate some aspects of Evangelical praxis within an Orthodox framework."[1] Daniel J. Lehmann highlighted the presence of an Antiochian Orthodox mission at Wheaton College.[2] In his article, he quoted Peter Gillquist as having told him:

> We'll use the same low-pressure, aggressive evangelism approach: knock on doors, make phone calls, give witness to students. All of us have a sense of territorial imperative. St. Paul had it in bringing the Christian faith to Israel. Our fathers

were evangelicals, and our desire is to bring the fullness of faith we have found in the church to our roots.[3]

As Lehmann implied, evangelical Christians in Wheaton were about to get a taste of their own medicine, Orthodox style. Gillquist consciously brought his evangelical fervor with him during his quest for the New Testament Church: "The true evangelical never sees this commission as reduced to preaching and witnessing alone, but presses on to baptism and the teaching of the holy faith as well, to the building of the Church."[4]

This same sense of mission had been present earlier when Gillquist's group shifted from the New Covenant Apostolic Order (NCAO) to the EOC. "Our name is aptly descriptive. We are *evangelical*, ardent tellers forth of the glorious gospel of Jesus Christ. We are *orthodox*, insisting that our doctrine square with that biblical faith of the historic Church . . . . And we most assuredly are *Church!*"[5] By having found the church of Christ in the Orthodox tradition, Gillquist had placed his concern for evangelism within the context of tradition. The evangelical fervor remained as the EOC became the Antiochian Evangelical Orthodox Mission (AEOM). "Phase I had to do with the Orthodox immigrants coming to these shores . . . . Now it's time to break through the national barriers and spread this Old World Church throughout the New World. That's Phase II."[6] Not only did Gillquist speak of a "Phase II" for Orthodoxy in North America, his *Becoming Orthodox* served an implicit evangelistic goal as well. Far from simply recounting the spiritual journey of a group of evangelical Christians into the Antiochian Orthodox Church, Gillquist devoted one-third of the book's contents to apologetics, providing answers to typical Protestant objections against Orthodox Christianity.[7]

Because this evangelistic fervor, however, went hand-in-hand with the other anti-traditional elements of the EOC, tensions and difficulties were bound to happen. In fact, if one follows the trajectory of the Evangelical converts beyond 1987, one encounters three events that demonstrate precisely that the EOC had initially viewed and used the Orthodox tradition in a manner consistent with American Christian restorationism: the Orthodox Study Bible, the remarriage of Joseph Allen, and the Ben Lomond crisis. Analyzing these three events demonstrates that the AEOM encountered anti-syncretism from the Antiochian Archdiocese and underwent a subsequent deconversion from their pre-conversion identity, which had included a purposeful liturgical syncretism and self-proclaimed dual identity as simultaneously Evangelical and Orthodox Christian.

THE ORTHODOX STUDY BIBLE

One of the most significant projects to develop out of the AEOM was the *Orthodox Study Bible*, a publication of the New King James Version of the Psalms and the New Testament, with Orthodox commentary and prayers and a lectionary.[8] Although Gillquist and the editors chose to use the New King James Version in order to be able to publish through Thomas Nelson in a way that avoided copyright issues, the criticisms centered not on the failure to provide an actual Orthodox translation based on a group of Orthodox scholars, but on the commentary and prayers the editors inserted. Ephrem Lash, a noted translator of Orthodox liturgical texts, critiqued the study bible on several points.[9] Lash not only highlighted translation difficulties with the New King James Version, he expressed concern about the

feel of the publication, noting that prayers to the Theotokos (Mary, the Mother of God) were omitted, the lectionary
contained errors, and the commentary at one point included
a blanket statement against any and all spontaneity in the
early church. The latter point might be marshaled to demonstrate that the former EOC clergymen had overzealously
worked to put their past behind them, since EOC parishes
did utilize spontaneity at times, especially regarding prophe-
cies and disciplines they believed came to them from God in
order to lead their congregants. The lack of Marian devotion,
however, does possibly show that the former EOC members
had yet to come to terms fully with Orthodox liturgics and
prayer life. Despite critiques such as these, *The Orthodox
Study Bible* has sold over 75,000 copies and received the endorsement of the Standing Conference of Orthodox Bishops
in America (SCOBA).[10] In 1992, on the eve of the study Bible's
publication, Gillquist even claimed, "I will not say that there
were, and in some cases still are, no barriers or obstacles to
be overcome [for Western intra-Christian converts entering
Orthodoxy]. I will say dogmatically, however, that the wedding of these two cultures has worked."[11]

THE JOSEPH ALLEN AFFAIR

The timing of that claim (March 1992) proves intriguing
not only in light of the publication of the study Bible, but
also in light of a controversy that was tearing through the
Antiochian Orthodox Christian Archdiocese of North
America (AOCANA) at the time, the Joseph Allen affair. On
November 4, 1991, Fr. Joseph Allen sent a letter to his parish,
St. Anthony Orthodox Church, in which he addressed some-
thing that had "provoked so much talk, judgement [sic] and

gossip"—his remarriage.[12] Allen, whose wife had died, stated
he needed to remarry because he could not imagine living
any other way and informed the parish that it was up to his
bishop, and his bishop alone, who was Metropolitan Philip,
to decide whether Allen could remain a priest. In February,
17 clergy, former clergy of the EOC, not including Gillquist,[13]
signed a letter addressed to Metropolitan Philip, asking him
"not to permit this violation of the Scriptural and Canonical
tradition of the Church . . . should reinstatement occur, we believe it would seriously hamper the fulfillment of your desire
for Orthodox unity in America and the bringing in of new
churches."[14] In other words, one month prior to Gillquist's
claim that the integration of the EOC had "worked," nearly
20 former EOC clergy were attempting to hold their metropolitan bishop to Orthodox canonical standards.

The reason for the concerns across the entire Antiochian Archdiocese were due to several aspects of the case.
First, the Orthodox tradition interprets St. Paul's admonition
in 1 Timothy 3:2 to apply to the entire life of the cleric. No
priest or bishop may have been married more than once.[15]
Second, Allen's second wife, Valerie, was a divorcée. Moreover, Allen had counseled her and her previous husband,
Gregory Maloof, through their divorce. During that time,
Allen suspended (Gregory) Maloof from serving within the
altar as an assistant, excommunicated him until the divorce
settlement was agreed upon, and advocated for a settlement
that heavily favored Valerie Maloof.[16] Once people learned of
the relationship between Allen and Valerie Maloof and their
impending wedding, the situation divided the parish and the
archdiocese. At one point, Maloof took it upon himself to
write to Metropolitan Philip in a desperate attempt to defend
his reputation and seek proper resolution.[17] The situation

also came to involve the Orthodox Church in America (OCA), because Allen was the professor of pastoral theology at St. Vladimir's Seminary and the seminary fired him once the case came to light.[18]

Metropolitan Philip responded in a manner that could have only come across to some as giving the former EOC clergy a taste of their own medicine. He answered the letter from the former EOC clergymen by writing them: "the depth of my disappointment . . . exceeds the joy which I experienced when I received you . . . you have aligned yourselves with some of the very same scribes and pharisees who condemned me . . . because I had the courage and <u>compassion</u> to receive you."[19] He outlined several points in his defense, relating to the theme of taking on pharisees and scribes (in an attempt to label those who disagreed with him as legalists), challenged their knowledge of the tradition (demanding to know, by mail, what canons and Scriptures he violated) and noted, "I thought you were going to missionize America. Except for Peter Gillquist, unfortunately, you have not done much."[20] Fr. John Weldon Hardenbrook then wrote to Philip, stating that they would be willing to take up the task of explaining which doctrines and canons had been violated "if you believe it would be of service."[21] Rogers, who had been so authoritarian in Indiana, took it upon himself to write up such a report, because, as he put it, "my heart and conscience would not let me rest."[22] The letters did not solve the situation, with people other than the former EOCers likewise raising concerns,[23] prompting Philip to issue a letter to the all the clergy of the diocese ordering them "to cease any further discussion and communication regarding this matter."[24] Moreover, Philip removed the Antiochian Archdiocese's seminarians from St. Vladimir's Seminary (so that they then had to attend either

St. Tikhon's Seminary in Pennsylvania or Holy Cross in Brookline, Massachusetts) and suspended several clergymen who refused to serve with Allen at the same altar.[25] Allen wrote a small paperback defending his position and Metropolitan Philip maintained Allen's assignment at the parish.[26]

What makes the case important to the conversion of the EOC leaders is not so much the behaviors of Allen and/ or Metropolitan Philip, but how the EOC leaders themselves responded to the situation. The way in which Allen groomed his relationship with Valerie and how Metropolitan Philip supported Allen's marriage to her challenged both poles of EOC emphasis (obedience and rigoristic living) by placing them in tension with one another. Without intending to reduce all former EOC leaders into one of two groups, one can observe that in general, the response of the former EOCers broke down precisely along that fault line.

On the one hand, the seventeen signers of the letter to Metropolitan Philip clearly emphasized moralistic Christian living: "A major reason we and our faithful came to Orthodoxy was the refuge it provided against the doctrinal and moral relativism of our times."[27] To these signers, the Orthodox tradition was seen as a means of breaking from the pluralistic chaos around them, in keeping with the EOC's desire to restore the New Testament church and avoid a "parachurch" existence. Therefore, the Joseph Allen affair challenged one of the core ways in which the EOC had existed within (and utilized) the American anti-traditional tradition of restorationism. Here, before their very eyes, was evidence that the moral relativism affecting the larger society could deeply affect the Orthodox Church as well, to the point where a priest and professor of pastoral theology and a leading archbishop could be seen as engaging in (and defending) unethical conduct within the ministry. Although others within the Archdiocese also believed ethical and canonical violations had occurred, what uniquely hit the signers of the letter to Metropolitan Philip was that the Orthodox moral tradition was supposed to have been the means by which they broke from the moral chaos around them, indeed, even from that anti-traditional tradition itself.

On the other hand, the former EOC clergy who did not sign the letter emphasized obedience, questioning, "who were we to be talking about what was traditional and canonical when we had been there for such a short time?"[28] The EOC had established a strict authoritarian structure as a means of furthering a rigoristic Christian life and to break from the relativistic chaos they saw around them, as so many American restorationist movements had done before them. For these EOC converts, which would include Gillquist, the emphasis upon obedience and authority was primary and therefore, they felt the former EOC leaders had no right to question and challenge the authority of Metropolitan Philip. There were priests within the Antiochian Archdiocese who decided not to challenge Metropolitan Philip further because they felt, in light of the suspensions and "disciplinary actions" Philip had already enacted in some cases, that there was no way to win the battle and so losing their priesthood and livelihood was not worth the stand.[29] For at least some of the former EOC clergy who did not sign the letter, however, the reason was not fearing a loss of livelihood but rather obedience. In fact, in light of the timing of his claim that the integration of the EOC into the Antiochian Archdiocese had "worked," it would appear that Gillquist was demonstrating that very obedience.

THE BEN LOMOND CRISIS

The Ben Lomond crisis would likewise raise the question of obedience and directly confront the anti-traditional tendencies latent within a former EOC parish in Ben Lomond, California. The crisis itself is better documented than the Joseph Allen affair, with some key documents online and one brief scholarly treatment having been published about a decade ago.[30] Not too long after the Joseph Allen affair, the AEOM realized the former EOC leadership had differing views on issues and could no longer function the way it used to function. In 1995, the AEOM requested that Metropolitan Philip disband the AEOM as an independent vicariate and integrate the parishes into the archdiocesan structure, which he agreed to do.[31] This placed Ben Lomond under the direct supervision of Bishop Basil, and then, in 1995, under the direct supervision of a new bishop, Bishop Joseph.

The parish encountered a series of difficulties that precipitated a division, beginning in September of 1996, when Bishop Joseph informed Hardenbrook that he (Bishop Joseph) would need to relocate or laicize many of its 29 clergymen and regularize the parish's liturgical practices.[32] On November 14, a Thursday, Bishop Joseph met with the parish clergy and informed them that none of them could exist as "part-time" clergy so those who were working secular jobs either needed to cease that work, with the possibility of being transferred, or accept to be laicized.[33] Many clergy interpreted this as a rejection of the Pauline model of a worker-priest.[34] On Holy Friday during the following spring, Bishop Joseph visited the parish and informed them he did not want to laicize any of the clergy after all, even though Hardenbrook had been meeting with the clergy for months to help with their discernment.[35] Bishop Joseph then asked Hardenbrook, after the meeting, to join him for lunch but since it was Holy Friday, Hardenbrook was keeping a strict fast, in conformity with Orthodox praxis. In fact, Hardenbrook and his parish had been emphasizing the ascetic tradition within Orthodox Christianity, including keeping the liturgical fasts, and this invitation to lunch affected Hardenbrook's view of Bishop Joseph.

The relationship continued to worsen. In August 1997, Bishop Joseph issued a directive regarding liturgical conformity, which affected the Ben Lomond parish because the parish had been utilizing some Russian and Greek liturgical musical settings and practices and following the advice of Fr. David Anderson's understanding of liturgical history.[36] For Hardenbrook and his fellow clergy ("the Presbytery") at that time, it was difficult. "We have tried, as American Orthodox, to embrace as our own the best that the various Orthodox traditions have to offer, rather than simply copy one particular expression of Orthodox worship."[37] What the clergy had articulated was the syncretistic approach to liturgics that had always exemplified the EOC and stood as a testament to its existence as a "restoration" of the New Testament church. The anti-traditional tradition was alive and well in Ben Lomond. A small group within the parish, however, disagreed with this statement and turned to Bishop Joseph, hoping he would follow through on enforcing the changes.[38] As with Bishop Antoun's 1993 letter on Metropolitan Philip's behalf, a stalemate was reached regarding the liturgical developments but the tensions remained and were, in fact, about to explode.

On February 6, 1998, Bishop Antoun informed Fr. David Anderson by phone that Anderson was being transferred to an Antiochian parish in Chicago.[39] Anderson had been on loan from the OCA to serve the Ben Lomond community and reminded Antoun of this. Anderson also had an elderly mother who was unable to care for herself and the parish was caring for her, something Anderson believed he could neither afford nor do if transferred to Chicago. For most of the clergy of Ss. Peter and Paul in Ben Lomond, it was too much. Hardenbrook called emergency meetings in which he described tensions that had been building and, for the meeting of the priests, went so far as to chair the meeting himself and reduce the priest-representative for Metropolitan Philip to the role of an observer.[40] The resulting decision was that they faxed a letter, outlining their grievances, and requested a release from Metropolitan Philip in order to join the OCA.[41] Two days later, Metropolitan Philip sent a fax in which he "laicized" both Anderson and Hardenbrook and suspended the other signers of the petition.[42] These final actions caused a rupture within the community between those who wished to follow the bishops (the minority) and those who wished to pursue things as they had been doing (the majority). Eventually, the majority formed a splinter group and sought refuge at a local parish of the OCA, where they did not formally join the OCA parish but only used the building to hold their own liturgies. Spiritual courts were granted but not successful for the Ben Lomond clergy. Metropolitan Philip also sued the parish for the buildings, a suit he won because the court noted it could not decide on internal church matters, the Orthodox Church was hierarchical, and therefore the hierarchy possessed control of church properties.[43] When the OCA bishop, Bishop Tikhon, requested that the majority-splinter group worship together with the OCA parish, a few joined the OCA parish but most of the group decided to look elsewhere, hoping to preserve their strong sense of community.

At that point, Hardenbrook and his supporters sought a haven under the missionary presence of the Jerusalem Patriarchate in America in which they formed a parish and eventually some of the clergy were able to serve as Orthodox clergy once again.[44] Metropolitan Philip dictated that even though the churches of Jerusalem and Antioch were in communion with one another, none of his clergy were to serve together with any of the former EOC members who were now serving as clergy under the Patriarch of Jerusalem.[45] The Jerusalem Patriarchate has since removed itself from the jurisdictional scene in North America, having transferred its parishes to the Greek Orthodox Archdiocese of North America. The Greek Orthodox Archdiocese has created a vicariate for Palestinian/Jordanian Communities in the United States. Despite the fact that the AOCANA is in full communion with the Greek Orthodox Archdiocese of North America, Metropolitan Philip has decreed that the clergy of the Antiochian Archdiocese are not to concelebrate with the clergy of this vicariate.[46]

What makes this event important for understanding the EOC conversions is that the crisis shows how the Ben Lomond parish's anti-traditional tendencies, forged in its restorationist past, remained even after Orthodoxy. Lucas claimed the willingness of Hardenbrook's group to break from the Antiochian Archdiocese "betrays the group's Protestant and congregational roots."[47] In light of the Antiochian bishops' abrupt heavy-handedness and inconsistent reasoning, the personal difficulties faced by working clergy and David Anderson, and the EOC's own history of authoritarianism (which was hardly congregational), such an assessment proves too simplistic, but Lucas made an important observation.

There were clearly elements to the Ben Lomond crisis that displayed a continuity with the EOC's previous placement within the anti-traditional tradition. Syncretism, a concern Bernstein had raised when he left the EOC in 1981, had continued within the Ben Lomond community, only represented through liturgical syncretism. Toward this end, Ss. Peter and Paul Orthodox Church, had specifically sought Anderson's guidance, and utilized Orthodox practices and musical settings from differing traditions and periods in church history, including practices based on attempts at what might be considered "historical reconstruction," which itself clearly demonstrates a restorationist tendency.[48]

Another feature of the community had been an emphasis on monasticism and the ascetic tradition within Orthodox Christianity. The clergy wore cassocks regularly, in contrast to the Western clergy shirts and suits preferred by Metropolitan Philip. In his defense, Hardenbrook even cited, as one of his grievances, a time when Bishop Antoun derided "Elder Ephraim," an Orthodox monk who has been founding monasteries in America based on a highly rigoristic, fundamentalist approach to Orthodoxy.[49] Hardenbrook remarked, "One can easily see why the Antiochians have never raised up a monastery over the last 100 years in North America."[50] One can see in this emphasis a continuation of the efforts of the old EOC to foster a strict Christian moral life, in contrast to the prevalent morality in the surrounding society. The former EOC's authoritarianism likewise played a role. Although a minority within the community accepted the oversight of Metropolitan Philip and Bishops Antoun and Joseph, the majority remained loyal to their leader from their EOC days. The prior bonds of authority remained stronger.

CONCLUSION

If one steps back and surveys all three difficulties in the integration process (the study Bible, the Joseph Allen affair, and the Ben Lomond crisis), a deconversion from the EOC's prior restorationism is firmly established. The study Bible's commentary and prayers evidenced a hesitancy to embrace the prayers of the Orthodox Church asking for the intercessions of Mary and the saints. In some places, oversimplifications seemed intended to present an apologia for how the EOC converts experienced the Orthodox Church (e.g., a lack of liturgical spontaneity).

The Joseph Allen affair demonstrated the EOC's emphasis upon a rigoristic approach to the Christian life, to the degree that 17 former EOC leaders were willing to challenge the metropolitan's decision to waive the traditional Orthodox teaching concerning clerical remarriage and dismiss the ethical questions arising from the specifics. One can see this within the very letter itself, in which they claimed that a central reason they had turned to Orthodoxy was to avoid the moral relativism they saw in society at large. Their response was more than merely objecting to Metropolitan Philip's decision and Allen's behavior (and indeed, Antiochian clergy and laity who had not been members of the EOC objected as well). Their response was directly related to their journey grounded in the anti-traditional tradition. It is just as telling to note that some former EOC leaders accepted the decision out of obedience. When no other Orthodox jurisdiction had been willing to accept them as a cohesive unit, Metropolitan Philip had been, and for that, he earned the strong loyalty of many of the former EOC leaders. The obedience and loyalty that EOC leaders professed to one another and that members owed to the leaders was, in some cases, transferred to Metropolitan Philip. This loyalty may be seen in the clergy who, like Gimmaka, did not believe they were to question Philip on this. It may also be seen in Gillquist's writings. His narratives of the EOC's conversion are sanitized and give such a prominence to Metropolitan Philip that the instrumental work of Fr. Thomas Hopko is completely ignored.[51] He said the conversion ("wedding") had "worked" even while the Joseph Allen affair was tearing through the archdiocese.

The Ben Lomond crisis highlighted the previous restorationist existence of the EOC as well. Hardenbrook, who had written against Metropolitan Philip's decision regarding Allen encouraged his parish to pursue a more ascetic approach to the Orthodox faith than was typically followed within the Antiochian Archdiocese. His parish also retained and developed syncretistic liturgical practices, many of which were intended as reinstating previous historic practices. The majority of the parish also remained loyal to Hardenbrook, who had been a key leader for them while in the EOC. Even when they finally had to leave the Antiochian Archdiocese, they sought to remain a rather independent, cohesive group, though they did find a way to remain within the Orthodox Church and currently reside within the Greek Archdiocese.

The emphases and practices that characterized the EOC were utilized by the EOC when they looked to the Orthodox tradition. By latching onto the aspects of the Orthodox tradition that already characterized their particular expression of restorationism, the EOC conversion set the stage for a confrontation between an anti-traditional tradition of a restored church and the lived tradition of the Orthodox Church. The Antiochian Archdiocese embodied an anti-syncretistic approach and expected the former EOC members to adhere to Antiochian praxis, something that was only successfully done after much difficulty.

CONCLUSION

EXAMINING EACH OF THE CONVERTS studied here demonstrates that American restorationism, itself an anti-traditional tradition, is being utilized as a means to turn to the Eastern Orthodox tradition. At first glance, this might have seemed counterintuitive, especially in light of the number of Protestant converts to Orthodoxy. How could a church that includes many of the sorts of things objectionable to Protestants (the use of incense, extensive chanting, crossing and bowing, prostrating, praying before icons, kissing icons, receiving blessings, use of relics, etc.) be seen as the primitive church that must be re-established in our midst? As noted in the introduction, Amy Slagle has already suggested the importance of the American context as an answer to this question, highlighting novelty creation and the acceptance of the language of the spiritual marketplace. Within this spiritual marketplace, theological arguments for tradition were given by many of her interviewees. What I hope to have done here is to have noted both how important the theological component is for many converts and the manner by which they are embarking upon their theological journeys. Throughout the twentieth century, restorationism led converts to view Orthodox Christianity as the truest expression of Christianity.

In order to reach that conclusion, of course, the converts first had to connect the primitive church to the Eastern

Orthodox Churches. For these exemplary converts, Orthodoxy became viewed as the primitive church principally through two means: (1) relying upon and emphasizing the Eastern character of many early sources themselves and (2) assuming that the Church established in the New Testament era was not simply to be restored, but could still be found. The first point is best understood, however, not so much as a geographical category, but as a theological one. For the Eastern aspect should be understood, actually, as a heightened primitivism, of primitivism pressed to an extreme in order to emphasize a Christianity that is pre-Western Christianity as we know it.

This emphasis on Easternism as a theological category may be seen in each of the converts discussed above.[1] Certainly, it is easy to see in Toth's works. He constantly played the "Eastern" card against the (Western) Roman Catholic Church. For him, this was an easy card to play because he could appeal to his fellow Carpatho-Rusyn's Eastern Orthodox heritage as well as point out the heavy-handedness of Western Catholicism. Morgan, too, emphasized Eastern Christianity. Admittedly, we have fewer sources to rely upon in his case, but he saw Western Christianity as caught up in a system that simply did not allow for African Americans to establish themselves truly as a part of historical Christianity. For Berry, it was early African monasticism and Christianity that was important, not the early monasticism of Benedict of Nursia. For Gillquist and the leaders of the Evangelical Orthodox Church (EOC), it was the Christianity of Justin Martyr (aka "the philosopher"), Ignatius of Antioch, and the Ecumenical Councils that were important. As with Toth, the leaders of the EOC also came to view the *filioque* as important. The prerogatives of the papacy were also important to the EOC, but seems to have been so precisely because they accepted a conciliar view from their reading of the Ecumenical Councils. In other words, when these converts looked "East," they did so as part of their act of looking to the past, as part of their search for the early church to which they believed we ought to return.

This is where the second point becomes important as well for understanding the kind of restorationism these converts displayed. For these converts did not simply seek to recreate the early Church but also believed it could be found. Of course, the converts studied here did cover quite a range on this point. Toth appealed to the historical church of the Carpatho-Rusyns' ancestors and theologically, he prioritized the Byzantine Church of the first nine centuries, seeing the *filioque* as a significant breaking point. Because of this approach, which was shaped primarily through Old World concerns (especially the status of the *unia* and a thriving Russophilism amongst Slavic people at the time), Toth's approach would not require the effort of overcoming intermediate centuries as one finds in the other converts. For with Morgan, Berry, and Gillquist, there is a need to account for the move from an ancient Christianity to a contemporary expression. In Toth's case, that was not as necessary since the union agreements with Rome were not that far into the past and the Orthodox Church that had existed in the early seventeenth century amongst the Carpatho-Rusyns was the same Orthodox Church (ecclesiologically and doctrinally) that continued to exist in late nineteenth- and early twentieth-century Russia.

For Morgan, Berry, and Gillquist, however, there was most definitely a need to make the move from an ancient form of Christianity to the contemporary Orthodox Church. What is interesting is that this jump received little attention in their theological argumentation. Certainly, the fact that they tended to emphasize sources important to the Orthodox Churches themselves played a key role. Additionally, however, one can determine that concerns important to each of these converts were seen as addressed by Eastern Orthodoxy. Morgan sought to address racism as a fundamentally religious problem and initially did so by joining a restorationist movement, only to find an Orthodox Church open and welcoming to him, with a claim to be the (then) contemporary existence of the early church. Berry connected a desire for otherworldly Christianity and racial catholicity to the spirituality of African slaves and early African monasticism, which he was able to do because of what he found expressed in the liturgics and iconography of the Orthodox Church. Gillquist and the EOC were at the opposite end of what one could find in Toth, for Gillquist and the EOC leaders initially believed they *could* and *did* reestablish the New Testament Church through a "Charismatic Apostolic Succession." Bold as that claim certainly was, they also saw the Orthodox Churches as continuations of the New Testament Church. The EOC might have claimed to be the pure form of Orthodoxy, the "Green Berets" of Orthodoxy,[2] but they also believed they needed to be seen as a member of the Orthodox Churches. The Orthodox Churches, though not seen as such special forces of spirituality, had (according to the EOC) maintained a structured liturgical form of worship, a fidelity to the Seven Ecumenical Councils, an Ignatian ecclesiology, and the uninterpolated Nicene Creed and therefore were a continued existence of New Testament Church.

By connecting the primitive Church to the Orthodox Church, these converts engaged in a restorationism that became the road to entering a church that emphasizes a lived tradition. This shift was not an easy one, and in the cases of three of the four, led to varying levels of deconversion from the anti-traditional tradition of restorationism. Toth's case did not require such a deconversion, as his conversion to Orthodoxy was as an Eastern Christian under Rome to the Orthodoxy of his ancestors, but each of the other three did enter a restorationist movement prior to becoming Orthodox. The transitions from their restorationist movements into Orthodoxy varied from nearly seamless (in the case of Morgan) to challenging (in the case of Berry) to contentious and difficult (in the case of the leaders of the EOC who had entered with Gillquist).

In fact, one way of examining the trajectory of the EOC is to view it as a clash of traditions. Restorationism is an anti-traditional tradition in America and the New Coventant Apostolic Church (NCAO) turned EOC was initially simply one more example of that. As such, it exhibited a strong belief in its own authority (allegedly divinely established directly by the Holy Spirit), a brazen confidence in its own mission (to bring real Orthodoxy to America), syncretistic liturgical creations, and an emphasis on a moral purity that would separate itself from the surrounding degenerate culture.

When this group encountered actual Orthodox Christians, including clergy, they encountered Christians who did not share the EOC's restorationist assessment of Orthodoxy's relationship to the New Testament Church. Orthodox Christians did not hold to a "spiritual" view of apostolic succession, but rather believed the spiritual apostolic succession resided within a succession that was historically verifiable. Orthodox Christians did not believe liturgics could be merely created from an idea in one's mind, nor that liturgical practices were to be a matter of attempting to recreate what seemed to be the exact practices of a past epoch. Orthodox Christians also already had established diocesan structures and a hierarchy. Orthodox Christians could also fall prey to the same moral struggles the EOC saw besetting American culture. In sum, Orthodox Christianity already had a history and already existed in a manner Orthodox theologians considered a "lived tradition."

Because of this lived tradition, the Antiochian Archdiocese expressed a clear anti-syncretistic approach to liturgics and church discipline. The EOC was forced to deconvert from American restorationism as much as it had to convert to Orthodox Christianity. Orthodox challenged the EOC's *Orthodox Study Bible* and forced the EOC to accept both the hierarchical leadership of the Antiochian Archdiocese and the Antiochian liturgical practices. Although in the case of the Joseph Allen affair one might note that non-EOC-converts likewise objected to Metropolitan Philip's decision, the way in which the former EOC leaders handled the issue was consistent with their restorationist background. In this way, that event was consistent with the deconversion the EOC leaders had to undertake in other ways, with the Ben Lomond crisis perhaps exhibiting the struggle most fully.

These conversions of Gillquist and the EOC, as well as those of Morgan and Berry, suggest that when one discusses religious conversion, one needs to account for a conversion that is neither a shift from one major religious system to another on the one hand (such as going from Islam to Christianity) nor merely "denominational switching" on the other.[3] Rather, one ought to consider these conversions as conversions to tradition, which are more significant than interdenominational hopping but not as drastic as changing religious systems all together. Certainly, in each case assessed here, the convert (and those converting with them or inspired by them later) converted from a restorationist view to the "lived tradition" of Orthodox Christianity. Even in Toth's case, there was a clear understanding (and apology for) a separate tradition, indeed, *the* tradition, from which all others, including Roman Catholicism, were heretically derived.[4] In fact, the Orthodox understanding of Tradition/traditions is what enabled the converts studied here to make their turn to tradition in a manner that is more than mere denomination switching. To the extent they could find their questions answered in earlier Eastern Christian sources, they could identify with the essential "Tradition" and see that as existing within the "traditions" of their contemporary Orthodox Churches.

This use of American restorationism to enter into the Orthodox tradition may also help explain how someone like Peter Berger could conflate arguing for a Christianity that is neither Catholic nor Protestant with mere defensiveness. Once one realizes that exemplary converts have utilized American restorationism to argue for the theological and historical priority of the Orthodox Church, one can better understand such an emphasis of otherness not as merely defensive tactics, but as a platform from which to engage American pluralism and evangelize.

This was certainly the result of the efforts of Fr. Peter Gillquist. After becoming Orthodox, Gillquist actively shared his story with evangelicals. One family that was influenced by him was the Mathewes-Green family. Gary and Frederica Mathewes-Green had been lapsed Christians who renewed their faith and joined the Protestant Episcopal Church.[5] The couple subsequently became disenchanted with the

Protestant Episcopal Church's increasingly liberal decisions and soon looked to both the Roman Catholic Church and the Orthodox Church. Gary soon began reading Orthodox materials and reached out to Gillquist, who helped guide the Mathewes-Green family into the Antiochian Archdiocese.[6] As part of this process, Frederica Mathewes-Green "re-encountered a history lesson . . . For the first thousand years, the thread of Christian Unity was preserved worldwide through battering waves of heresies . . . This unity was so consistent that I could attribute it to nothing but the Holy Spirit."[7] Following Gary Mathewes-Green's ordination, Gillquist spoke to the local paper in which he made similar arguments, claiming that the Orthodox Church had not "negotiated" concerning doctrine and was the only church to remain unchanged: "Looking for a good non-denominational church? How about one that started before there were denominations?"[8] Far from being merely defensive, utilizing American restorationism as a means of arguing for Orthodox Christianity has become the basis of engaging American pluralism. It did not affect only the former EOC members in their own conversions, but has become part of how they have continued to engage America. Frederica Mathewes-Green herself has become a prolific author of American Orthodoxy and has further extended this kind of engagement—prioritizing the early Church, which is seen as continued in the Orthodox Church, as a tradition in which one may find refuge from the denominational and moral chaos of much of American society.

In this way, Frederica Matthewes-Green's case is not all that different from the case of Frank Schaeffer, who likewise serves as a post-Gillquist example of one who has utilized restorationism to engage American pluralism, though Schaeffer was not directly dependent upon Gillquist or the EOC in his conversion. On December 16, 1990, Frank Schaeffer entered the Orthodox Church, by way of the Greek Orthodox Archdiocese of North America. He had spent much time as a writer and film director wrestling with problems and concerns within the American culture and Western culture more broadly. Schaeffer came from a family tradition of reflecting upon cultural issues and Christianity's engagement with Western society. His own father, Francis Schaeffer, was one of the most influential evangelical authors in the world during the 1970s and 1980s and an opponent of theological modernism and an advocate of a more traditional Protestantism.[9] Frank Schaeffer became convinced the Orthodox Church provided a corrective to the problems in Western culture.[10] He came to this conclusion only after coming to see Protestantism itself as part of the problem in Western culture.[11] As with the converts studied here, it was a turn to history that inspired Schaeffer to look to the Orthodox, which he recounted in his book *Dancing Alone*.[12] According to Schaeffer, Protestants "live, as I did, before my conversion to Orthodoxy, from one day to the next, spiritually rooted in nothing beyond their own emotions and feelings and their own subjective denominational, or personal, interpretations of the Scriptures."[13] When he turned to history to solve his dilemma, he cited three historical factors: the eleventh-century schism between Western and Eastern Christianity, the "failed attempt" to reform the Western church, and the Enlightenment and Romantic movements.[14] The latter two were seen as a direct result of the first:

At its heart the Great Schism is not an historical event but a continuing battle between Augustinianism and scholasticism, on the one hand, and the tradition of the historical Church, on the other. At stake is the most important religious question of all: the nature of the character of God. The difference of opinion, between the Eastern Orthodox Church and the Western Roman Church came, I believe, to glaring fruition approximately five hundred years after the Schism of A.D. 1054. The date was A.D. 1517, and the 'new Augustine,' Martin Luther, was about to complete what Augustine began.[15]

According to Schaeffer, the East–West divide within Christianity was not just a theological divide, but a theological-cultural divide, a division that sent the two churches down irreconcilable paths, a division that led to the problems and flaws he saw within Western society as a whole. In this scheme, the Reformation and its aftermath forever changed the direction Western society has gone, and it was a journey that had long since passed the "wrong way" sign. Like the other converts studied here, Schaeffer utilized an American restorationism to enter the Orthodox Church. Although Schaeffer did not formally enter or found a restorationist movement like Berry or Gillquist, he did prioritize a particular epoch in church history saw an East–West divide as part of that process, enabling him to see the continued Eastern Christian existence as a continuation of that prioritized historical church.

It would be a mistake, however, to think that this kind of engagement with American pluralism has occurred only recently, starting in the 1980s and 1990s. In addition to the cases of Toth and Morgan, one might call to mind Ingram Nathaniel Washington (Fr. Nathaniel) Irvine, who was much less successful in bringing in other converts but who nonetheless made an argument on behalf of the early church of the Seven Ecumenical Councils.[16] Although we do not have enough source material to discuss their own conversions, it would also seem possible that George Royce McCollouch (Fr. Boris) Burden and Fr. Michael Gelsinger likewise utilized the American restorationist model to engage American pluralism in their efforts to acquire official governmental recognition for Orthodox Christianity (especially recognition from the Selective Service).[17] In light of what has been shown in the exemplary converts investigated here, an inquiry into the extent by which Orthodox Christianity has utilized American restorationism to engage American pluralism is certainly appropriate.

What can be said for sure, is that American restorationism has been the path for many intra-Christian conversions into American Orthodoxy. Many converts, at least many intra-Christian converts, to Orthodox Christianity have joined the Orthodox Churches because they have prioritized an earlier expression of Christianity and have identified the Orthodox Churches as continuations of that earlier church. The precise, historical parameters of that earlier church could vary (from the first few centuries so important to the EOC converts to the later periods emphasized by Toth), but in their efforts to bypass Western Christian encrustations, Easternness functioned as a theological category rather than strictly geographical. This assisted the converts in finding their concerns addressed not only in the primitive past, but also in the continued Eastern Christian tradition, which they found faithfully expressed in Orthodox Christianity.

Through such a process, Christians in America have utilized the anti-traditional tradition of restorationism to turn to a more traditional form of Christianity. This use of restorationism has inspired Protestants to embrace things such as icons, incense, structured liturgical worship, and asking saints for their intercessions. Furthermore, the converts examined here are the exemplars. Thousands of others have followed them, making their stories an ecclesial, Eastern-focused subcategory of American restorationism. Far from establishing unAmerican fortresses, Orthodox jurisdictions and parishes have enabled and encouraged an American expression of religion. True, most American restorationists will continue to seek to reinvent, or reestablish, the New Testament Church, but some will use that primitive impulse to examine Patristic sources and conclude that the "restoration" of the New Testament church is best fulfilled in a church that already exists and lays claim to those very same sources—the Orthodox Church.

NOTES

Introduction

1. For a detailed assessment of Nicholas Bjerring, see my article, "A Catholic, Presbyterian, and Orthodox Journey: The Changing Church Affiliation and Enduring Social Vision of Nicholas Bjerring," *Zeitschrift fur Neuere Theologiegeschichte/Journal for the History of Modern Theology* 14:1 (2007), 49–80.
2. Bjerring, "Which the True Church: A Roman Catholic Savant Renounces Rome," *The Sun*, January 12, 1870.
3. I realize that restorationism and primitivism are often used interchangeably, but for my purposes here, I distinguish between those movements that seek to restore, or re-embody, an ancient order versus those that may be seeking a nostalgic retreat into the past.
4. Edward Shils, *Tradition* (1981, rpr., Chicago: University of Chicago Press, 2006), 2.
5. Ibid., 3.
6. Ibid., 10–11.
7. Ibid., 115. I am indebted here to Shils' phrase "anti-traditional tradition."
8. Martin E. Marty, "Tradition," *Religion and Intellectual Life* 2:1 (1984), 14–16. Marty himself accepted this, arguing for change

based on looking at the tradition like a giant Rubik Cube, from which one may choose a square to propel change.

9. Wilbur Zelinsky, "The Uniqueness of the American Religious Landscape," *Geographical Review* 91:3 (2001), 571.

10. On this, see Richard T. Hugh and C. Leonard Allen, *Illusions of Innocence: Protestant Primitivism in America, 1630–1875* (Chicago: University of Chicago Press, 1988); Richard T. Hughes, ed., *The American Quest for the Primitive Church* (Urbana: University of Illinois Press, 1988); and Theodore Dwight Bozeman, *To Live Ancient Lives: The Primitivist Dimension in Puritanism* (Chapel Hill: University of North Carolina Press, 1988).

11. Ibid.

12. R. Laurence Moore, *Religious Outsiders and the Making of Americans* (New York: Oxford University Press, 1986), xi.

13. Ernest Lee Tuveson, *Redeemer Nation: the Idea of America's Millenial Role* (Chicago: University of Chicago Press, 1980).

14. Ibid., 2.

15. Ibid., 7. "The movement of the Revelation is in its way *progressive.*"

16. Conrad Cherry, ed., *God's New Israel: Religious Interpretation of American Destiny*. Rev. ed. (Chapel Hill: University of North Carolina Press, 1998).

17. Larry Witham, *A City Upon a Hill: How Sermons Changed the Course of American History* (New York: Harper Collins, 2007), 19, 282.

18. Lewis R. Rambo, *Understanding Religious Conversion* (New Haven and London: Yale University Press, 1993), 171.

19. *Britannica Book of the Year 1995* (Chicago: Encyclopedia Britannica, 1995), 275. Orthodox growth was 2.41% and next was evangelical Protestantism with a growth rate of 1.33%. However, it must be noted that not all jurisdictions in America have experienced this. At a 2004 evangelization conference, Fr. Jonathan Ivanoff noted that the Orthodox Church in America (OCA) had declined in membership. Papers from the conference may be downloaded from http://www.oca.org/DOdept.asp?SID=5&LID=5 (accessed February 14, 2009).

20. In this way, the converts studied here may serve as yet one more example questioning the "secularization" thesis so popular not

too long ago. See, for example, Peter Berger, "Some Further Thoughts on Religion and Modernity," *Sociology* 49 (2012), 313–316; Rodney Stark, "Secularization," *Sociology of Religion* 60:3 (1999), 249–273; Craig Calhoun, Mark Juergensmeyer, and Jonathan VanAntwerpen, *Rethinking Secularization* (New York: Oxford University Press, 2011).

21. "2008 U.S. Religious Landscape Survey," The Pew Forum on Religion and Public Life, accessed January 22, 2011, available at http://religions.pewforum.org/pdf/report-religious-landscape-study-full.pdf.

22. "2008 American Religious Identification Survey," Trinity College, accessed January 22, 2011, available http://www.americanreligionsurvey-aris.org/reports/ARIS_Report_2008.pdf.

23. Alexei D. Krindatch, "The Orthodox Church Today," Patriarch Athenagoras Orthodox Institute, accessed January 23, 2011, available at http://www.hartfordinstitute.org/research/OrthChurchFullReport.pdf.

24. Ibid.

25. Amy Slagle, *The Eastern Church in the Spiritual Marketplace: American Conversions to Orthodox Christianity* (DeKalb, IL: Northern Illinois University Press, 2011). On this, Slagle's work resonates with some earlier work on female converts to Orthodox Judaism. See Lynn Davidman, *Tradition in a Rootless World: Women Turn to Orthodox Judaism* (Berkeley and Los Angeles: University of California Press, 1991); and Debra Renee Kaufman, *Rachel's Daughters Newly Orthodox Jewish Women* (New Brunswick: Rutgers, 1991). Davidman outlined the importance of individual choosing, describing ways in which two Orthodox synagogues had reached out to individuals and sought to make Orthodox Judaism more appealing. Although one synagogue stressed choice making within a pluralistic culture, the "tradition" of Judaism as a response to feminism within late twentieth-century America was something highlighted by both communities. Kaufman described her subjects as "post-feminists," who found a feminine identity within Orthodox Judaism.

26. Slagle, 87.

27. Ibid., 8–9, 87, 90.

28. The Antiochian Orthodox Christian Archdiocese of North America (AOCANA) is an Orthodox jurisdiction in America that has its roots in early Syrian and Lebanese Orthodox immigrants to America.

29. Darren E. Sherkat, "Tracking the 'Other': Dynamics and Composition of 'Other' Religions in the General Social Survey, 1973–1996," *Journal for the Scientific Study of Religion* 38:4 (1999), 557.

30. Ibid., 553, 554.

31. Ibid., 555.

32. Peter L. Berger, "Orthodoxy and the Pluralistic Challenge," in the *Orthodox Parish in America: Faithfulness to the Past and Responsibility for the Future*, edited by Anton C. Vrame (Brookline, MA: Holy Cross Orthodox Press, 2003), 39.

33. Ibid., 41.

34. Elizabeth H. Prodromou, "Religious Pluralism in Twenty-First-Century America: Problematizing the Implications for Orthodox Christianity," *Journal of the American Academy of Religion* 72:3 (2004), 742.

35. Ibid., 744. Concerning the inclusivity of the Judeo-Christian construct, Prodromou cited Mark Silk, "Notes on the Judeo-Christian Tradition in America," *American Quarterly* 36:1 (1994), 65–85.

36. Ibid., 745.

37. Alexei D. Krindatch, "Eastern Christianity in North American Religious Landscape: Ethnic Traditionalism versus Civic Involvement and Social Transformations," Report for *Research on Orthodox Religious Groups in the United States*, Hartford Institute for Religion Research, available at http://hirr.hartsem.edu/research/krindatch.pdf (accessed October 12, 2011); Alexander Agadjanian and Victor Roudometof, "Introduction: Eastern Orthodoxy in a Global Age—Preliminary Considerations," in *Eastern Orthodoxy in a Global Age: Tradition Faces the Twenty-First Century*, ed. Victor Roudometof, Alexander Agadjanian, and Jerry Pankhurst (Walnut Creek, CA: AltaMira Press, 2005), 9.

38. See Saloutos, 100 and Scourby, 42. GAPA was a reactionary response to the American Hellenic Educational Progressive Association, a Greek-American effort to help immigrants adjust to their American life.

39. See Nicholas Ferencz, *American Orthodoxy and Parish Congregationalism* (Piscataway, NJ: Gorgias Press, 2006), 167–186. Ferencz discussed Greek Catholic societies as well since many Carpatho-Rusyn Greek Catholics converted to Orthodox Christianity in America.

40. See for example Alice Scourby, *The Greek Americans* (Boston: Twayne Publishers, 1984), 33–34; Theodore Saloutos, "Cultural Persistence and Change: Greeks in the Great Plains and Rocky Mountain West, 1890–1970," Pacific *Historical Review* 49 (1980), 85–88 and Karel D. Bicha, "Hunkies: Stereotyping the Slavic Immigrants, 1890–1920," *Journal of American Ethnic History* 2:1 (1982), 16–38. For the religious dimension to such situations, see Peter Carl Haskell, "American Civil Religion and the Greek Immigration: Religious Confrontation Before the First World War," *St. Vladimir's Theological Quarterly* 18:4 (1974), 166–192. A similar occurrence may yet be seen in recent Orthodox immigrants to Canada. Canadian Orthodox immigrants appear to hold endearing views of iconography that relate to cultural branding in order to further cohesion among the immigrants themselves. See Mariana Mastagar, "Icons and the Immigrant Context," *Fieldwork in Religion* 2:2 (2006), 146–169.

41. John McGuckin, "Eschaton and Kerygma: The Future of the Past in the Present Kairos, The Concept of Living Tradition in Orthodox Theology," *St. Vladimir's Theological Quarterly* 42:3–4 (1998), 228. The concept of "living tradition" is actually drawn from German Romanticism. See Brandon Gallaher, "'Waiting for the Barbarians': Identity and Polemicism in the Neo-Patristic Synthesis of Georges Florovsky," *Modern Theology* 27:4 (2011), 669. The concept was largely adapted from the Slavophiles, with Aleksei Khomiakov (1804–1860) a prime example. The Slavophiles were heavily dependent on Johann Adam Möhler (1796–1838) of the Catholic Tübingen School.

42. On this latter point, one should consider Vladimir Lossky, *Of the Image and Likeness of God* (Crestwood, NY: St. Vladimir's Seminary Press, 1974), 141–168. Lossky sees tradition as "the unique mode of receiving the revealed Truth, of recognizing it in its scriptural, dogmatic, iconographic and other expressions and also of expressing it anew" (168). Of course, this distinction between Tradition and traditions raises the issue

of criteria for determining the difference. See John Behr, *The Mystery of Christ: Life in Death* (Crestwood, NY: St. Vladimir's Seminary Press, 2006), 49.

43. See, for example, John Breck, *Scripture in Tradition: the Bible and its Interpretation in the Orthodox Church* (Crestwood, NY: St. Vladimir's Seminary Press, 2000), 4, where he describes the relationship as "Scripture *in* Tradition" (emphasis in the original). Behr offers, instead, that "Tradition is the continuity of the interpretive engagement with the scriptures in the contemplation of Christ, as delivered ('traditioned') by the apostles " (*The Mystery of Christ*, 68).

44. See, for example, Thomas Fisch, ed., *Liturgy and Tradition: Theological Reflections of Alexander Schmemann* (Crestwood, NY: St. Vladimir's Seminary Press, 1990).

45. See, for example, the numbers given in Timothy Ware, *The Orthodox Church* (London: Penguin, 1997), 6. Numbers of adherents in the United States of America may be readily found at http://hirr.hartsem.edu/research/orthodoxsummary.html (accessed March 8, 2008). Global figures may also be found in Ronald Roberson, *The Eastern Christian Churches: A Brief Survey*, 7th rev. ed (Rome: Orientalia Christiana, 2007). Another source for global information is the database available through the Center for the Study of Global Christianity at http://www.globalchristianity.org, the database of which is continually updated.

46. As noted below, the Oriental Orthodox are those churches that have their roots in disagreeing with the Fourth Ecumenical Council at Chalcedon in 451. Although this disagreement led to schism, there has been some recent rapproachement between the two groups.

47. See Luke 1:26–38.

Chapter 1

1. The term Uniate refers to those Christians who would trace their heritage to the Union of Brest of 1596 and similar union agreements with the See of Rome (such as the Union

of Užhorod in 1646). Some contemporary Eastern Catholics may take offense at the term "Uniate" despite the fact that during the time covered in this chapter, Uniates would use the term "non-Uniate" pejoratively! At times, secondary literature will use phrases such as "Greek Catholics" or "Byzantine Rite Catholics" to refer to the same group, though these carry their own intriguing characteristics. I have chosen to use the term "Eastern Catholic."

2. This encounter has been recounted numerous times. Although far from all-inclusive, the following list should suffice: Keith S. Russin, "Father Alexis G. Toth and the Wilkes-Barre Litigations," *St. Vladimir's Theological Quarterly* 16:3 (1972), 132–133; Constance J. Tarasar, 50–51; James Jorgenson, "Father Alexis Toth and the Transition of the Greek Catholic Community in Minneapolis to the Russian Orthodox Church," *St. Vladimir's Theological Quarterly* 32:2 (1988), 127–128; Mark Stokoe, in collaboration with Leonid Kishkovsky, *Orthodox Christians in North America, 1794–1994* (Syosset, NY: Orthodox Christian Publications Center, 1995), 26–27; Peter G. Kochanik, *Rus' i pravoslavie v sievernoi Amerikie; k XXV lietiiu Russkago pravoslavnago obshchestva vzaimopomoshchi, 1895–1920* (Wilkes-Barre, PA: Russian Orthodox Catholic Mutual Aid Society, 1920), 20–21; "Primiernoe i muzhestvennoe vysuplenie otsa Aleksiya Tovta na zashchitu pravoclavnych 'i russko narodnych' idealov," *Svit* 62 (May 1959), 18–19. Konstantin Simon notes that one will not find any reference to this encounter in Ireland's correspondence. See Konstantin Simon, "Alexis Toth and the Beginnings of the Orthodox Movement among the Ruthenians in America (1891)," *Orientalia Christiana Periodica* 54:2 (1988), 391.

3. See Keith Russin, 134. The reader should note that I use the term Carpatho-Rusyn rather than other designations, such as Carpatho-Russian, Carpatho-Ukrainian, or Greek Catholic Hungarians in an attempt both to designate the traditional geographic and national locale of the people and to allow for a better recognition of any ulterior motives that may lie behind those other designations. For several essays relating

to the issue of designation, see Paul Robert Magocsi, *Of the Making of Nationalities there is no End*, Vol. 2, *Speeches, Debates, Bibliographic Works* (Columbia, NY: Columbia University Press, 1999). Accordingly, I have used the Library of Congress's transliteration system for Carpatho-Rusyn names and sources. I have chosen to use the Russian transliteration system for Russian and Russian Orthodox names and sources. However, exceptions have been made in cases where the spelling of a name has become standardized across many (or all) of the sources used here. For example, I use "Toth" rather than "Tovt." I humbly ask the reader to bear with me in this endeavor and sincerely apologize for any confusion caused. For place names I have largely adopted the contemporary spellings for convenience.

4. Documents relating to the canonization, including liturgical service materials, may be found in Alexis Toth, *The Orthodox Church in America and other writings by Saint Alexis, Confessor and Defender of Orthodoxy in America*, trans. George Soldatow (Minneapolis, AARDM Press, 1996). See also John Kowalczyk, "The Canonization of Fr. Alexis Toth by the Orthodox Church in America," *St. Vladimir's Theological Quarterly* 38:4 (1994), 424–431.

5. "Autocephalous" is a technical term meaning "self-headed" or "self-governing."

6. Thomas F. Sable, "Lay Initiative in Greek Catholic Parishes in Connecticut, New York, New Jersey, and Pennsylvania (1884–1909)," (doctoral dissertation, Graduate Theological Union, 1984), 124.

7. See Simon, "Alexis Toth," 412.

8. On this, see Joel Brady, "Transnational Conversions: Greek Catholic Migrants and Russky Orthodox Conversion Movements in Austria-Hungary, Russian and the Americas (1890–1914)" (doctoral dissertation, University of Pittsburgh, 2012). Brady's dissertation highlights the transnational aspect of Carpatho-Rusyn conversions, from Britain to South America.

9. Athanasius B. Pekar, *The History of the Church in Carpathian Rus'*, trans., Marta Skorupsky (New York: Columbia University Press, 1992), 107, 110, 144–161. See also "Assassinate Bishop

Who Led Secession from Rome," *The Christian Century* (October 13, 1948), 1069; drew Sorokowski, "Ukrainian Catholics and Orthodox in Czechoslovakia," *Religion in Communist Lands* 15:1 (1987), 54–68; Andrij Yurash, "Orthodox-Greek Catholic Relations in Galicia and their Influence on the Religious Situation in Ukraine," *Religion, State & Society* 33:3 (2005), 185–205, especially 190.

10. Pekar, 107.

11. Americanists were those who believed that all Roman Catholics in America should conform to a single Catholic ethos, or culture. Two prominent Americanists were Archbishops John Ireland and James Gibbons (of Baltimore). Prominent opponents included Archbishop Michael Corrigan of New York City and Bishop Bernard McQuaid of Rochester, New York. Americanism had become a point of contention in the 1890s. For more on Americanism, see Robert D. Cross, *The Emergence of Liberal Catholicism in America* (Cambridge: Harvard University Press, 1958); James Hennesey, *American Catholics* (New York: Oxford University Press, 1981); Thomas T. McAvoy, *The Americanist Heresy in Roman Catholicism* (Notre Dame: Notre Dame University Press, 1963).

12. No document of the union itself exists. Pekar notes that the "act of union" often cited by historians is, in fact, simply a 1652 request from Carpatho-Rusyn clergy, asking for their bishop-elect to be confirmed. See Pekar, *The History of the Church in Carpathian Rus'*, 38. For a further discussion, see also Michael Lacko, "The Union of Užhorod," *Slovak Studies* 6 (1966), 7–190. An English translation of this document is available in Walter C. Warzeski, *Byzantine Rite Rusins in Carpatho-Ruthenia and America* (Pittsburgh: Byzantine Seminary Press, 1971), 272–273. The intra-Western Christian disputes centered on the Thirty Years' War. See Lawrence Barriger, *Good Victory: Metropolitan Orestes Chornock and the American Carpatho-Russian Orthodox Greek Catholic Diocese* (Brookline, MA: Holy Cross Orthodox Press, 1985), 8.

13. Pekar, 84.

14. Ibid., 89.

15. Pekar believed the Orthodox movement would have been abated simply with a cessation of Magyarization. See Pekar, *The History of the Church in Carpathian Rus'* 110. While I agree that forced Magyarization (including public trials and imprisonment for converting to Orthodoxy) played a vital role, I am skeptical that the movement can be dismissed, en masse, so easily. Regardless, this set the stage for religious violence in the region during the twentieth century.

16. Pekar, 5, 84–100.

17. Maria Mayer, *The Rusyns of Hungary: Political and Social Developments, 1860–1910*, trans., János Boris (New York: Columbia University Press, 1997) 3–11, where she introduces these three movements. Mayer discusses all three throughout this work. Russophilism was a form of Slavophilism that believed Slavic peoples were to be led by Russia and the tsar. Ukrainophilism and Rusynophilism were expressions of nineteenth century nationalism, with their proponents propagating a national agenda for the Ukrainian people and the Carpatho-Rusyn population (which used the term *Rusyn* when speaking nationalistically).

18. Pekar, 101. Concerning Louis Kossuth and the Kossuth Rebellion, see Deák István, *The Lawful Revolution: Louis Kossuth and the Hungarians, 1848–1849* (New York: Columbia University Press, 1979) and Louis Kossuth, *Memories of My Exile*, trans. Ferencz Jausz (New York: D. Appleton and Company, 1880). For the 1848 pan-Slavic conference in Prague, see Lawrence D. Orton, *The Prague Slav Conference of 1848* (Boulder, CO: East European Quarterly, 1978).

19. Emperor Francis I established the eparchy in 1815, and Pope Paul VII declared it canonically established on September 22, 1818. Despite this, it was not until June of 1821 that a bishop was consecrated.

20. Pekar, 75, 78.

21. Simon, "Alexis Toth," 390.

22. Richard Renoff, "Seminary Background and the Carpatho-Russian Celibacy Schism: A Sociological Approach," *Diakonia* 10:1 (1975), 56.

23. See Bohdan P. Procko, "The Establishment of the Ruthenian Church in the United States, 1884–1907," *Pennsylvania*

History 42 (1975), 139, 143 n26, 149 n48, 150, and 152. For a source that exaggerated the number of immigrants to two to three million, see Greek Catholic Union, *Opportunity Realized: The Greek Catholic Union's First One Hundred Years, 1892-1992* (Beaver, PA: Greek Catholic Union of the U.S.A., 1994), 5.

24. Konstantin Simon, "The First Years of Ruthenian Church Life in America," *Orientalia Christiana Periodica* 60 (1994), 188. Further background information may be found in Konstantin Simon, "Before the Birth of Ecumenisn: the Background Relating to the Mass 'Conversion' of Oriental Rite Catholics to Russian Orthodoxy in the U.S." *Diakonia* 20:3 (1986), 128-151.

25. Ibid. See also Greek Catholic Union, 6-7.

26. See Jorgenson, 122. See also Simon, "Alexis Toth," 389-390.

27. Ibid., 188-189.

28. Thomas J. Shelley, "Dean Lings's Church: The Success of Ethnic Catholicism in Yonkers in the 1890's," *Church History* 65:1 (1996), 32.

29. Ibid., 36 n.22.

30. Indeed, Eastern European immigrants could occur encounter difficulties even when the immigrants were clearly Western Rite Roman Catholics. See Victor R. Greene, "For God and Country: the Origins of Slavic Catholic Self-Consciousness in America," *Church History* 35:4 (1963), 446-460. Greene recounts the difficulties faced in a Polish community in Chicago and charts its division into separate parishes.

31. For a summary of Ireland's prejudiced views of Eastern Rite Roman Catholics, see Marvin R. O'Connell, *John Ireland and the American Catholic Church* (St. Paul: Minnesota Historical Society Press, 1988), 269-271. O'Connell mentions the fallout between Ireland and Toth and notes the irony of Ireland's prejudiced dislike of Eastern Rite Catholics despite his work on behalf of African Americans.

32. Simon, "Alexis Toth," 391-392. Given Simon's depiction of this reaction from Ireland, I find it odd that Simon claims Ireland "took little notice of the incident" (391).

33. O'Connell, 270.

34. Simon, "The First Years," 206.

35. Simon, "First Years," 192. It is worth noting that this proposed solution came in correspondence with Ryan since both bishops reacted negatively (and strongly) to Volans'kyĭ's presence. On the Americanist controversy, see Gerald P. Fogarty, *The Vatican and the Americanist Crisis; Denis J. O'Connell, American Agent in Rome, 1885–1903* (Rome: Gregorian University, 1974) and Thomas Timothy McAvoy, *The Americanist Heresy in Roman Catholicism, 1895–1900* (Notre Dame: Notre Dame University Press, 1963).
36. Ibid., especially 193–194.
37. Simon, "First Years," 226.
38. Ibid., 232.
39. Rusin, 134. The claim that Toth had already considered Orthodoxy is elicited from Russin's usage of court transcripts that were, I was informed by the Luzerne county clerk, lost in a 1972 flood from Hurricane Agnes. Russin cited the transcript as *Testimony: Greek Catholic Church et. al. v. Orthodox Greek Church et. al.* (Court of Common Pleas, Luzerne County, Wilkes-Barre, Pennsylvania, 1894).
40. Russin, 134. Simon notes that the "Reverend Dzubay" mentioned by Toth is likely not Fr. Alexander Dzubay, the colleague of Toth's who later became an Orthodox priest and bishop and then reverted to Roman Catholicism, which will be discussed below, but Canon Joseph Dzubay of Prešov. See Simon, "Alexis Toth," 392 n15.
41. Mayer discussed a letter available in the "Slovak State Archives" from Toth to Valyĭ, dated December 16, 1889 (200–201). In this letter, Toth referred to his exchange with Ireland and listed some religious grievances experienced by the Carpatho-Rusyns in America. This letter also mentioned a previous letter dated December 5, 1889, which has been lost. It is unknown whether Toth was including a reference to this letter as well when he mentioned writing three letters. Toth claimed that following his exchange with Ivan Valyĭ and "Reverend Dzubay," he made up his mind to follow through on something he had long considered—converting to Orthodox Christianity. See Rusin, 134. The minutes from the meeting of the clergy can be found in Kochanik, *Rus' i pravoslavie*

v sievernoi Amerikie, 481–484. John Slivka provides an English translation in John Slivka, *Historical Mirror: Sources of the Rusin and Hungarian Greek Rite Catholics in the United States of America, 1884–1963* (Brooklyn, 1978), 3–5. Slivka actually used the version Kochanik published in *Svit,* which he gave as: Archbishop Peter Kochanik, "Pravoslavije v Siv. Ameriki," *Svit* (1920), 12–32. Simon also quotes from the Kochanik's transcript in "The First Years."

42. Some sources mistakenly place this meeting two months before Toth's encounter with Ireland, which then prompts them erroneously to give 1890 as the year of that encounter (rather than 1889). Simon, possibly following Slivka, gave the year as 1890. See Simon, "Alexis Toth," 393 and Slivka, 6. Fr. Nicholas Ferencz, giving a more recent summary of Toth's encounter with Ireland and conversion gives both dates. See Nicholas Ferencz, *American Orthodoxy and Parish Congregationalism* (Piscataway, NJ: Gorgias Press, 2006). He explicitly writes 1890 (148) but then later says Toth arrived in Minneapolis in 1889 (149). Toth himself referred to the encounter with Ireland as having occurred in 1889, so the clergy meeting occurred in 1890. Alexis Toth, "The Archpriest John Naumovich as Viewed by the Uniate Viestnik" in *Archpriest Alexis Toth: Selected Letters, Sermons, and Articles,* trans. and ed., George Soldatow, Vol. 4 (Minneapolis: AARDM Press, 1988), 3.

43. Slivka, 4–5 and Kochanik, *Rus' i pravoslavie v sievernoi Amerikie,* 482–484.

44. Incidentally, trusteeism was not just a problem within the Eastern Catholic and Orthodox Churches. In addition to Ferencz's work, which takes note of this, see other Catholic works, such as Terrence Murphy, "*Trusteeism* in Atlantic Canada: the struggle for leadership among the Irish *Catholics* of Halifax, St John's, and Saint John, 1780–1850," in *Creed and Culture : the Place of English-speaking Catholics in Canadian society, 1750–1930,* ed. by Terrence Murphy and Gerald J. Stortz, 126–151 (Montreal: McGill University Press, 1993) and Patrick W. Carey, *People, Priests, and Prelates: Ecclesiastical Democracy and the Tensions of Trusteeism* (Notre Dame, IN: Notre Dame University Press, 1987).

45. Kochanik, *Rus' i pravoslavie v sievernoi Amerikie*, 483, Qtd. in Simon, "The First Years," 213.
46. For reflections on the significance of this, see Thomas F. Sable and Nicholas Ferencz. The importance of the lay ownership of parish property and lay trusteeship in general will be discussed further below.
47. Qtd. in Mayer, 202.
48. On the point of Toth's actions taking advantage of a situation (Carpatho-Rusyn discontent and consideration of Orthodoxy) see Brady, 132–135.
49. Qtd. in Mayer, 203. Mayer's presentation corrects Simon's, who had thought the report had not been authored by Toth but Mayer found the report together with his letter in the archives of the Prešov eparchy.
50. See Alex Simirenko, *Pilgrims, Colonists, and Frontiersmen: An Ethnic Community in Transition* (New York: Free Press of Glencoe, 1964), 42 and Sable, 110–111. Sable mistakenly claims that Nicholas was the bishop. Vladimir was actually the bishop at the time, with Nicholas beginning his tenure in America in 1892, though he had been consecrated bishop of the Aleutian Islands and Alaska on September 29, 1891. See Tarasar, 30–31. It should be noted that Bishop Vladimir was recalled primarily because of unresolved infighting at the cathedral in San Francisco in October of 1891. On this, see Terence Emmons, *Alleged Sex and Threatened Violence: Doctor Russel, Bishop Vladimir, and the Russian in San Francisco, 1887–1892* (Stanford, CA: Stanford University Press, 1997).
51. Russin, 131. Russin relied upon an account available in Very Reverend John Dzubay, ed., *Diamond Jubilee Album* (St. Mary's Russian Orthodox Greek Catholic Church, Minneapolis, Minnesota 1962), 21.
52. Ibid.
53. Per Carpatho-Rusyn tradition, Mlinar knew himself only as Orthodox. "They tell me I'm a Uniate; what sort of Uniate? When I never heard anything about it, I always held myself for an Orthodox Christian," qtd. in Simon, "Alexis Toth," 401, from Kochanik, *Rus' i pravoslavie v sievernoi Amerikie*, 490.

54. Kochanik, *Rus' i pravoslavie v sievernoi Amerikie,* 490. My quotation is taken from Simon, "Alexis Toth," 401. Simon quoted (in English translation) from two sections of the letter (see pp. 397 and 401). Taken together, they amount to a translation of about half the letter and contain the most important portions. The letter is included as part of *The Archpriest John Naumovich as Viewed by the Uniate Viestnik,* written by Toth and available in translation in Alexis Toth, *Selected Letters, Sermons, and Articles,* trans. George Soldatow,Vol. 4 (Minneapolis: AARDM Press, 1988), 9–10. An Igumen is typically the head of a monastic community, though in the Russian Orthodox tradition, the title may sometimes be given to any priest-monk for honorary purposes.

55. Jorgenson, 132, Russin, 135. Jorgenson notes that there is no record of how Toth and the parishioners were received, but correctly claims that likely it was through a profession of faith, without any re-ordination of Toth himself.

56. Russin, 135 and Simon, "Alexis Toth," 404.

57. Vladimir to Toth, September 12, 1891. This letter is available (in Russian) in Kochanik, *Rus' i pravoslavie v sievernoi Amerikie,* 491. This letter is mentioned in secondary sources as evidence of Vladimir's respect for Toth. See Simon, "Alexis Toth," 404–405.

58. See Simon, "Alexis Toth," 406 and Tarasar, 51.

59. Simon, "Alexis Toth," 407.

60. Russin, 140.

61. Russin, 140–141 and Simon, "Alexis Toth," 410. Simon added, "Toth fails to explain how, as an acknowledged Orthodox priest, he celebrated for and presumably communicated church members who were still Uniate Catholics." Here, Simon anachronistically presupposed his post-Vatican II experience for that of late nineteenth-century Eastern Catholics. Likely, Toth alone consumed the Eucharistic gifts of consecrated bread and wine that day. Infrequent communion by the laity was the norm at the time, not the exception.

62. Russin produced the petition on 141–142. The petition may also be found in "GREEK CATHOLIC CHURCH et. al. v. ORTHODOX GREEK CHURCH et. al.," *Atlantic Reporter*

46 (1900), 74. According to Toth himself, the sermon lasted an hour and a half. See "From the History of the Orthodox Church in Wilkes-Barre," in Alexis Toth, *Selected Letters, Sermons, and Articles*, trans. George Soldatow, Vol. 1 (Minneapolis: AARDM Press, 1978), 79–80.

63. Toth to Bishop Nicholas, August 14/26, 1896 in Soldatow, *Selected Letters, Sermons, and Articles*, vol. 1, 49–50.

64. See Toth to Bishop Nicholas, December 16/28, 1896, in Soldatow, *Selected Letters, Sermons, and Articles*, vol. 1, 67. The consistency of Toth's approach whenever he described meeting with prospective converts should also caution against Constantine Simon's doubt of Toth's veracity. Though again, the Supreme Court of Pennsylvania accepted Toth's outline of the events even while ruling against him.

65. Soldatow, *Selected Letters, Sermons, and Articles*, vol. 3, 1 (1–2).

66. Ibid., p. 3 (9–10).

67. Ibid., p. 5 (13). *Kalakuts* is a derogatory term referring to a group of Slavic people in the region of Chelm (Kholm) and Podlachia (Podlasie) who accepted Roman Catholicism and adopted a Polish self-identity despite retaining their Ukrainian language. Toth claimed that the East–West divide occurred in the ninth century in other places as well. He seemed to be unaware of the 879–880 reunion council that healed the rift between Rome and Constantinople.

68. Ibid., 25–26 (63, 70–71).

69. Although Rome and the Eastern Churches did separate in 869, a reunion council in 8789–880 revoked the 869 council and healed the division. Ironically, however, the 869 council is considered the eighth ecumenical council by the Roman Catholic Church, and this likely shaped Toth's views. Most scholars date the separation of the Roman Catholic Church from the Eastern Churches in 1054, when Cardinal Humbert, hotheaded a papal legate, slammed a bull of excommunication upon the altar of Hagia Sophia, the main Orthodox Christian temple in Constantinople. This act, brazen as it was, however, did not become the touchstone it now is until the crusades, which were truly the final rupture between the churches.

70. Ibid., 29 (79).
71. Ibid., 1-2 (6-8).
72. See John Douglas Strickland, *The Making of Holy Russia—The Orthodox Church and Russian Nationalism Before the Revolution* (Jordanville, NY: Holy Trinity Publications, 2013). Interestingly, Nicholas Bjerring had also adopted "Orthodox patriotism." See my article, "A Catholic, Presbyterian, and Orthodox Journey," 64. Toth, however, did not use the imagery and culture of the Israelites to make sense of Russian history and culture, as was common amongst "Orthodox patriots." For more on this aspect of "Orthodox patriotism," see Daniel Rowland, "Moscow—The Third Rome or the New Israel?" *The Russian Review* 55 (1996), 591-614.
73. I assume, here, that this is likely the immediate reaction of most contemporary readers, given the secondary literature on ethnoreligiocity. See for example, Paul Mojzes, *Yugoslavian Inferno: Ethnoreligious Warfare in the Balkans* (New York: Continuum, 1994), where Mojzes analyzed the conflict in the Balkans and relegated religion to a secondary factor, falling in line behind nationalism. It may be worth noting, though, that even Paul Mojzes was later still willing to speak of the "specifically religious factor." See Paul Mojzes, "The Role of Religious Leaders in Times of Conflict in Multinational and Multi-Religious Societies: A Contribution Toward Interreligious Dialogue in Macedonia," *Journal of Ecumenical Studies* 39:1-2 (2002), 83.
74. Soldatow, *Selected Letters, Sermons, and Articles*, vol. 3, pp. 23 (67-68). Toth used *ksendzes*, the Polish word for priest, here and consistently used this term as a derogatory term when discussing Roman Catholic priests. He would also make a similar maneuver by referring to Roman Catholic church buildings as *kostels* rather than churches.
75. One should not dismiss this remark by Toth as mere anti-Semitism or, more properly speaking, anti-Judaism (since Palestinian Orthodox are also Semites). Mayer provided examples of the Hungarian government using Jewish agents to

undermine the Orthodox movement in Hungary in 1904. See Mayer, 138 and 140. Mayer presented these are being unexceptional, suggesting the Hungarian government had a history of paying Jews to help settle Christian religious affairs according to its liking. In one of his footnotes to his translation of Toth, Soldatow also cited some examples of Poles and Russians paying Jews to work toward their own cause. See Toth, *Selected Letters, Sermons, and Articles*, vol. 3, p. 37 n. 2.

76. See Michael Oleksa, *Orthodox Alaska: A Theology of Mission* (Crestwood, NY: St. Vladimir's Seminary Press, 1998), 173–174.

77. Soldatow, *Selected Letters, Sermons, and Articles*, vol. 3, p. 32 (97).

78. A more balanced account of Kuntsevych would be that the man persecuted Orthodox Christians, but certain abuses cannot be attributed to him. For such an account, see the recent Polish work by Antoni Mironowicz, *Prawoslawie i unia za panowania Jana Kazimierza* ["Orthodoxy and Union during the reign of King John Casimir"] Dissertationes Universitatis Varsoviensis 443 (Bialystok: Orthdruk, 1997). For an example of what can be verified, see the letter from the Lithuanian chancellor Leo Sapiega to Kuntsevych, dated March 12, 1622, in Alphonse Guépin, *Un apotre l'union des églises au XVII siècle: Saint Josaphat et l'église Greco-Slave en Pologne et en Russie*, vol. 1, Paris: the religious library of H. Oudin, 1897, supporting works, 1–10. Guépin included a second letter as well. Unfortunately, all accounts in Western languages, including that by Guépin, are panegyric in nature and heavily biased. See Theodosia Boresky, *The Life of St. Josaphat Martyr of the Union, Archbishop of Polotsk, Member, Order of St. Basil the Great* (NY: Comet Press, Books, 1955); Johann Looshorn, *Der heilige Märtyrer Josaphat Kuncewicz, Erzbischof von Polozk* (Munich: P. Zipperer's Bookstore, 1898) and Athanasius B. Pekar, *Saint Josaphat (1580–1623)* (Stamford, CT: Publications of Basilian Fathers, 1967).

79. Soldatow, *Selected Letters, Sermons, and Articles*, vol. 3, p. 34. There is no corresponding Slavic text in the later 1907

version. In section seven of the 1907 version, the text is much shorter, suggesting that Toth condensed this portion.

80. See Toth to Bishop Nicholas, August 21, 1897, in Soldatow, *Selected Letters, Sermons, and Articles*, vol. 3, 67, where he says the faithful in Pottsville and Sheppton "have worked only 2–3 days a week. These work shortages will continue in places where work depends on soft coal as long as the strike continues there." The reader, however, should not conclude that because of the dangerous work and poor pay, Slavic immigrants were completely at the mercy of larger powers and incapable of fending for themselves. On this, see Victor R. Greene, *The Slavic Community on Strike: Immigrant Labor in Pennsylvania Anthracite* (Notre Dame and London: Notre Dame University Press, 1968). Although acknowledging their poverty, Greene's central purpose was to argue against mistakenly believing the Slavic immigrants had been disorganized and incapable of seeking to improve their status by unionization.

81. See Toth to Bishop Nicholas, December 28, 1896, in Soldatow, *Selected Letters, Sermons, and Articles*, vol. 1, p. 74.

82. Mayer, 13. Amongst this second generation of Russophilists, Mayer also mentioned Aleksander Dukhnovych (1803–1865), Aleksandr Mitrak (1837–1913), Ivan Sil'vai (1838–1904), Anatolii Kralyts'kyĭ (1835–1894), Viktor Kimak (1840–1900), and Kyril Sabov (1838–1914). The two leading proponents of the Russophile movement from the generation before were Adolf Dobrians'kyĭ (1817–1901) and Ivan Rakovs'kyĭ (1815–1885). See Pekar, 102.

83. Toth, Alexis, *Gde iskati (glyadati) pravdu?* (1907), 82–91. Concerning the question of beards, Toth argues that neither Christ nor the apostles shaved themselves, nor did the great luminaries of the Church such as Moses and King David or St. Nicholas of Myra or Basil the Great (82–83). Soldatow's translation omits these supplement pages, suggesting that earlier versions of the pamphlet did not yet contain them.

84. Ibid., 108–112. As with the supplement sections, Soldatow's translation omits it, presumably because it did not yet exist in the version used by Soldatow.

85. See Toth to Bishop Nicholas, March 12, 1896, Soldatow, *Selected Letters, Sermons, and Articles*, vol. 1, 17.
86. See Toth to Bishop Nicholas, March 12, 1896, Soldatow, *Selected Letters, Sermons, and Articles*, vol. 1, 27.
87. See Toth to Bishop Nicholas, July 5/17, 1896 in Soldatow, *Selected Letters, Sermons, and Articles*, vol. 1, 42.
88. Toth to Bishop Nicholas, December 16/28, 1896 in Soldatow, *Selected Letters, Sermons, and Articles,* vol. 1, 69. A little less than a year later, as the idea began to take shape, Toth argued that "Orthodox Galician" would not be appropriate name for such a paper, but rather *Svit* (Light) or *Zarya* (Dawn). See Toth to Bishop Nicholas, March 3/15, 1897, in Soldatow, *Selected Letters, Sermons, and Articles*, vol. 3, 66.
89. See "GREEK CATHOLIC CHURCH et al. v. ORTHODOX GREEK CHURCH et al.," 72–77. The Lutheran case's bearing on the Wilkes-Barre suit is described on 75.
90. See "GREEK CATHOLIC CHURCH et al. v. ORTHODOX GREEK CHURCH et al.," 77, where the supreme court noted, "This case has taken a very great latitude and a vast amount of testimony that was really irrelevant to the issue has gone in, and by reason of this vast amount of testimony, and by reason of the great width and breadth of the case, and of the discussion thereon, it has been dragged along for a very great length of time."
91. Ibid., 75.
92. Harvard Law Review Association, "Judicial Intervention in Disputes over the use of Church Property," *Harvard Law Review* 75:6 (1962), 1154–1158.
93. Ibid., 1145–1149.
94. Ibid., 1157–1158. "Yet, while most state courts professed adherence to *Watson*, and while judicial interference with hierarchically organized churches decreased markedly after *Watson*, the implied-trust doctrine persisted in most states."
95. Simon, "Alexis Toth," 411.
96. See Toth to Bishop Nicholas, March 12, 1896, in Soldatow, *Selected Letters, Sermons, and Articles*, vol. 1, 17.
97. Simon, "Alexis Toth," 407.
98. Toth recounts this in a lengthy letter to Nicholas when describing the troubles he (Toth) had had to endure from the

Russians up to that point. See Toth to Nicholas, March 12, 1896, in Soldatow, *Selected Letters*, vol. 1, 23.

99. Sable discusses these on 118–122. Like Toth, Hotovitsky would later be canonized by the Orthodox Church. In his case, this was due to martyrdom by Bolsheviks. No official report of his martyrdom exists, though oral reports do. He had been spied upon and arrested several times before dying a martyr's death due to sufferings undergone while in exile.

100. See Sable, 122.

101. Willard Sunderland, "Peasant Pioneering: Russian Peasant Settlers Describe Colonization and the Eastern Frontier, 1880's–1910's," *Journal of Social History* 34:4 (2001), 895–922.

102. Toth to Bishop Nicholas, March 12, 1896, in *Selected Letters, Sermons, and Articles*, vol. 1, 21.

103. See Toth to Bishop Nicholas, March 12, 1896, in *Selected Letters, Sermons, and Articles*, vol. 1, 22.

104. Toth to Bishop Nicholas, December 10, 1897, in Soldatow, *Selected Letters, Sermons, and Articles*, vol. 4, 18.

105. See "Bishop Stephen (Alexander Dzubay)," in Tarasar, 132.

106. See Toth to Bishop Nicholas, December 10, 1897, in Soldatow, *Selected Letters, Sermons, and Articles*, Vol. 4, 19. Fr. Ambrose Vretta served the Russian Mission in America from 1892–1896. See Oliver Herbel, "An Old World Response to a New World Situation: Greek Clergy in the Service of the Russian Mission to America," *LOGOS: A Journal of Eastern Christian Studies* 53:3–4 (2012), forthcoming.

107. See Toth to Bishop Nicholas, December 27/January 8, 1898, in Soldatow, *Selected Letters, Sermons, and Articles*, Vol. 4, 26.

108. Bishop Nicholas's letter, dated January 10/22, 1896, is available in the *Amerikanskiĭ Russkiĭ Viestnik*, of February 13, 1896 (page 2 of the Cyrillic).

109. Bishop Nicholas's letter is also available in *Svoboda* 6 (1896).

110. See Toth to Bishop Nicholas, March 12, 1896 in Soldatow, *Selected Letters, Sermons, and Articles*, vol. 1, 20–21.

111. See Toth to Bishop Nicholas, December 27, 1897/January 8, 1898, in Soldatow, *Selected Letters, Articles, and Sermons*, vol. 4, 25, where Toth thanks Bishop Nicholas for the award.

112. See "Autobiography of Father A. Toth," taken from a church record book in Wilkes-Barre, in Soldatow, *Selected Letters,*

Sermons, and Articles, vol. 1, 13. A *palitsa*, or an *epigonation*, is a diamond-shaped vestment piece worn by bishops and certain priests on their right side. In the Russian practice, the *palitsa* is awarded to priests for extensive and/or exemplary service, though in the Greek practice, it signifies a priest who may have an advanced degree and, more typically, a priest who has been blessed to hear confessions (which in the Russian/Slavic practice is assumed of all ordained priests). This award is not to be confused with the similar rectangular vestment piece called a *nabedrennik*, which hangs also on the right side. The *nabedrennik* is not utilized in the Greek tradition and in the Slavic tradition, when a priest has been awarded both, is worn on the left side. Russian bishops do not wear the *nabedrennik*.

113. See Platon, "A Wreath Upon the Grave of Mitered Archpriest Fr. Alexis Georievich Toth" (*"Venok na mogilu mitrofornago protoiereya o. Aleksiya Georievicha Tovta"*) in *Amerikanskiĭ Pravoslavnyĭ Viestnik* 13:10 (May 28/15, 1909), 177–182, in Soldatow, *The Orthodox Church in America and other writings*, 153–157.

114. See *Amerikanskiĭ Pravoslavnyĭ Viestnik* 13:10 (May 15/28, 1909), 375–377. This memorial has been translated by Soldatow. See "The Bat'ko of the American Rus," in *The Orthodox Church in America and other writings by Saint Alexis, Confessor and Defender of Orthodoxy in America* (Minneapolis, AARDM Press, 1996), 168–169.

115. See "To the memory of Fr. Alexis Toth," in *The Orthodox Church in America and other writings by Saint Alexis, Confessor and Defender of Orthodoxy in America* (Minneapolis, AARDM Press, 1996), 164–165.

116. Simon, "The First Years," 227.

117. For further discussions of the intra-Roman Catholic struggles and this later group of Rusyn converts, see Simon, "The First Years," especially 215–232; Gerald P. Fogarty, *"The American Hierarchy and Oriental Rite Catholics, 1890-1907,"* Records of the American Catholic Historical Society 85 (1974), 17–28; and Lawrence Barriger's, *Good Victory: Metropolitan Orestes Chornock and the American Carpatho-Russian Orthodox*

Greek Catholic Diocese, cited above, and *Glory to Jesus Christ! A History of the American Carpatho-Russian Orthodox Church* (Brookline, MA: Holy Cross Orthodox Press, 2000).

118. For an overview of the difficulty Catholic immigrants faced, see Chester Gillis, "American Catholics: Neither out Far nor in Deep," in *Religion and Immigration*, ed. by Yvonne Yazbeck Haddad, Jane I. Smith, and John L. Esposito, 33–52 (Walnut Creek, CA: AltaMira Press, 2003).

Chapter 2

1. The Repose of Mary, the Mother of God (specifically, Jesus, the Son of God).

2. Gavin White, "Patriarch McGuire and the Episcopal Church," *Historical Magazine of the Protestant Episcopal Church* 38:2 (1969), 126. Exactly why this seems "improbable" is hard to say, leaving the reader to wonder which aspect(s) made the story all the more improbable.

3. "The First African American Orthodox Priest," *Epiphany* 15:4 (1996), 88.

4. Ibid. The biography in *Epiphany* is quite truncated. Better biographies may be found in Dellas Oliver Herbel, "Reverend Raphael Morgan," in *African American National Biography* (New York: Oxford University Press, 2008) and Matthew Namee, "Father Raphael Morgan: The First Orthodox Priest of African American Decent in America," *St. Vladimir's Theological Quarterly* (2009), 447–459.

5. Two early biographies provide a basic outline. See Frank Lincoln Mather, ed., *Who's Who of the Colored Race: A General Biographical Dictionary of Men and Women of African Descent*, vol. 1, 1915 (1915; rpr., Detroit: Gale Research, 1976), 226–227 and Monroe N. Work, ed., *Negro Year Book: an Annual Encyclopedia of the Negro, 1921–1922* (Tuskegee, AL: Negro Year Book Publishing, 1922), 213. Mather's phraseology leads me to the conclusion that he had correspondence of some sort with Morgan, since he gives explanations from Morgan himself rather than merely describing what he knew from other sources.

6. Presently, there is no way of determining Morgan's exact year of birth. 1869 is used as an estimate. This was ascertained by an examination of ship lists, which included dates of births, ages, racial information, and often the names of close relatives for passengers. The passenger list from the *S.S. Joseph J. Cuneo*, which sailed from Port Antonio, Jamaica to Philadelphia, arriving on October 28, 1914, indicates a date of 1869. The 1911 ship, *S.S. Patris*, which departed Piraeus, Greece and arrived in New York City on November 16, 1911, indicates 1871. A special thanks to Matthew Namee for providing the ship lists from his personal database. Namee acquired these lists from Ancestry.com.

7. Mather, 226.

8. See Edward B. Reuter, *The Mulatto in the United States* (Boston: R.G. Badger, 1918), 183–184, where he writes, "Father Raphard [*sic*] of Philadelphia, the one Negro Priest in the Greek Catholic Church, is a dark man, but not a full-blooded Negro." See also Richard Newman, *Words Like Freedom: Essays African-American Culture and History* (West Cornwall, CT: Locust Hill Press, 1996), 110.

9. Ibid. Work simply notes that Morgan traveled to Liberia, omitting any reference to Ferguson.

10. Both Work and Mather make the claim that Morgan studied at these institutions. Katharine Higgon, an archivist assistant at King's College sent an email to me on January 25, 2006, in which she noted that despite extensive investigation on her part, she was unable to locate any mention of one Robert Josias Morgan as a student in any department. Gavin White had received a similar reply during his research for his 1969 article on George Alexander McGuire. See White, 126. I have not yet searched any archival holdings for St. Aidan's Theological College, Birkenhead.

11. For Morgan's ordination date, see George F. Bragg, *History of the Afro-American Group of the Episcopal Church* (1922; repr. New York: Johnson Reprint Corporation, 1968), 273.

12. Mather, 226. That he was an honorary curate means that there must have been a priest who had oversight over his actions in the parish. A curate was often a deacon or priest-in-training.

13. White, 126. He is listed as being at Hoffman Hall in Nashville, Tennessee in Frederick Ebenezer John Lloyd, *The American Church Clergy and Parish Directory* (Uniontown, PA: Frederick E.J. Lloyd, 1905), 200. During the first four months of 1901, he served as rector of St. Philip's Episcopal Church in Richmond, Virginia. This information had been available on the parish website at http://stphilips.thediocese.net. Unfortunately, the link is no longer active. The current history link is quite truncated: http://www.stphilipsrva.org/About_Us/History_of_St_Philip_s/ (accessed November 29, 2012).

14. See White, 127, where he noted, "There can be no doubt that McGuire knew all about Morgan and it is very probable that he knew him personally. It is just possible that it was Morgan who first introduced McGuire to the Episcopal Church in Wilmington; it was almost certainly Morgan who introduced McGuire to the idea of Eastern episcopacy."

15. White, 111 and 126.

16. A list of the rectors of St. Thomas Episcopal Church may be found at http://www.accst.org/about_us/history/rectors.html.

17. See "The McGuire Lesson," *The Living Church* (June 25, 1921), 250. In at least one other instance, Bragg specifically calls himself a friend of McGuire. See *Church Advocate* 17:5 (1908), 1.

18. Mather, 226. The phrase, "pillar and ground of truth" is a reference to 1 Timothy 3:15, where St. Paul claimed the household of God, which is the Church, is the pillar and ground of truth.

19. Gavin White, 126, citing *Church Advocate*, March, 1898. White's essay was reprinted in Randall K. Burkett and Richard Newman, eds., *Black Apostles: Afro-American Clergy Confront the Twentieth Century* (Boston: G.K. Hall, 1978).

20. Peter F. Anson, *Bishops at Large* (London: Faber and Faber, 1964), 91.

21. Ibid., 93.

22. Ibid., 96.

23. Ibid., 108. Terry-Thompson did include some photocopies of official correspondence in the opening pages of his book.

24. Ibid., 127.

25. "Christmas is Celebrated by the Greek Christians," *Philadelphia Inquirer*, January 8, 1906. It should be noted that it

was not until 1915 that Vilatte formally established what he called the "American Catholic Church" (Anson, 124). Although that may be the case technically, the manner in which Vilatte had already been operating and the fact that Morgan was using the name publicly, suggests that Vilatte had already begun calling his church by that name as early as 1906.

26. *Amerikanskiĭ Pravoslavnyĭ Viestnik* October and November Supplement (1904), 380–382.

27. Ibid., 380.

28. See Bryn Geffert, *Eastern Orthodox and Anglicans* (Notre Dame, IN: University of Notre Dame Press, 2010). Morgan did not specifically mention any pre-trip awareness but one would think he must have been at least generally informed.

29. Allison Blakely, "The Negro in Imperial Russia: A Preliminary Sketch," *Journal of Negro History* 61:4 (1976), 353.

30. Ibid., 354. The most famous example may be General Ivan Hannibal, who became a general under Peter the Great after being brought from Africa in 1707.

31. *Amerikanskiĭ Pravoslavnyĭ Viestnik*, October and November Supplement (1904), 381–382.

32. Ibid., 382.

33. Ibid., 381.

34. Ibid.

35. Ibid., 382.

36. Ibid.

37. Paul G. Manolis, *Raphael (Robert) Morgan the First Black Orthodox Priest in America* (Athens, NP: 1981), 6.

38. Ibid. The documents themselves may be found in Manolis, 14–21. A more summarized version, without the documents may be found in a Greek article by Bishop Makarios of Rirogtas. See Bishop Makarios of Rirogtas, "O protos mauros orthodoxos iereas: Raphala Robertos Morgkan." *Orthodoxi Marturia* 50 (1996), 72–75.

39. Ibid., 7, 14–15. In the Orthodox Church, a man desiring to be a priest must be ordained a deacon first. The reader is reminded that although it is the practice of the Russian Orthodox Church to chrismate converts who had already received a Trinitarian baptism, the Greek Orthodox Church rebaptized

such converts, a practice started in response to Roman Catholic rebaptism of Orthodox Christians. The Roman Catholic Church has since ceased this practice. To this day, Constantinople and the Greek Orthodox Church officially sanction rebaptism, but in America, the Greek Orthodox Archdiocese regularly extends leniency, or *economia*. In this regard, the Greek Orthodox Church in America follows the Slavic practice of recognizing Trinitarian baptisms, but does so while trying to keep to the letter of the law for Constantinople. During Morgan's time, such leniency, or expediency, was not yet the standard practice in America. To enter the Greek Orthodox Church, a Western Christian had to accept an Orthodox baptism in place of any Western baptism given previously, even if that baptism had been Trinitarian. See John Erickson, "On the Cusp of Modernity: The Canonical Hermeneutic of St Nikodemos the Haghiorite (1748-1809)," *St Vladimir's Theological Quarterly* 42:1 (1998), 45-66 and Timothy (Kallistos) Ware, *Eustratios Argenti: A Study of the Greek Church under Turkish Rule* (Oxford: Clarendon Press, 1964), 65-107.

40. Mather, 226.
41. Manolis, 8-9. It should be noted that being granted the right to hear confessions was an honor and is not normally granted to a priest in the Greek tradition until some time has passed following his ordination. By contrast, in the Slavic tradition, a priest may hear confession immediately upon ordination.
42. Ibid. The antimension, which means, "instead of table," is a cloth that must reside on the altar, or table being used as an altar, during an Orthodox Divine Liturgy. It contains depictions of the four evangelists in the corners and the laying of Christ in the tomb. A relic from a saint is sewn into the cloth and the cloth is signed by the bishop, providing episcopal approval for the priest and community in question to serve the Eucharistic liturgy.
43. Vilatte himself had, in fact, argued in an autobiography on behalf of the Old Catholic Church on the basis that Protestants had not only removed the "Roman errors, but also a part of the primitive deposit of faith," qtd. in Anson, 92.
44. Ibid., 9.

45. Ibid., 10–11. Concerning Cartier, Bragg lists the initials as "A. V. C." See *History of the Afro-American Group*, 273. However, the records in Constantinople (available in Manolis) and the archives of the Episcopal Church both list his initials as "A. C. V." and so that is what I have used here. As for Cartier himself, he had been ordained a deacon and then priest in 1895 and eventually died a Protestant Episcopal priest in South Carolina in 1917. See Bragg, *History of the Afro-American Group*, 273, for the dates of his ordination (under Bishop Quintard). Concerning A. C. V. Cartier's later career, I am reliant upon correspondence with Glen Colliver, archivist for the Protestant Episcopal Diocese of Pennsylvania.

46. See "Deacon Suspended," *Gleaner*, June 4, 1908.

47. Charlotte Selina Morgan against Robert Josiah Morgan is case number 72 of the March Term of 1909 from the Court of Common Pleas of Delaware County, Pennsylvania. The presiding judge was Andrew J. Dalton. According to the divorce records, the marriage was a difficult one. From the testimonies of Charlotte and a witness, it seems almost certain that Fr. Raphael Morgan was abusive, though it is possible that Charlotte was also an unstable person, making a bad situation even worse. Their marriage consisted of years of separations and reunions. The children were split between them, with their son remaining with her and the daughter remaining with him. See also "30 Years Later," *Chester Times*, March 21, 1939.

48. Ship list from S.S. Patris, Sailing from Piraeus to Ellis Island, October 29, 1911. Matthew Namee, who kindly provided me with the ship lists he obtained through an Ancestry.com search, first noted this in his biography of Morgan. See Namee, 453.

49. Mather, 226.

50. For references to a lecture in 1901 and again in 1902, see, "West Africa," *Gleaner*, October 9, 1901 and "Port Maria, A Lecture," *Gleaner*, October 7, 1902. The 1911 trip is evidenced by his name in the passenger list for the *S.S. Patris*, which sailed from Athens to Ellis Island. This trip was likely for the purposes of some official visit, since the archbishop of Athens and the synod of Greece would have been overseeing the Greek Orthodox parishes in America at this time.

51. For some references to his speaking engagements and lectures, see the following: "Shipping News," *Gleaner*, July 16, 1913; "Priest is now on Visit to His Native Land," *Gleaner*, July 22, 1913; "Some Interesting Church Notes and Services," *Gleaner*, August 9, 1913; "Father Raphael," *Gleaner*, August 15, 1913; "Father Raphael," *Gleaner*, August 22, 1913; "Father Raphael," *Gleaner*, August 28, 1913; "Current Items," *Gleaner*, September 10, 1913; "General Notes," *Gleaner*, September 12, 1913; "Current Items," *Gleaner*, October 24, 1913; "Happenings in the Parishes," *Gleaner*, October 30, 1913; "A Lecture Given," *Gleaner*, July 15, 1914. Morgan had already attracted some minor attention in Jamaica, as evidenced by a 1908 article. See "Deacon Suspended," *Gleaner*, June 4, 1908.

52. "Late News from Port Antonio," *Gleaner*, November 2, 1914.

53. Ibid. Although Bishop Raphael was a bishop in the Russian Orthodox diocese of the Aleutian Islands and North America, archivist Alex Liberovsky informed me that the archives in Syosset contain no record of this correspondence. It is possible that it exists somewhere in the archives of the Antiochian Archdiocese in Pennsylvania, but presently their archives are in need of further organization.

54. "Mass on Warship," *Gleaner*, December 27, 1913.

55. See "Mr. Marcus Garvey in U.S.," *Gleaner*, October 4, 1916 and "Letter Denouncing Marcus Garvey," in Robert A. Hill, ed., *The Marcus Garvey and Universal Negro Improvement Association Papers*, vol. 1, *1826–August 1919* (Berkeley, Los Angeles, and London: University of California Press, 1983), 106–107. Robert A. Hill cites the *Jamaican Times*, October 7, 1916.

56. The literature on Garvey is extensive. For a starting point, the following may prove helpful: Robert A Hill, ed., *The Marcus Garvey and Universal Negro Improvement Association Papers*, vol. I–VII, IX. (Berkeley, Los Angeles, London: University of California Press, 1983–1995); Randall K. Burkett, *Garveyism as a Religious Movement: The Institutionalization of a Black Civil Religion* (Metuchen, N.J.: Scarecrow Press, 1978); Edmund David Cronon, *Black Moses: The Story of Marcus Garvey* (Madison: University of Wisconsin Press, 1955).

57. Of the 13, I have only been able to verify the existence of a few: Henry J. Booth, who arrived in 1911 from Kingston, Aldred Campbell, who arrived from Jamaica in 1906, Hubert Barclay, who arrived in 1915 from Clarendon, Phillip Hemmings, who is listed in the 1920 census, and S.C. Box, who arrived to the United States by way of England. There is no reason to doubt the existence of the others. It seems that the signers were not people of high social stature, which would explain the difficulty in researching them. Philip Hemmings would later join Garvey's movement. One signer, H.S. Boulin, later joined Garvey's movement and worked covertly as a federal agent. See Robert A. Hill, *The Marcus Garvey and Universal Negro Improvement Association Papers*, vol. XI, The Caribbean Diaspora (Durham, NC: Duke University Press, 2011), 730. There was no mention of Morgan in Boulin's file in the FBI archives, since they cover a later period of Boulin's life.

58. "Mr. Marcus Garvey in U.S.," *Gleaner*, October 4, 1916.

59. Mather, 226.

60. *Boyd's Philadelphia City Directory* (Philadelphia: C.E. Howe, 1916), 1209. I am indebted to Fr. Anastasius Bandy, the late archivist and historian for Annunciation Greek Orthodox Church in Philadelphia, for this observation. Morgan was also listed in the directories for 1907, 1909, and 1910. It is possible he died in Philadelphia, though responses from both Mount Lawn Cemetery and Joy Hill Cemetery Company revealed no listing for Morgan. Another logical (and perhaps more likely) burial place, Eden Cemetery, has not yet responded to several attempts at correspondence. It is possible that Morgan did return to Jamaica in 1916 in order to serve the local Syrian/Lebanese population.

61. The phrase *filioque* means "and the Son" and referred to the origin of the Holy Spirit. The phrase was originally used to combat Arianism in Spain in the sixth century but did not become a church-wide concern until it was added to many Western recitations of the Nicene-Constantinopolitan Creed in the ninth century and received papal blessing in the eleventh. The Eastern Churches disputed both the theology as well

as the lack of ecumenical concensus for the addition and to this day, they do not include it.

62. See http://netministries.org/frames.asp?ch=ch26904&st=NY& name=African%20Orthodox%20Church%20Inc.&city= New%20York%20City (accessed November 29, 2012).

63. Byron Rushing strongly argued against the idea that the African Orthodox Church had its origins in Garvey's UNIA. See Byron Rushing, "A Note On the Origin of the African Orthodox Church," *The Journal of Negro History* 57:1 (1972), 37–39. Gavin White and Warren C. Platt, while acknowledging some influence from Garvey, also emphasized McGuire's independence. See White, 120; Platt, 477. Juan Williams has recently argued the reverse, placing the impetus on McGuire's encounter with the UNIA. Juan Williams, *This Far by Faith: Stories from the African American Religious Experience* (New York: Harper Collins, 2003), 180–181.

64. See Richard Newman, *Words Like Freedom: Essays African-American Culture and History* (West Cornwall, CT: Locust Hill Press, 1996), 110. Newman stated that Morgan and McGuire did, in fact, know each other, but I have been unable to do any more than locate them within the same social circle. He may have had access to records which I have not yet obtained or are no longer extant. See Newman, 132 n.15.

65. Irvine himself had been a convert. See Dellas Oliver Herbel, "Turning to Tradition: Intra-Christian Converts and the Making of an American Orthodox Church" (doctoral dissertation, Saint Louis University, 2009), 162–196.

66. Richard Newman, "Archbishop Daniel William Alexander and the African Orthodox Church," *The International Journal of African Historical Studies* 16:4 (1983), 617.

67. Ibid., 619.

68. Qtd in. Newman, 620.

69. Newman, 624.

70. Archbishop Daniel William Alexander to Metropolitan Isidore, October 16, 1934, African Orthodox Church Records, RG 005, Archives and Manuscripts Department, Pitts Theology Library, Emory University.

71. Ibid.

72. Metropolitan Isidore to Archbishop Daniel William Alexander, September 17, 1935, African Orthodox Church Records, RG 005, Archives and Manuscripts Dept., Pitts Theology Library, Emory University.

73. F.B. Welbourn, *East African Rebels, A Study of Some Independent Churches* (London: SCM Press, 1961).

74. Spartas, qtd. in Welbourn, 77.

75. Newman, 622. See also Theodore Natsoulas, "Patriarch McGuire and the Spread of the African Orthodox Church to Africa," *Journal of Religion in Africa* 12 (1982), 100.

76. Natsoulas, 100.

77. Newman, "Archbishop Daniel William Alexander," 625.

78. Ibid.

79. For information on their formal conversion in 1946, as well as persecution in the 1950s and an overview of Orthodox mission work in Africa during the twentieth century, see Stephen Hayes, "Orthodox Mission in tropical Africa," *Missionalia* 24:3 (1996), 383–398. Originally available at http://hayesfam. bravehost.com/ORTHMISS.HTM [a currently broken link], his essay may now be found at http://www.orthodoxytz.com/ OrthodoxMission.asp (accessed November 29, 2012). Although Orthodoxy expanded in Africa due to the initiative of Africans themselves, Hayes also discussed the efforts of Greek missionary-priest Fr. Nicodemus Sarikas. For a brief discussion of Spartas leaving the Orthodox Church, see Allan H. Anderson, *African Reformation: African Initiated Christianity in the 20th Century* (Trenton, NJ: Africa World Press, 2001), 146.

80. Ibid.

81. John Binns, *An Introduction to the Christian Orthodox Churches* (New York: Cambridge University Press, 2002), 14.

Chapter 3

1. This narrative derives from my discussions with Berry on August 13, 2006. A reference to this story, but not the story itself, may be found in Father Moses Berry, "An Encounter

with a Saint," *Again* 17:2 (1994), 26. Except when citing Berry's writings or another interview, my presentation here derives from our discussions in August 2006 and November 2007. For a short summary of Berry's life, see also Mike Penprase, "Religious Mission Expanding," *Springfield News-Leader*, October 15, 1998.

2. As in the case of Raphael Morgan, the reader is reminded that upon ordination, a priest receives a saint's name, by which he is thereafter known within his ministerial capacity. Saints' names are taken by anyone baptized and/or chrismated (anointed with chrism) in the Orthodox Church, but in reality, only those of the clergy tend to become public identities.

3. Fr. Moses Berry, in personal discussions with the author, August 13, 2006. See also, Berry, "An Encounter with a Saint," 26.

4. Berry, "An Encounter with a Saint," 26.

5. Paisius Altschul, ed., *An Unbroken Circle: Linking Ancient African Christianity to the African-American Experience* (St. Louis: Brotherhood of St. Moses the Black, 1997), 66–67. Incidentally, Wallace White, Berry's great-grandfather, was also the only member of Company D not to receive a military pension, though Berry notes his great-grandfather was not resentful, but thankful for what he did have.

6. Ibid., 67.

7. Ibid., 68.

8. Father Moses Berry, "Lost Heritage," *Epiphany* 15:4 (1996), 74.

9. "Lost Heritage of African Americans," 67.

10. Fr. Moses Berry, in discussion with the author, August 13, 2006.

11. A highly informative history of HOOM may be found in Phillip Charles Lucas, *The Odyssey of a New Religion: the Holy Order of MANS from New Age to Orthodoxy* (Bloomington, IN: Indiana University Press, 1999). MANS was an acronym standings for the Greek words mysterion, agape, nous, and sophia. A brief history may be found in Hieromonk Jonah (Paffhausen), "The Doors of Repentance: The Journey of the Holy Order of MANS/Christ the Saviour Brotherhood and the St. Herman of Alaska Brotherhood into the Canonical

Orthodox Church," *AGAIN* 23:1 (2001), 23–26. Jonah Paff-hausen was subsequently elevated to the episcopacy and is now a retired metropolitan of the Orthodox Church in America.

12. See Lucas, 46.

13. Berry, in discussion with the author, November 9, 2007. In 1979, Berry went to Harlem as a youth director for St. Philips's Episcopal Cathedral, under the pastorate of the notable African American social activist and minister, Rev. M. Moran Weston. Fr. Moses Berry, in discussion with the author, November 9, 2007.

14. Fr. Moses Berry, in discussion with the author, November 9, 2007. At a deanery meeting in December 2007, at which I was present, Archbishop Job decided to merge the two parishes. Fr. Christopher Phillips, the rector of Christ the Good Shepherd, became the pastor of the joint community.

15. Fr. Seraphim died in 1982 and in 1984, ROCOR suspended Podmoshensky from the priesthood on charges of homosex-uality and threatening the life of his bishop. However, Pod-moshensky had already been "evangelizing" HOOMS as early as 1982.

16. Certificate No. 330 from The New Valaam Theological Acad-emy, dated 12/25 day of September, 1985, issued to Rev. Karl Berry, available in the archives of Fr. Moses Berry (henceforth, AFMB).

17. Hieromonk Jonah, 24. At the time, Abbot Herman was Berry's spiritual director. See Abbot Herman to Fr. Moses Berry, Sep-tember 11/24, 1988 and Abbot Herman to Fr. Moses Berry, September 11/24, 1993. AFMB. Orthodox Christians con-tinue to call Easter by the name Pascha, the Greek word for "Passover."

18. Abbot Herman Podmoshensky to Fr. Moses Berry, September 11/24, 1988, AFMB. Again, the reader is reminded that the first date is from the Julian Calendar, used by Orthodox to determine Pascha (Easter) and the surrounding ecclesiastical year. Since 1900, the calendars have differed by thirteen days.

19. Abbot Herman Podmoshensky to Fr. Moses Berry, September 11/25, 1993, AFMB. Underline and grammatical shifts were in the original. This letter actually contained many phrases

contrasting the world and Christ the Savior Brotherhood's Orthodox faith.

20. Podmoshenky's outlook has also been called "traditionalist" or a "catacomb ecclesiology." See Paffhausen, 24.
21. Discussions with the author, November 2007.
22. "An Encounter with a Saint," 26–27. Berry expanded upon this in personal discussions with the author, August 13, 2006.
23. "An Encounter with a Saint," 26.
24. Ibid., 27.
25. Ibid.
26. Berry, "An Encounter with a Saint," 27. Berry expanded upon this in personal discussions with the author, August 13, 2006
27. "An Encounter with a Saint," 27. The reference to "New Calendar" versus "Old Calendar" is a reference to the fact that some Orthodox Churches, including the majority in America, have adopted the later Gregorian calendar for determining its liturgical cycle except for that of Pascha (Easter).
28. See Thelma Michaila Altschul, "31st and Troost: An Orthodox Mission Flowers in the Inner City," *AGAIN* 17:2 (1994), 24–25. The parish is pastored by Paisius Altschul, editor of the book *Unbroken Circle*. It's website contains information on the conferences of St. Moses the Black. See http://www.stmaryofegypt. net. The parish eventually left Pangratios Vrionis' jurisdiction and is now within the Serbian Orthodox Church.
29. Paisius Altschul, ed., *An Unbroken Circle: Linking Ancient African Christianity to the African-American Experience* (St. Louis: Brotherhood of St. Moses the Black, 1997), xiii.
30. Farajajé-Jones was later removed from the Orthodox priesthood when he advocated alternative sexual mores. He subsequently became a Muslim and changed his name to Ibrahim Abdurrahman Farajajé. Farajajé continued to explore the connection(s) between African American spirituality and African spirituality.
31. This purpose for the Brotherhood of St. Moses the Black may be found on the brotherhood's website: http://www. mosestheblack.org/ (accessed December 19, 2012).
32. This collection is the book, *An Unbroken Circle*, cited in the note above.

33. 65–73 and 164–166.
34. For example, see Father Paisius Altschul, *Wade in the River: The Story of the African Christian Faith* (Kansas City: Crossbearers Publishing, 2001); Jerome Sanderson, *Saint Moses the Ethiopian* (Indianapolis: Christ the Saviour Brotherhood, 2001); Jerome Sanderson and Carla Thomas, *Saints of Africa* (Indianapolis: Christ the Saviour Brotherhood, 2006).
35. Berry, "Full Circle: A Final Word from the Brotherhood of St. Moses the Black," in *An Unbroken Circle*, 164.
36. "Lost Heritage," 76. In Mark 9:29, Jesus informs his disciples that the reason they could not exorcise a demon was because it could not be removed except by "prayer and fasting."
37. Berry spoke at length about this during our discussions in August, 2006.
38. Berry, "Full Circle,"165.
39. Ibid.
40. See Hieromonk Jonah, 24.
41. Fr. Moses Berry, in discussion with the author, November 9, 2007. Berry remains thankful for what Podmoshensky did and still loves the man, but feels "misled" nonetheless and believes Podmoshensky led them astray by advocating for Pangratios's group rather than guiding them directly into canonical Orthodoxy.
42. See "Rediscovering Africa's Ancient Christian Heritage," *The Orthodox Church* 42:7/8 (2006), 16–17. Metropolitan Herman, metropolitan of the Orthodox Church in America (OCA), recognized the importance of the work of the Brotherhood of St. Moses the Black, and wrote to Archbishop Nathaniel of Detroit and the Romanian Episcopate, "I invoke God's blessing upon all those who have organized the Conference and all those who will attend." Metropolitan Herman to Archbishop Nathaniel, June 16, 2006.
43. Albert Raboteau, *A Sorrowful Joy* (New York and Mahwah, N.J.: Paulist Press, 2002).
44. Ibid., 35.
45. Theotokos literally means "God-bearer," or "birth-giver of God." This is a traditional Christian reference to Mary still used by Orthodox today.

46. Raboteau, 41.
47. Ibid., 42.
48. Albert Panteleimon Raboteau, afterword to *An Unbroken Circle*, 162.
49. Ibid.
50. Ibid.
51. Ibid.
52. Ibid., 163.
53. Albert J. Raboteau, "American Salvation: The Place of Christianity in Public Life," *Boston Review* (April/May, 2005), available at http://bostonreview.net/BR30.2/raboteau.html (accessed December 21, 2012).
54. This can be seen in several stories in: Virginia Nieuwsma, *Our Hearts' True Home* (Ben Lomond, CA: Conciliar Press, 1996). See also Frederica Mathewes-Green, "Men and Church," *Word* (December 2007), available at http://www.antiochian.org/node/17069 (accessed December 12, 2012).
55. Dr. Carla N. Thomas kindly presented the outline of her own religious journey through email correspondence, March, 2010.
56. Carla N. Thomas, *Unbroken Circle*, 133–139.
57. James H. Cone, "America: A Dream or A Nightmare?" *Journal of the International Theological Center* 13:2 (1986), 264.
58. Ibid., 271.
59. And here I am taking for granted that readers realize a key difference. Berry and the Brotherhood of St. Moses the Black emphasize an otherworldly, suffering Christian spirituality. In contrast, Malcolm X saw Christianity as a driving force in racial suppression and was willing to use "any means necessary" to achieve his goal, which was not steps toward full integration but the furthering of black nationalism. See Derek Q. Reeves, "Beyond the River Jordan: An Essay on the Continuity of the Black Prophetic Tradition," *The Journal of Religious Thought* 47:2 (1991), 48.
60. Raboteau, *Canaan Land: A Religious History of African Americans* (New York: Oxford University Press, 2001), 89.
61. This answer should not surprise us, since Raboteau himself pointed out a similar problem with scholarship that tended to dichotomize earlier African American thought between W. E. B. Du

Bois and Booker T. Washington, who disagreed on how best
to respond to the racial situation. "This disagreement between
DuBois and Washington reveals a sometimes overlooked fact:
African-American opinion has never been unanimous. The various perspectives . . . reflected their differences in class, education,
residence, and religion." Raboteau, *Canaan Land*, 78.

Chapter 4

1. Peter E. Gillquist, *Becoming Orthodox: A Journey to the Ancient Christian Faith* (Brentwood, TN: Wolgemuth & Hyatt,
   1989), 146–152.
2. A parachurch organization is a faith-based organization that
   is not under the direct oversight of any one tradition, denomination, or church. Such entities may be businesses, non-profit
   organizations, or even private associations.
3. The version of the EOC conversion journey described in this
   book is the one to which he referred me when I asked in telephone conversations (in 2007 and again in 2009) about his
   journey. He had mentioned a "great documents" file but did
   not have it readily available either time. Unfortunately, the
   possibility for follow-up conversations no longer exists, as Fr.
   Peter Gillquist died on July 1, 2012.
4. It should be noted that although I provide a "fuller" picture
   here, many former members of the Evangelical Orthodox
   Church and the Orthodox Church into which they converted
   (the Antiochian Orthodox Christian Archdiocese of North
   America) are uncomfortable discussing events related to the
   Evangelical Orthodox Church's integration into Orthodox
   Christianity. The reasons for their hesitancy are varied, rang-
   ing from not wishing to discuss painful events to a fear of re-
   prisal from fellow Orthodox clergy, including Metropolitan
   Philip, the leading Antiochian bishop in America. For this
   reason, much of the correspondence I cite below will not cite
   any particular archive. In those cases, obtaining the materials
   was difficult and in those cases, I had to agree not to name
   those who provided them.

5. See http://evangelicalorthodox.org/site/our-churches/ (accessed January 18, 2013).
6. Gillquist, "Evangelicals Turned Orthodox," *Christian Century* 109:8 (1992), 242.
7. Ibid.
8. The evangelical background centered on the Campus Crusade for Christ and the Christian World Liberation Front. Evangelicalism in the Berkeley area was a dynamic enterprise in the 1960s. For more information on this background, including those who would develop into leaders in the Evangelical Orthodox Church, see Adam Scott Parsons, "Everyday Apocalyptic: Radical Politics and Evangelical Society, 1969-2000" (doctoral dissertation, Syracuse University, in progress).
9. Peter E. Gillquist, "Presiding Bishop's Corner," *AGAIN* 2:4 (October–December 1979), 2.
10. Ibid.
11. *Becoming Orthodox*, 20–21.
12. Ibid., 21.
13. George Peter Liacopulos noted that another member who was present thought about fifty-five men had gathered. See George Peter Liacopulos, "A Comparative Study of Selected Orthodox Missiological Approaches Emerging in Contemporary American Society" (doctoral dissertation, Princeton Theological Seminary, 1995), 168. This is the same number given by Ron Grove, who was allowed to spend time with the newly formed Evangelical Orthodox Church and participated in their liturgical life to quite an extent and got to know its members and leaders. See Ron Grove, "Authenticity and Discipline in Isla Vista: A Study of the Evangelical Orthodox Church," paper delivered at the Southwest Anthropological Association in Santa Barbara, March 21, 1981.
14. Gillquist, "Presiding Bishop's Corner," *AGAIN* 2:4 (October–December, 1979), 29.
15. Ibid., 21, emphasis in the original.
16. Bill Counts, *The Evangelical Orthodox Church and the New Covenant Apostolic Order* (Berkeley: The Spiritual Counterfeits Project, 1979), 2–3.

17. Liacopulos, 169, citing *AGAIN* 1 (October–December 1978), 12 and 13.

18. Gillquist, *Becoming Orthodox*, 33–34.

19. Ibid., 39–44.

20. Ibid., 44–49.

21. Ibid., 38. Ron L. Zell, who served as the EOC's "deacon of music" claimed the EOC lost a lot of people from this, more than Gillquist and others indicated. Zell made this point in discussions with the author on February 13, 2013.

22. This was relayed to me in conversations and emails by Fr. James (Arnold) Bernstein, Fr. Ted Wojcik, and Ron Zell. Zell in particular remembered the phrase "Charismatic Apostolic Succession" being important and repeated often.

23. Ron Grove, "An Orthodox Perspective on the EOC," unpublished paper for an anthropology class, dated September, 1983. Grove offered this as a supplement to his conference paper given two years earlier.

24. Ibid.

25. Ibid. Grove asked about this practice and was told kitchen elements were "part of" the living room elements and therefore equally the body of Christ, though he was also told that the kitchen elements in this way were like *antidoron*. Antidoron is what remains from the loaf of bread after the celebrant removes the portion that is to be consecrated within the liturgy itself. As Grove noted, "At the least, the EOC is confused about Orthodox eucharistic practices."

26. See Grant Wacker, "Playing for Keeps: The Primitivist Impulse in Early Pentecostalism," in *The American Quest for the Primitive Church*, ed. by Richard T. Hughes (Urbana, IL: University of Illinois Press, 1988), 196–219.

27. I am not the first scholar to have discussed this. Bruce Wollenberg analyzed the group and noticed a "lust for authority." See Bruce Wolenberg, "The Evangelical Orthodox Church: A Preliminary Appraisal," *Christian Century* 97:23 (1980), 701–702.

28. Counts, 4.

29. See Robin Fornoff, "Ex-members call Glen Park church a cullt," *Post-Tribune*, March 30, 1980; "Healing by faith called

extremist," March 30, 1980; " 'Prophet' now calls church a cult," *Post-Tribune*, March 31, 1980.; and "Members confirm some church extremes," April 2, 1980.

30. According to Fornoff's findings in "Healing by faith called extremist," Rogers once ordered a diabetic to cease his medication because Rogers believed he had healed the man. When a parishioner noted that the man was showing symptoms consistent with diabetes, she was removed from the community and "shunned." Fred Rogers followed the majority of the Evangelical Orthodox Church in the Antiochian Orthodox Christian Archdiocese of North America and currently serves St. Barnabas Orthodox Church in Lexington, South Carolina, as Fr. Gregory Rogers.

31. See Richard Ballew, Kurt Speier, and John Sommer to Carol Barnett, May 11, 1979. In this letter the three men wrote, "How could the integrity of your commitment dissolve so quickly, so easily? The Lord hasn't changed his mind. We haven't changed ours. This behavior [questioning whether to join] is so unlike you, Carol. It seems as though someone has bewitched you. Whoever they are, they will bear their own judgment." Notice that according to this letter, the Lord's "mind" or decision and theirs is one and the same.

32. The description of what I outline here may be found in Ron Zell to Dr. Howard, February 7, 1984, and Ronald L. Zell to Bishop Maximos of Pittsburgh, February 18, 1984. Both letters contained the same outline of events, though the letters differed slightly in phrasing. "Dr. Howard" refers to Dr. Thomas Howard, author of *Evangelical is Not Enough*, and one of the collaborators with Gillquist and others in support of an effort by Robert E. Webber in 1977 to call evangelicals to a more historically conscious and liturgical expression of Christianity.

33. Qtd. in Counts, 4.

34. Ibid.

35. Peter E. Gillquist, "Believing What is Right," *AGAIN* 2:1 (January–March 1979), 1, 7.

36. For example, Fr. Mel Gimmaka, who had been a bishop within the EOC and currently serves as a priest at St. Innocent

Orthodox Church in Everson, Washington, claimed in a phone conversation on January 19, 2013, that the extent of the authoritarian behavior varied from location to location and that the parishes in California and Gary, Indiana are not necessarily representative of every EOC parish, though he acknowledged that the use of spiritual courts and an emphasis on authority was an aspect of the EOC as a whole. Recent scholarship has also cautioned against using the label "cult," pointing out the role news media and pop culture have had in providing definitions of "cult" over the years. See, for example, Lynn S. Neal, "They're Freaks! The Cult Sterotype in Fictional Television Shows, 1958–2008," *Nova Religio* 14:3 (2011), 81–107 and Joseph Laycock, "Where Do They Get These Ideas? Changing Ideas of Cults in the Mirror of Popular Culture," *Journal of the American Academy of Religion* 81:1 (2013), 80–106.

37. Although Gillquist wrote the book that has become the standard narrative for the group, others have published similarly sanitized and selectively edited accounts. For example, Fr. Gregory Rogers, who was Bishop Fred Rogers of the EOC parishes in Gary, Indiana, has posted a short narrative online, available at http://www.christisrisen.org/evang-to-orthodox.html (accessed January 21, 2013).

38. Richard T. Hughes and C. Leonard Allen, *Illusions of Innocence: Protestant Primitivism in America, 1630–1875* (Chicago: University of Chicago Press, 1988), 79.

39. Ibid., 205. This irony is a central theme highlighted throughout the monograph.

40. Rev. Gene Selander to the Executive Committee of the National Association of Evangelicals, October 3, 1984. National Association of Evangelical Papers (SC-113), Wheaton College Special Collections, Wheaton, Illinois. See also John G. Turner, *Bill Bright & Campus Crusade for Christ* (Chapel Hill: University of North Carolina Press, 2008), 212–213.

41. Jack Sparks, *The Mindbenders: A Look at Current Cults* (Nashville: Thomas Nelson, 1977).

42. Documents from the case, including the retraction published by Thomas Nelson in major newspapers across the country

may be found at http://www.contendingforthefaith.org/libel-litigations/mindbenders/ (accessed March 1, 2013).

43. Peter E. Gillquist, "Presiding Bishop's Corner," *AGAIN* 2:1 (January–March 1979), 2.

44. Liacopulos, 182 and 187. In particular, Liacopulos cited Mike Reagan, "What Orderly Living Means to Me," *AGAIN* 1 (July–September 1978), 11 and Jon E. Braun, "Share the Vision," *AGAIN* 14 (1991), 28–29.

45. On this, see Dean M. Kelley, *Why Conservative Churches are Growing: A Study in Sociology of Religion* (New York: Harper and Row, 1972).

46. See, for example, Lawrence R. Iannaccone, "Why strict churches are strong," *American Journal of Sociology* 99 (1994), 1180–1211 and Rodney Stark and Roger Finke, *Acts of faith* (Berkeley: University of California Press, 2000).

47. See Joseph B. Tamney and Stephen D. Johnson, "The Popularity of Strict Churches," *Review of Religious Research* 39: 3 (1998), 209–223; Joseph B. Tamney, "Does Strictness Explain the Appeal of Working-Class Conservative Protestant Congregations?" *Sociology of Religion* 66: 3 (2005), 283–302; and Gary D. Bouma, "The Real Reason One Conservative Church Grew," *Review of Religious Research* 50 (2008), 43–44.

48. See George Vecsey, "New Group Combines Evangelism and Orthodoxy: Ritual and Tradition 'A Spiritual Super Race,'" *New York Times*, March 11, 1979.

49. See "New church body formed," *Chicago Tribune*, March 11, 1979.

50. Vecsey, March 11, 1979.

51. Ibid.

52. In addition to the correspondence I cite here, I base my account on a corroborating telephone conversation on January 19, 2013, with Bernstein, who is now known as Fr. James Bernstein and is a priest in the Antiochian Orthodox Christian Archdiocese of North America. Jeremiah Crawford, friends with Bernstein, also left the EOC at this time and currently serves as a deacon within the Orthodox Church in America.

53. Robert Guio to Arnold Bernstein, October 12, 1981.
54. Arnold Bernstein to Robert Guio, an undated letter written sometime before Guio's October 12 letter.
55. Undated letter of Arnold Bernstein to Robert Guio. This letter would have been written sometime in mid-October.
56. Peter Gillquist, "Evangelicals Turned Orthodox," *Christian Century* 109:8 (1992), 242–245.
57. Peter E. Gillquist, "Presiding Bishop's Corner," *AGAIN* 3:3 (July–September 1980), 2. Here, Gillquist was responding to Wollenberg, cited above for critiquing the EOC as merely another form of American primitivism. Gillquist took Wollenberg's assessment seriously, arguing that the task for the EOC was not simply restoring the New Testament church within the EOC, but getting the EOC to enter into communion with the Orthodox Churches, also seen as expressions of the New Testament Church.
58. Weldon Hardenbrook and Terry Somerville, "Parachurch or Parasite?" *AGAIN* 4:2 (1981), 2.
59. Peter E. Gillquist, "Editorial: Christless Church or Churchless Christ?" *AGAIN* 5:3 (1982), 2. Emphasis is in the original.
60. Gillquist, *Becoming Orthodox*, 61.
61. Billy A. Melvin to Peter Gillquist, December 21, 1984. National Association of Evangelical Papers (SC-113), Wheaton College Special Collections, Wheaton, Illinois.
62. Two members who wrote to the executive committee were Gene Selander and Donald B. Patterson. Selander had been involved with the Campus Crusade for Christ and feared that the authoritarianism of the EOC meant the EOC leaders had "become what they once opposed—and perhaps even more severe." He also expressed concerns regarding transubstantiation and consubstantiation as well as apostolic succession. See Gene Selander to the NAE Executive Committee, October 3, 1984. Patterson expressed concern over the EOC's authoritarianism and lack of charity toward other evangelicals. See Donald B. Patterson to Billy A. Melvin, November 19, 1984. Both letters may be found in: National Association of Evangelical Papers (SC-113), Wheaton College Special Collections, Wheaton, Illinois.

63. Peter Gillquist."The Response of Peter E. Gillquist, Presiding Bishop of the Evangelical Orthodox Church to the Four Questions Posed by the Board of Administration of the National Association of Evangelicals." National Association of Evangelical Papers (SC-113), Wheaton College Special Collections, Wheaton, Illinois.

64. Ibid., 4.

65. Ibid., 5.

66. Billy A. Melvin to Peter Gillquist, April 10, 1985. National Association of Evangelical Papers (SC-113), Wheaton College Special Collections, Wheaton, Illinois.

67. This event was shared with me by Fr. Ted Wojcik in an email exchange. Bishop Dmitri led the committee and Frs. John Meyendorff and Michael Prokurat also served on the committee.

68. See Ron Zell to Bishop Maximos of Pittsburgh, February 18, 1984, cited above. In conversations with the author, on February 13, 2013, Zell stated that on more than one occasion, he had been told by Greek Orthodox clergy that his case was known by the Greek Orthodox hierarchs.

69. Gillquist recounted their moods as "varying degrees of despair" (*Becoming Orthodox*, 152).

70. Fr. Thomas Hopko was visiting Holy Cross Seminary at the time and verified that they were "dejected." He stated that the EOC had a meeting with Archbishop Iakavos. Gillquist mentioned a meeting (151) but did not mention Archbishop Iakavos' declaration. Hopko admitted to standing outside, not too far from the door, which, because of the loudness of Iakavos and others, enabled him to hear much of the meeting (in conversation on January 25, 2013).

71. Gillquist, *Becoming Orthodox.*, 153–157.

72. Ibid., 157.

73. Gillquist stressed Philip's role even more in *Metropolitan Philip: His Life and His Dreams* (Nashville: Thomas Nelson, 1991), 255–272.

74. The entirety of this narrative was recounted to me by Fr. Thomas Hopko on January 25, 2013.

75. According to Hopko, "I was involved in at least 25 hours of formal dialogue and discussion during the visit, not counting

conversations during meals, traveling, informal gatherings and periods of relaxation." Thomas Hopko, "Reflections on the EVANGELICAL ORTHODOX CHURCH and its entry into full communion with the Orthodox Church," Report Sent to Metropolitan Maximos, Metropolitan Philip, and Metropolitan Theodosius, February 1986, p. 1. The report is available in the personal archives of Fr. Thomas Hopko.

76. Ibid. Hopko made many suggestions throughout the report, noting a lack of "living Orthodox involvement" (3), or that "living Tradition."

77. Ibid. See p. 2 where Hopko worte "In evaluating the EOC one must be careful to test what the church is doing now, and not what it may have done in earlier days" (emphasis in the original).

78. Ibid., 4.

79. This can be seen in proposal "J" on p. 9, where Hopko recommended liturgical harmony "with all Orthodox churches."

80. Hopko had outlined a regularized step-by-step approach to reception of the EOC clergy and laity in proposals C through G on page 8.

81. It is worth noting that Hopko had written that "each local community, however, should have only one archpriest or protopresbyter, and not more than one presbyter per fifty or so people, unless missionary efforts require it." Metropolitan Philip chose, rather, to bring the EOC clergy into the Antiochian Archdiocese *en masse* and only later to press for a redistribution of the EOC clergy, an issue that would affect things later in Ben Lomond, California.

82. Metropolitan Philip to Metropolitan Theodosius, October 12, 1986.

83. Ibid.

84. Metropolitan Theodosius to Metropolitan Philip, January 30, 1987.

85. Metropolitan Philip to Metropolitan Theodosius, February 2, 1987.

86. Metropolitan Philip to Metropolitan Theodosius, April 8, 1987.

87. V. Rev. John Meyendorff to Metropolitan Theodosius, April 15, 1987. Though unstated in the letter, one of the central reasons

was almost certainly financial, as the seminary would have had difficulty making up for the lost revenue brought in from the attendance of the Antiochian seminarians. The Antiochian Archdiocese paid for the students' tuition in full.
88. Metropolitan Philip to V. Rev. John Meyendorff, April 21, 1987.
89. Metropolitan Theodosius to the OCA Synod, April 29, 1987.
90. Metropolitan Theodosius to Metropolitan Philip, April 29, 1987.
91. Metropolitan Theodosius to Metropolitan Philip, April 29, 1987 [Letter 2].
92. Metropolitan Philip to Metropolitan Theodosius, June 2, 1987.
93. To use the words of Fr. James Bernstein from our conversation on January 19, 2013.

Chapter 5

1. Liacopulos, 203–203. Liacopulos notes the adoption of methodologies from the Church Growth Movement.
2. Daniel J. Lehmann, "Evangelizing the Evangelicals," *Christian Century* 105:30 (1988), 916–917.
3. Ibid.
4. Peter E. Gillquist, "Presiding Bishop's Corner," *AGAIN* (n.d., October–December 1981?), 2.
5. Peter E. Gillquist, "Presiding Bishop's Corner," *AGAIN* 2:1 (January–March 1979), 2.
6. Peter E. Gillquist, "Editorial: Phase II," *AGAIN* 11:4 (December 1988), 2.
7. See pages 65–131.
8. *The Orthodox Study Bible: New Testament and Psalms, New King James Version*, Peter E. Gillquist, Project Director, Alan Wallerstedt, Managing editor (Nashville: Thomas Nelson Publishers, 1993). The study Bible is now available with a complete Old Testament, but one that has simply adopted the New King James translation and tweaked certain passages to make them conform with the Septuagint rendering, since the Septuagint is the liturgical Scriptures of the Orthodox Churches.

9. Ephrem Lash, Review of *The Orthodox Study Bible* in *Sourozh* 54 (1993), 42–49.
10. See Matthew Francis, "*The Orthodox Study Bible* and Orthodox Identity in North America," *Canadian Journal of Orthodox Christianity* 2:2 (2007), 37–55, available at http://www.cjoc.ca/pdf/Vol%202%20S1%20Francis.PDF (accessed February 15, 2009).
11. Peter E. Gillquist, "Sealed: Five Years Later," *AGAIN* 15:1 (March 1992), 6.
12. V. Rev. Joseph Allen to St. Anthony Orthodox Church, November 4, 1991.
13. Among the signers was Fr. James Bernstein, who had reconciled with many of his former EOC colleagues. The rest, however, were former EOC leaders who had entered as a group with Gillquist to form the AEOM.
14. Letter of Former EOC Clergy to Metropolitan Philip, February 7, 1992.
15. Canon three of the Quinisext Council, which met in 692, between the Fifth and Sixth Ecumenical Councils, to update canon law, legislated this traditional interpretation.
16. The details of this case may be found in H. Keith Mephodie Sterzing, "Orthodox Bishop Claims to Apply the Canons—Orthodox Question Application," unpublished article, January 28, 1993. This article underwent at least two significant revisions and he sent copies to Metropolitan Philip, Joseph Allen, and the board of trustees of the Antiochian Archdiocese, asking for any corrections on matters of fact to be sent to him. Sterzing attempted to get the article published on some Orthodox websites. To the best of my knowledge, no website published it and Sterzing himself seems not to have published the piece. As late as December, 1994, Sterzing was attempting to publish his researched exposé on the website for the Orthodox Church in America's Diocese of the West. It seems the copies that exist were those distributed in person or by mail.
17. Gregory Maloof to Metrpolitan Philip, April 6, 1992. Clergy defending Allen and Metropolitan Philip had been spreading rumors that Maloof had been unable to consummate his marriage to Valerie.

18. This is also documented in Sterzing's report.
19. Metropolitan Philip to the Seventeen Former EOC Clergy-man, February 24, 1992. Emphasis in the original.
20. Ibid. Given his words to Metropolitan Theodosius a few years earlier, that "no bishop alone can express the mind of the entire Church," one might expect that some former EOC members found Philip's position in the Joseph Allen affair ironic but I have not seen evidence of this yet at this point, suggesting they either had forgotten or had not actually seen the written correspondence between the two metropolitans in 1986–1987.
21. Fr. John Weldon Hardenbrook to Metropolitan Philip, March 4, 1992.
22. Fr. Gregory Rogers to Metropolitan Philip, March 16, 1992.
23. See for example, Rev. Joseph Abud to Metropolitan Philip, March 30, 1992. In addition, Sterzing had received a copy of the letter from someone and took it upon himself to verify that one of Philip's lines of defense was inaccurate. Philip had written that Metropolitan George Khodre of Mount Lebanon had done something similar for one of his priests. In fact, Metropolitan George had laicized the priest in question (Fr. Elias Abou Saba), whose wife had died in a car bomb, according to Orthodox canon law. Saba moved into another diocese and was accepted as a priest in that diocese by a different bishop. In that case, however, Sabba's second wife was not a divorcée and therefore not someone Sabba had counseled and guided through a divorce to her husband immediately prior to their marriage. Furthermore, the Sterzing-Khodre correspondence demonstrates that Sabba's case was an exception that proved the Orthodox canonical rule.
24. Metropolitan Philip to the Clergy of the Antiochian Archdiocese, April 9, 1992.
25. See Sterzing's report.
26. For the book, see Joseph Allen, *Widowed Priest: A Crisis in Ministry* (Minneapolis: Light and Life, 1994).
27. Letter of Former EOC Clergy to Metropolitan Philip, February 7, 1992. It is worth noting that Fr. James Bernstein was one of the signers. His support for a firm moral and ethical stance help him reconcile with the former EOC leaders he had left

back in 1981. Although shunned by the EOC at that time, the Joseph Allen affair enabled him to reestablish relationships.

28. In conversation with Fr. Mel Gimmaka, January 19, 2013.

29. One priest (from the diocese of Toledo and the Midwest) shared with me, for example, that a group of priests had agreed to gather and decide upon a course of action. When the meeting began and only eight priests were present, they ended the meeting and disbanded, knowing that Philip could too easily suspend and replace such a small number.

30. Charles Philip Lucas has produced a short summary and analysis of the difficulties found in Ben Lomond at the time. See "Enfants Terribles: The Challenge of Sectarian Converts to Ethnic Orthodox Churches in the United States." *Nova Religio* 7:2 (2003), 5–23. A synopsis of the events, which is heavily dependent on Lucas' article, may be found at http://orthodoxwiki.org/Ben_Lomond_Crisis (accessed January 22, 2013). In addition, a handful of primary sources are available at http://benlomond.wordpress.com/ (accessed January 22, 2013). Any citations to sources from that website will contain a reference to the document's webpage.

31. See "Fr. John Weldon Hardenbrook's Defense," a transcript of his defense at a spiritual court during the Ben Lomond crisis, available at http://benlomond.wordpress.com/1998/05/26/fr-john-weldon-hardenbrooks-defense/ (accessed January 24, 2013). According to Hardenbrook, EOC leadership had been in the practice of committing themselves to one another in strict loyalty "to death." He came to believe this was no longer possible and others agreed and believed it was time for the AEOM to cease to exist as a continuation of the old EOC.

32. This was actually the second time this issue was raised. In 1993, Bishop Antoun, who often assisted Metropolitan Philip directly, wrote on Metropolitan Philip's behalf, informing Hardenbrook that he and his clergy needed to be trained liturgically, so as to conform to practices within the archdiocese and be prepared to be called to serve elsewhere as needed. Hardenbrook and Jon Braun asked Bishop Basil to intercede and nothing further came of that particular request at that time. See "Fr. John Weldon Hardenbrook's Defense."

33. Ibid. A corroborating account of these events was given to me by Fr. Don Berge, in a conversion on January 24, 2013. Lucas also provides a similar outline of events, see "Enfants Terribles," 8–10.
34. Fr. Don Berge, in conversation on January 24, 2013.
35. Although this could have meant he preferred transfers over laicization, Hardenbrook understood the event to place the entire difficulty upon his (Hardenbrook's) shoulders. See "Fr. John Weldon Hardenbrook's Defense."
36. Published as "Bishop Joseph's Vision for Ben Lomond," in *Grapevine*, the title given to the parish newsletter.
37. The Presbytery to Ss. Peter and Paul Orthodox Church, August 28, 1997. Lucas had given the timing as May, but this note to the parish, which I have obtained, clearly is dated August 28 and discussed the liturgical changes as having just been received and made available in the parish newsletter, the *Grapevine*. Anderson was a priest who had graduated from St. Vladimir's Seminary and was on loan from the OCA to assist the Ss. Peter and Paul Orthodox Church in Ben Lomond, California.
38. Lucas, "Enfants Terribles," 9; confirmed in "Fr. John Weldon Hardenbrook's Defense."
39. Lucas, "Enfants Terribles," 9 and Request for Transfer to the OCA by the Ben Lomond Presbytery, February 12, 1998, available at http://benlomond.wordpress.com/1998/02/12/initial-request-of-clergy-for-release-to-the-oca/#more-7 (accessed January 24, 2013).
40. Thomas Zell, "Once AGAIN," *AGAIN Magazine* 21:1 (Winter 1999), 1–2.
41. Request for Transfer to the OCA by the Ben Lomond Presbytery, February 12, 1998, available at http://benlomond.wordpress.com/1998/02/12/initial-request-of-clergy-for-release-to-the-oca/#more-7 (accessed January 24, 2013).
42. Metropolitan Philip to Petitioning Presbytery, February 14, 1998, available at http://benlomond.wordpress.com/1998/02/14/archpastoral-directive-depositions/#more-29 (accessed January 24, 2013). The claim to laicize Anderson is quite peculiar, since Anderson was simply a priest the OCA had loaned to the Antiochian Archdiocese. Technically, Metropolitan Philip

could only renege the loan and send Anderson back to the OCA, where it would be up to Metropolitan Theodosius to decide what to do with Anderson (whether to discipline him or assign him to an OCA parish).

43. See *The Opinion of the Superior Court of Santa Cruz for Metropolitan Philip v. Steiger* (2000) 82 Cal. App. 4th 923 [98 Cal. Rptr. 2d 605] available at http://law.justia.com/cases/california/caapp4th/82/923.html (accessed January 22, 2013).

44. Fr. David Anderson, however, returned not to the OCA, but to the Roman Catholic Church, and serves as an Eastern Catholic priest.

45. Archpastoral Directive, May 2, 2003.

46. Archpastoral Directive, August 7, 2008. This was seen as a restatement of the earlier 2003 directive. One of the puzzling aspects to this directive, however, was Philip's contention that "it has been clear since the disintegration of Orthodox unity which existed in North America since 1917, that the Arabic-speaking Orthodox people in North America have been exclusively under the pastoral care of the Self-Ruled Antiochian Archdiocese of North America. Similarly, the Greek speaking Orthodox people . . . have always been under the pastoral care of the Greek Orthodox Archdiocese of America." There never was jurisdictional unity in America prior to 1917 even though one could argue there should have been. See Matthew Namee, "The Myth of Past Unity," paper delivered at St. Vladimir's Seminary, June 20, 2009, available at http://www.orthodoxdetroit.com/stvladimirswebinar.htm (accessed January 25, 2013). More puzzling, though, is the reference to languages and ethnicities, since the overwhelming majority of the Ben Lomond parishioners were former members of the EOC and, therefore, not ethnically Arab. Such a phyletistic approach is at odds with the narrative so often portrayed (of a metropolitan who unites and sees no room for ethnic division). See, for example, Bishop Joseph's words claiming Metropolitan Philip never forgets that "we are an Orthodox Christian community, rather than a member of this or that ethnicity." See "Metropolitan PHILIP in View of His Bishops," available at http://www.antiochian.org/node/18574 (accessed January 24, 2013). Likewise, this was a

theme in Gillquist's book *Metropolitan Philip: His Life and His Dreams. See, especially, Philip's 1984 sermon where he himself decried ethnic jurisdictionalism.*

47. Ibid., 11.

48. Hopko stated that some of the practices were so unusual by contemporary liturgical standards that one could not always concelebrate when visiting (in conversation, January 25, 2013).

49. Archimandrite Ephraim, who served as an abbot for a time at the Philotheou Monastery on Mount Athos, is a divisive person. An Orthodox watchdog site has listed him, though no specific charges are mentioned (as is the case for other clergy and monastics who have been convicted of various crimes). See http://pokrov.org/display.asp?ds=Person&id=464 (accessed January 26, 2013). One of the Ephraimite monasteries is currently being sued in a lawsuit that highlights the ways in which Elder Ephrem's form of monasticism has become disruptive. See http://gotruthreform.org/nevins-demand-letter-and-important-attachments (accessed February 9, 2013).

50. See "Fr. John Weldon Hardenbrook's Defense." This same emphasis on monasticism was cited by Fr. James Bernstein in my conversation with him, when he mentioned that many of the former EOC members had seen transitioning to the Antiochian Archdiocese as an opportunity to relax their previous rigorism but Hardenbrook and many in Ben Lomond were taken by the ascetic traditions of Orthodoxy.

51. Although *Becoming Orthodox* is a book-length narrative, it was not the only time Gillquist wrote of the EOC conversion. Another prominent narrative may be found in *Metrpolitan Philip*, 255–272.

Conclusion

1. In this way, they fit within the a larger trend amongst Orthodox to polemicize against the West. On this, see (again) Brandon Gallaher, "'Waiting for the Barbarians'" as well as the forthcoming: George Demacopoulos and Aristotle Papanikoloau,

Orthodox Constructions of the West (New York: Fordham University Press, 2013).

2. This term was apparently frequent in Ron Zell's experience. Zell had been the EOC's deacon of music. See Chapter 4.

3. These are the only two possibilities from which to choose according to Lewis R. Rambo's otherwise helpful assessment (see *Understanding Religious Conversion*, 13–14). Incidentally, allowing for a third category, one between changing whole religious systems and denominational switching, might also allow for a better way of categorizing many Protestant conversions to Roman Catholicism as well. Although clearly beyond the scope of this study, an emphasis on the early historical church and tradition have played roles in Protestant conversions to Roman Catholicism within America. For example, Scott Hahn highlights the importance of tradition in his journey, citing it as the difference between Roman Catholicism and Protestantism. See "The Scott Hahn Conversion Story," available at http://www.catholiceducation.org/articles/apologetics/ ap0088.html (accessed March 1, 2013). While acknowledging that one ought not to reduce conversions from Evangelicalism to Roman Catholicism down to one factor, Scot McKnight highlighted the importance of tradition, noting that in the 1980s many evangelicals began looking to history and suggesting that the authority of tradition was important to many. See Scot McKnight, "From Wheaton to Rome: Why Evangelicals Become Roman Catholic," *Journal of the Evangelical Theological Society* 45:3 (2002), 459, 468.

4. This is an important point in light of John Erickson's recent article highlighting the liberal aspects of Slavophilism. See John H. Erickson, "Slavophile Thought and Conceptions of Mission in the Russian North American Archdiocese, Late 19th-Early 20th Century," *St. Vladimir's Theological Quarterly* 56:3 (2012), 245–268. Erickson's point is generally correct, and one may see how that approach could affect non-Orthodox in my article on Nicholas Bjerring. This makes Toth's more exclusivist view of Russophilism all the more notable.

5. Specifically, Gary became an atheist and Frederica declared herself a Hindu. She had a conversion experience on their honeymoon, before a statue of Mary, while visiting a church in Dublin

and he began rethinking atheism. For a summary of their journey and more concerning Frederica Matthewes-Green, see my
dissertation, "Turning to Tradition: Intra-Christian Converts
and the Making of an American Orthodox Church," (doctoral
dissertation, Saint Louis University, 2009), 213-223.

6. On January 30, 1993, the Mathewes-Green family and 14 others
became Orthodox and core members of a newly founded mission parish. Mathewes-Green Christmas Letter, February
1993. According to a letter from Frederica Mathewes-Green to
Nancy Waggener, the Mathewes-Green family had made the
decision by July 1992.

7. Mathewes-Green, "In the Passenger's Seat," in *Our Hearts' True
Home*, 11-24, edited by Virginia Nieuwsma (Ben Lomond,
CA: Conciliar Press, 1996), 18.

8. Frank P. Somerville, "Episcopal Priest takes a new path," *The
Sun*, February 1, 1993.

9. Francis Schaeffer's most monumental work may have been
his *A Christian Manifesto*. See Francis Schaeffer, *A Christian
Manifesto,* revised edition (Westchester, IL: Crossway, 1982).
Francis Schaeffer's main purpose in this work was to offer a
conservative, Protestant critique of Western culture, claiming
that Western culture had become increasingly pluralistic and
further removed from its Christian roots. The publisher sold
over 350,000 copies. See Gary North, "The Escalating Confrontation with Bureaucracy" in *Tactics of Christian Resistance*,
141-190, edited by Gary North (Tyler, TX: Geneva Divinity
School Press, 1983), 162.

10. By reaching this conclusion, the younger Schaeffer did something the older Schaeffer had been criticized for omitting—
offering a solution to the problems critiqued. Gary North
claimed that Francis Schaeffer "offers Christians little or no hope
in their ability to do anything substantial to reverse the drift of
humanism over the falls . . . . The fact remains that *Dr Schaeffer's
manifesto offers no prescriptions for a Christian society.* We mention that merely in the interests of clarity, for we are not sure that
anybody has noticed it up to now." See North, 164, 173.

11. See Frank Schaeffer, *Addicted to Mediocrity: Contemporary
Christians and the Arts* (Westchester, IL: Crossway Books,
1981) and its follow-up (written as he was preparing to enter

the Orthodox Church) *Sham Pearls for Real Swine: Beyond the Cultural Dark Age—A Quest for Renaissance* (Brentwood, TN: Wolgemuth and Hyatt, 1990).

12. Frank Schaeffer, *Dancing Alone: The Quest for Orthodox Faith in the Age of False Religion* (Brookline, MA: Holy Cross Orthodox Press, 1994). In addition to writing this book, he established a paper entitled *Christian Activist*, in which he wrote and published articles committed to sharing his view of Orthodox Christianity as an answer to Western problems.

13. Ibid., 9. This individual subjectivism might be what was referenced in the title of the book. The title was ambiguous and led one Orthodox reviewer to find it highly odd that a convert to a church that emphasizes community would choose such a title. See Vigen Guroian, "Dancing Alone—Out of Step with Orthodoxy," *Christian Century* 112:19 (1995), 608–610.

14. Ibid., 58.

15. Ibid., 72–73.

16. For a summary of Irvine, one may see my chapter in my dissertation, "Turning to Tradition: Intra-Christian Converts and the Making of an American Orthodox Church," 162–196. Irvine had a propensity for sticking to his dogmatic guns in a legalistic manner, which led to confrontations with two different Protestant Episcopal bishops before becoming Orthodox. Unfortunately, he was also financially untrustworthy and unstable and caused headaches for the Russian Mission, the full extent of which I have learned only since writing the dissertation. It was largely for this reason that his efforts to establish an English-language parish were slowed. He was able to help found Holy Transfiguration, an English language parish shortly before his death, and several converts did later join the Orthodox Church through this chapel.

17. Very little has been written on any of this. Again, the reader is forwarded to my article, "A Lesson to be Learned: Fr. Boris Burden's Failed Attempts to Foster Orthodox Jurisdictional Unity in America," *St. Vladimir's Theological Quarterly* 56:3 (2012), 317–334.

BIBLIOGRAPHY

Introduction

Agadjanian, Alexander and Victor Roudometof, "Introduction: Eastern Orthodoxy in a Global Age—Preliminary Considerations." In *Eastern Orthodoxy in a Global Age: Tradition Faces the Twenty-First Century*, edited by Victor Roudometof, Alexander Agadjanian, and Jerry Pankhurst, 1–26. Walnut Creek, California: AltaMira Press, 2005.

Behr, John. *The Mystery of Christ: Life in Death*. Crestwood, New York: St. Vladimir's Seminary Press, 2006.

Berger, Peter L. "Orthodoxy and the Pluralistic Challenge." In *The Orthodox Parish in America: Faithfulness to the Past and Responsibility for the Future*, edited by Anton C. Vrame, 33–42. Brookline, Massachusetts: Holy Cross Orthodox Press, 2003.

Bicha, Karel D. "Hunkies: Stereotyping the Slavic Immigrants, 1890–1920." *Journal of American Ethnic History* 2:1 (1982), 16–38.

Bjerring, Nicholas. "Which the True Church: A Roman Catholic Savant Renounces Rome." *The Sun*, January 12, 1870.

Bozeman, Theodore Dwight. *To Live Ancient Lives: The Primitivist Dimension in Puritanism*. Chapel Hill: University of North Carolina Press, 1988.

Breck, John. *Scripture in Tradition: the Bible and its Interpretation in the Orthodox Church.* Crestwood, New York: St. Vladimir's Seminary Press, 2000.

Brookline, Massachusetts. "Some Further Thoughts on Religion and Modernity." *Sociology* 49(2012), 313–316.

Calhoun, Craig, Mark Jurgensmeyer, and Jonathan VanAntwerpen. *Rethinking Secularization.* New York: Oxford University Press, 2011.

Cherry, Conrad ed. *God's New Israel: Religious Interpretation of American Destiny.* Revised edition, Chapel Hill: University of North Carolina Press, 1998.

Ferencz, Nicholas. *American Orthodoxy and Parish Congregationalism.* Piscataway, New Jersey: Gorgias Press, 2006.

Fisch, Thomas, ed. *Liturgy and Tradition: Theological Reflections of Alexander Schmemann.* Crestwood, New York: St. Vladimir's Seminary Press, 1990.

Gallaher, Brandon. "'Waiting for the Barbarians': Identity and Polemicism in the Neo-Patristic Synthesis of Georges Florovsky." *Modern Theology* 27:4 (2011), 659–691.

Haskell, Peter Carl. "American Civil Religion and the Greek Immigration: Religious Confrontation Before the First World War." *St. Vladimir's Theological Quarterly* 18:4 (1974),166–192.

Herbel, Dellas Oliver. "A Catholic, Presbyterian, and Orthodox Journey: The Changing Church Affiliation and Enduring Social Vision of Nicholas Bjerring." *Zeitschrift für Neuere Theologiegeschichte/Journal for the History of Modern Theology* 14:1 (2007), 49–80.

———. "A Lesson to be Learned: Fr. Boris Burden's Failed Attempts to Foster Orthodox Jurisdictional Unity in America." *St. Vladimir's Theological Quarterly* 56: 3 (2012), 317–334.

Hughes, Richard T. ed. *The American Quest for the Primitive Church.* Urbana: University of Illinois Press, 1988.

Hughes, Richard T. and C. Leonard Allen. *Illusions of Innocence: Protestant Primitivism in America, 1630–1875.* Chicago: University of Chicago Press, 1988.

Krindatch, Alexei D. "Eastern Christianity in North American Religious Landscape: Ethnic Traditionalism versus Civic

Involvement and Social Transformations." Report for *Research on Orthodox Religious Groups in the United States*, Hartford Institute for Religion Research. http://hirr.hartsem.edu/research/krindatch.pdf (accessed February 4, 2013).

———. "The Orthodox Church Today." Patriarch Athenagoras Orthodox Institute. accessed http://www.hartfordinstitute.org/research/OrthChurchFullReport.pdf (accessed February 5, 2013).

———. "Research on Orthodox Religious Groups in the United States." Hartford Institute for Religion Research. http://www.hartfordinstitute.org/research/orthodoxsummary.html (accessed February 5, 2013).

Lossky, Vladimir. *Of the Image and Likeness of God*. Crestwood, New York: St. Vladimir's Seminary Press, 1974.

Marty, Martin E. "Tradition." *Religion and Intellectual Life* 2:1 (1984), 7–16.

Mastagar, Mariana. "Icons and the Immigrant Context," *Fieldwork in Religion* 2:2 (2006), 146–169.

McGuckin, John. "Eschaton and Kerygma: The Future of the Past in the Present Kairos, The Concept of Living Tradition in Orthodox Theology," *St. Vladimir's Theological Quarterly* 42:3–4 (1998), 225–271.

Moore, Laurence R. *Religious Outsiders and the Making of Americans*. New York: Oxford University Press, 1986.

Pew Forum on Religion and Public Life. "2008 U.S. Religious Landscape Survey." http://religions.pewforum.org/pdf/report-religious-landscape-study-full.pdf (accessed February 5, 2013).

Prodromou, Elizabeth H. "Religious Pluralism in Twenty-First-Century America: Problematizing the Implications for Orthodoxy [sic] Christianity." *Journal of the American Academy of Religion* 72:3 (2004), 733–757.

Rambo, Lewis R. *Understanding Religious Conversion*. New Haven and London: Yale University Press, 1993.

Saloutos, Theodore. "Cultural Persistance and Change: Greeks in the Great Plains and Rocky Mountain West, 1890–1970," *Pacific Historical Review* 49:1 (1980), 77–103.

Scourby, Alice. *The Greek Americans*. Boston: Twayne Publishers, 1984.

Sherkat, Darren E. "Tracking the 'Other': Dynamics and Composition of 'Other' Religions in the General Social Survey, 1973–1996." *Journal for the Scientific Study of Religion* 38:4 (1999), 551–560.

Shils, Edward. *Tradition.* 1981. Reprint, Chicago: University of Chicago Press, 2006.

Silk, Mark. "Notes on the Judeo-Christian Tradition in America." *American Quarterly* 36:1 (1994), 65–85.

Slagle, Amy. *The Eastern Church in the Spiritual Marketplace: American Conversions to Orthodox Christianity.* DeKalb, Ilinois: Northern Illinois University Press, 2011.

Stark, Rodney. "Secularization." *Sociology of Religion* 60:3 (1999), 249–273.

Trinity College. "2008 American Religious Indentification Survey." http://commons.trincoll.edu/aris/files/2011/08/ARIS_Report_2008.pdf (accessed February 5, 2013).

Trumbell, Charles P. *Britannica Book of the Year 1995.* Chicago: Encyclopedia Britannica, 1995.

Tuveson, Ernest Lee. *Redeemer Nation: the Idea of America's Millenial Role.* Chicago: University of Chicago Press, 1980.

Witham, Larry. *A City Upon a Hill: How Sermons Changed the Course of American History.* New York: Harper Collins, 2007.

Zelinsky, Wilbur. "The Uniqueness of the American Religious Landscape." *Geographical Review* 91:3 (2001), 565–585.

St. Alexis Toth

Primary Sources

Kossuth, Louis. *Memories of My Exile.* Translated by Ferencz Jausz. New York: D. Appleton and Company, 1880.

Nicholas. Letter to the Editors. *Amerikanskiĭ Russkiĭ Viestnik.* February 13, 1896.

———. Letter to the Editors. *Svoboda* 6 (1896).

Platon, "A Wreath Upon the Grave of Mitered Archpriest Fr. Alexis Georievich Toth." In *The Orthodox Church in America and other Writings,* translated and edited by George Soldatow, 153–157. Minneapolis: AARDM Press, 1996. Originally published as

"*Venok na mogilu mitrofornago protoiereya o. Aleksiya Georievicha Tovta.*" *Amerikanskiĭ Pravoslavnyĭ Viestnik* 13:10 (May 28/15, 1909), 177–182.

Toth, Alexis. *Gde iskati (glyadati) pravdu?* 1907.

———. *Archpriest Alexis Toth: Letters, Articles, Papers, and Sermons.* Translated and edited by George Soldatow. 4 Vols. Chilliwack, British Columbia: Synaxis Press, 1978.

———. *Selected Letters, Sermons, and Articles.* Translated and edited by George Soldatow. Minneapolis: AARDM Press, 1982.

———. *The Writings of St. Alexis Toth, Confessor and Defender of Orthodoxy in America.* Translated and edited by George Soldatow. Minneapolis: AARDM Press, 1994.

———. *The Orthodox Church in America and other Writings.* Translated and edited by George Soldatow. Minneapolis: AARDM Press, 1996.

Secondary Sources

Annonymous. "GREEK CATHOLIC CHURCH et. al. v. ORTHODOX GREEK CHURCH et. al.," *Atlantic Reporter* 46(1900), 72–77.

———. "Assassinate Bishop Who Led Secession from Rome," *The Christian Century* (October 13, 1948), 1069.

Barriger, Lawrence. *Good Victory: Metropolitan Orestes Chornock and the American Carpatho-Russian Orthodox Greek Catholic Diocese.* Brookline, Massachusetts: Holy Cross Orthodox Press, 1985.

———. *Glory to Jesus Christ! A History of the American Carpatho-Russian Orthodox Church.* Brookline, Massachusetts: Holy Cross Orthodox Press, 2000.

Boresky, Theodosia. *The Life of St. Josaphat: Martyr of the Union, Archbishop of Polotsk, Member, Order of St. Basil the Great.* New York: Comet Press, Books, 1955.

Brady, Joel. "Transnational Conversions: Greek Catholic Migrants and Russky Orthodox Conversion Movements in Austria-Hungary, Russia, and the Americas (1890–1914)." Doctoral dissertation, University of Pittsburgh, 2012.

Carey, Patrick W. *People, Priests, and Prelates: Ecclesiastical Democracy and the Tensions of Trusteeism.* Notre Dame, Indiana: Notre Dame University Press, 1987.

Cross, Robert D. *The Emergence of Liberal Catholicism in America.* Cambridge, Massachusetts: Harvard University Press, 1958.

Dranichak, Julianna. "Alexander Dukhnovich and the Carpatho-Russian National Cultural Movement." Doctoral dissertation, University of New York, Binghamton, 1979.

Ferencz, Nicholas. *American Orthodoxy and Parish Congregationalism.* Piscataway, New Jersey: Gorgias Press, 2006.

Fogarty, Gerald P. "The American Hierarchy and Oriental Rite Catholics, 1890–1907." *Records of the American Catholic Historical Society* 85 (1974), 17–28.

Gillis, Chester. "American Catholics: Neither out Far nor in Deep." In *Religion and Immigration,* edited by Yvonne Yazbeck Haddad, Jane I. Smith, and John L. Esposito, 33–52. Walnut Creek, California: AltaMira Press, 2003.

Greek Catholic Union, *Opportunity Realized: The Greek Catholic Union's First One Hundred Years, 1892–1992.* Beaver, Pennsylvania: Greek Catholic Union of the U.S.A., 1994.

Greene, Victor R. "For God and Country: the Origins of Slavic Catholic Self-Consciousness in America," *Church History* 35:4 (1963), 446–460.

———. *The Slavic Community on Strike: Immigrant Labor in Pennsylvania Anthracite.* Notre Dame and London: Notre Dame University Press, 1968.

Guépin, Alphonse. *Un apotre l'union des églises au XVII siècle: Saint Josaphat et l'église Greco-Slave en Pologne et en Russie.* Volume 1. Paris: the religious library of H. Oudin, 1897.

Harvard Law Review Association, "Judicial Intervention in Disputes over the use of Church Property," *Harvard Law Review* 75:6 (1962), 1142–1186.

Haugh, Richard. *Photius and the Carolingians: The Trinitarian Controversy.* Belmont, Massachusetts: Nordland Publishing Company, 1970.

Hennesey, James. *American Catholics.* New York: Oxford University Press, 1981.

István, Deák. *The Lawful Revolution: Louis Kossuth and the Hungarians, 1848–1849.* New York: Columbia University Press, 1979.

Jorgenson, James. "Father Alexis Toth and the Transition of the Greek Catholic Community in Minneapolis to the Russian

Orthodox Church." *St. Vladimir's Theological Quarterly* 32:2 (1988), 119–137.

Kochanik, Peter G. "Pravoslavije v Siv. Ameriki," *Svit* (1920), 12–32.

———. *Rus' i pravoslavie v sievernoi Amerikie; k XXV lietiiu Russkago pravoslavnago obshchestva vzaimopomoshchi, 1895–1920.* Wilkes-Barre, Pennsylvania: Russian Orthodox Catholic Mutual Aid Society, 1920.

———. "Primiernoe i muzhestvennoe vysuplenie otsa Aleksiya Tovta na zashchitu pravoclavnych" i russko narodnych" idealov"," *Svit* 62(May 1959):18–19.

Kowalczyk, John. "The Canonization of Fr. Alexis Toth by the Orthodox Church in America." *St. Vladimir's Theological Quarterly* 38:4 (1994), 424–431.

Lacko, Michael. "The Union of Užhorod," *Slovak Studies* 6(1966), 7–190.

Looshorn, Johann. *Der heilige Märtyrer Josaphat Kuncewicz, Erzbischof von Polozk.* Munich: P. Zipperer's Bookstore, 1898.

Louth, Andrew. *Greek East and Latin West: The Church AD681–1071.* Crestwood, New York: St. Vladimir's Seminary Press, 2007.

Magocsi, Robert Paul. *Of the Making of Nationalities there is no End,* vol. 2, *Speeches, Debates, Bibliographic Works.* New York: Columbia University Press, 1999.

Mayer, Maria. *The Rusyns of Hungary: Political and Social Developments, 1860–1910.* Translated by János Boris. Edited with an introduction by Paul Robert Magocsi. New York: Columbia University Press, 1997.

McAvoy, Thomas T. *The Americanist Heresy in Roman Catholicism.* Notre Dame: Notre Dame University Press, 1963.

Mironowicz, Antoni. *Prawoslawie i unia za panowania Jana Kazimierza* ["Orthodoxy and Union during the reign of King John Casimir"] Dissertationes Universitatis Varsoviensis 443. Bialystok: Orthdruk, 1997.

Mojzes, Paul. *Yugoslavian Inferno: Ethnoreligious Warfare in the Balkans* (New York: Continuum, 1994.

———. "The Role of Religious Leaders in Times of Conflict in Multinational and Multi-Religious Societies: A Contribution Toward Interreligious Dialogue in Macedonia," *Journal of Ecumenical Studies* 39:1–2 (2002), 82–86.

Murphy, Terrence. "Trusteeism in Atlantic Canada: the struggle for leadership among the Irish Catholics of Halifax, St John's, and Saint John, 1780–1850." In *Creed and Culture: the Place of English-speaking Catholics in Canadian society, 1750–1930*, edited by Terrence Murphy and Gerald J. Stortz, 126–151. Montreal: McGill University Press, 1993.

O'Connell, Marvin R. *John Ireland and the American Catholic Church*. St. Paul: Minnesota Historical Society Press, 1988.

Oleksa, Michael. *Orthodox Alaska: A Theology of Mission*. Crestwood, New York: St. Vladimir's Seminary Press, 1998.

Orton, Lawrence D. *The Prague Slav Conference of 1848*. Boulder, CO: East European Quarterly, 1978.

Pekar, Athanasius B. *Saint Josaphat (1580–1623)*. Stamford, CT: Publications of Basilian Fathers, 1967.

———. *The History of the Church in Carpathian Rus*. Translated by Marta Skorupsky. Bio-bibliography by Edward Kasinec and Richard Renoff. New York: Columbia University Press, 1992.

Procko, Bohdan P. "The Establishment of the Ruthenian Church in the United States, 1884–1907," *Pennsylvania History* 42(1975), 137–154.

Renoff, Richard. "Seminary Background and the Carpatho-Russian Celibacy Schism: A Sociological Approach." *Diakonia* 10:1 (1975), 55–62.

Rowland, Daniel. "Moscow—The Third Rome or the New Israel?" *The Russian Review* 55 (1996), 591–614.

Russin, Keith S. "Father Alexis G. Toth and the Wilkes-Barre Litigations." *St. Vladimir's Theological Quarterly* 16:3 (1972), 128–149.

Sable, Thomas F. "Lay Initiative in Greek Catholic Parishes in Connecticut, New York, New Jersey, and Pennsylvania (1884–1909)." Doctoral dissertation, Graduate Theological Union, 1984.

Shelley, Thomas J. "Dean Lings's Church: The Success of Ethnic Catholicism in Yonkers in the 1890's," *Church History* 65:1 (1996), 28–41.

Simirenko, Alex. *Pilgrims, Colonists, and Frontiersmen: An Ethnic Community in Transition*. New York: Free Press of Glencoe, 1964.

Simon, Konstantin. "Before the Birth of Ecumenisn: the Background Relating to the Mass 'Conversion' of Oriental Rite

Catholics to Russian Orthodoxy in the U.S." *Diakonia* 20:3 (1986), 128–151.

———. "Alexis Toth and the Beginnings of the Orthodox Movement among the Ruthenians in America (1891)." *Orientalia Christiana Periodica* 54:2 (1988), 387–428.

———. "First Years *Orientalia Christiana Periodica*.

Sivrić, Ivo. *Bishop J.G. Strossmayer: New Light on Vatican I*. Chicago: Franciscan Herald Press, 1975.

Slivka, John. *Historical Mirror: Sources of the Rusin and Hungarian Greek Rite Catholics in the United States of America, 1884–1963*. Brooklyn, 1978.

Sorokowski, Andrew. "Ukrainian Catholics and Orthodox in Czechoslovakia," *Religion in Communist Lands* 15:1 (1987), 54–68.

Stokoe, Mark, in collaboration with Leonid Kishkovsky. *Orthodox Christians in North America, 1794–1994*. Syosset, New York: Orthodox Christian Publications Center, 1995.

Strickland, John Douglas. *The Making of Holy Russia—The Orthodox Church and Russian Nationalism Before the Revolutionn*. Jordanville, New York: Holy Trinity Publications, 2013.

Sunderland, Willard. "Peasant Pioneering: Russian Peasant Settlers Describe Colonization and the Eastern Frontier, 1880s–1910s," *Journal of Social History* 34:4 (2001), 895–922.

Tarasar, Constance J. and John H. Erickson, eds., *Orthodox America, 1794–1976*. Syosset, New York: Orthodox Church in America Department of History and Archives, 1975.

Warzeski, Walter C. *Byzantine Rite Rusins in Carpatho-Ruthenia and America*. Pittsburgh: Byzantine Seminary Press, 1971.

Yurash, Andrij. "Orthodox-Greek Catholic Relations in Galicia and their Influence on the Religious Situation in Ukraine," *Religion, State and Society* 33:3 (2005), 185–205.

Fr. Raphael Morgan

Primary Sources
Anonymous. "West Africa." *Gleaner*. October 9, 1901.

———. "Port Maria, A Lecture." *Gleaner*. October 7, 1902.

———. "Christmas is Celebrated by the Greek Christians," *Philadelphia Inquirer*, January 8, 1906.

———. "Deacon Suspended." *Gleaner*. June 4, 1908.

———. *Gleaner* Editor. "Current Items." *Gleaner*. September 10, 1913.

———. "Current Items." *Gleaner*. September 24, 1913.

———. "Father Raphael." *Gleaner*. August 15, 1913.

———. "Father Raphael." *Gleaner*. August 22, 1913.

———. "Father Raphael." *Gleaner*. August 28, 1913.

———. "General Notes." *Gleaner*. September 12, 1913.

———. "Happenings in the Parishes." *Gleaner*. October 30, 1913.

———. "Mass on Warship." *Gleaner*. December 27, 1913.

———. "Priest is now on Visit to His Native Land." *Gleaner*. July 22, 1913.

———. "Shipping News." *Gleaner*. July 16, 1913.

———. "Some Interesting Church Notes and Services." *Gleaner*. August 9, 1913.

———. "Late News from Port Antonio." *Gleaner*. November 2, 1914.

———. "A Lecture Given." *Gleaner*. July 15, 1914.

———. "Matters Dealt with in People's Parliament." *Gleaner*. November 14, 1916.

———. "Mr. Marcus Garvey in U.S.," *Gleaner*. October 4, 1916.

———. "30 Years Later." *Chester Times*. March 21, 1939.

Archbishop Isidore to Daniel William Alexander. September 17, 1935. African Orthodox Church/Daniel William Alexander Papers. Pitts Theology Library. Emory University. File 10/112.

Boyd's Philadelphia City Directory. Philadelphia: C. E. Howe, 1916.

Bragg, George F., ed. "Editorial." *Church Advocate* 17:5 (1908), 1.

———. "The McGuire Lesson," *The Living Church* (June 25, 1921), 250.

———., ed. "Robert Josias Morgan." In *History of the Afro-American Group of the Episcopal Church*, 273. Baltimore: Church Advocate Press, 1922.

Charlotte Selina Morgan v. Robert Josiah Morgan. Case 72 (Court of Common Pleas of Delaware County, Pennsylvania, March 1909).

Daniel William Alexander to Archbishop Isidore. May 21, 1935. African Orthodox Church/Daniel William Alexander Papers. Pitts Theology Library. Emory University. File 10/112.

———. September 4, 1935. African Orthodox Church/Daniel William Alexander Papers. Pitts Theology Library. Emory University. File 10/112.

Hill, Robert A., ed. *The Marcus Garvey and Universal Negro Improvement Association Papers*. Volume 1, *1826–August 1919*. Berkeley, Los Angeles, and London: University of California Press, 1983.

———., ed. *The Marcus Garvey and Universal Negro Improvement Association Papers*. Volumes 1–7, 9. Berkeley, Los Angeles, and London: University of California Press, 1983–1995.

Lloyd, Ebenezer John. *The American Church Clergy and Parish Directory*. Uniontown, Pa: Frederick E. J. Lloyd, 1905.

Mather, Frank Lincoln, ed. "Raphael, the Very Reverend." In Who's Who of the Colored Race, A General Biographical Dictionary of Men and Women of African Descent. Vol. 1, 1915, 226–227. 1915; Reprint, Detroit: Gale Research Company, 1976.

McGuire, George Alexander. "Patriarch's Address," The Negro Churchman 6 (1928), 3.

Morgan, Robert Josias. "Letter of a Deacon of the Anglican Church in America, Mr. R. J. Morgan, addressed to the public." *Amerikanskiĭ Pravoslavnyĭ Viestnik* (October–November Supplement, 1904), 380–382.

———. "Letter Denouncing Marcus Garvey." In The Marcus Garvey and Universal Negro *Improvement Association Papers*. Vol. 1, *1826–August 1919*, 106–107. Edited by Robert A. Hill and Carol A. Rudisell. Berkeley, Los Angeles, and London: University of Californian Press, 1983. Based on version found in *Jamaican Times*, October 7, 1916.

———. Letter to Marcus Garvey. In "Mr. Marcus Garvey in U.S.," *Gleaner*. October 4, 1916.

Phillips, Henry L. *Church of the Crucifixion, Philadelphia, PA, Semi-Centennial, May 1817-May 1897, A Historical Discourse*. Philadelphia, n.p., 1897.

Reuter, Edward B. *The Mulatto in the United States*. Boston: R. G. Badger, 1918.

Ship List. *S.S. Patris.* Piraeus, Greece to New York City. November 16, 1911.

———. *S.S. Joseph J. Cuneo.* Port Antonio, Jamaica to Philadelphia. October 28, 1914.

Work, Monroe N., ed. "Negro Priest in the Greek Catholic Church." In *Negro Year Book, an Annual Encyclopedia of the Negro, 1921–1922,* 213. Alabama: The Negro Yearbook Publishing Company, Tuskegee Institute, 1922.

Secondary Sources

Anonymous Editor. "The Saga of Jimmy Winkfield," *Ebony* (June, 1974), 64–70.

Anson, Peter F. *Bishops at Large.* London: Faber and Faber, 1964.

Barkan, Elazar. *The Retreat of Scientific Racism.* New York and Cambridge: Cambridge University Press, 1992.

Blakely, Allison. "The Negro in Imperial Russia: A Preliminary Sketch," *Journal of Negro History* 61:4 (1976).

Burkett, Randall K. *Black Redemption: Churchmen Speak for the Garvey Movement.* Philadelphia: Temple University Press, 1978.

———. *Garveyism as a Religious Movement: The Institutionalization of a Black Civil Religion.* Metuchen, New Jersey: Scarecrow Press, 1978.

Cronon, Edmund David. *Black Moses: The Story of Marcus Garvey.* Madison: University of Wisconsin Press, 1955.

Drape, Joe. *Black Maestro: The Epic Life of an American Legend.* New York: Morrow, 2006.

Fortescue, Adrian. *The Orthodox Eastern Church.* 1908; Reprint, Piscataway, New Jersey: Gorgias Press, 2001.

Geffert, Bryn. *Eastern Orthodox and Anglicans.* Notre Dame, Indiana: University of Notre Dame Press, 2010.

Hayes, Stephen. "Orthodox Mission in tropical Africa," *Missionalia* 24:3 (1996), 383–398.

Herbel, Dellas Oliver. "Reverend Raphael Morgan." In *African American National Biography,* Edited by Henry Louis Gates, Jr., and Evelyn Brooks-Higginbotham, Vol. 6. New York: Oxford University Press, 2008.

Hotaling, Ed. *Wink: The Incredible Life and Epic Journey of Jimmy Winkfield.* Camden, Maine: McGraw-Hill, 2004.

Lane, Roger. *Roots of Violence in Black Philadelphia, 1860-1900.* Cambridge and London: Harvard University Press, 1986.

Lewis, Rupert and Patrick Bryan, eds. *Garvey: His Work and Impact.* Trenton, New Jersey: Africa World Press, 1991.

Makarios, Bishop of Rirogtas. "O protos mauros orthodoxos iereas: Raphala Robertos Morgkan." *Orthodoxi Marturia* 50(1996), 72-75.

Manolis, Paul G. *Raphael (Robert) Morgan, the First Black Orthodox Priest in America.* Athens, n.p., 1981.

———. "The First African American Orthodox Priest." *Epiphany* 15:4 (1996), 88.

Namee, Matthew. "Father Raphael Morgan: The First Orthodox Priest of African Descent in America." *St. Vladimir's Theological Quarterly* 53:4 (2009), 447-459.

Natsoulas, Theodore. "Patriarch McGuire and the Spread of the African Orthodox Church to Africa," *Journal of Religion in Africa* 12:2 (1981), 81-104.

Newman, Richard. "Archbishop Daniel William Alexander and the African Orthodox Church," *The International Journal of African Historical Studies* 16:4 (1983), 615-630.

———. *Words Like Freedom: Essays African-American Culture and History.* West Cornwall, Connecticut: Locust Hill Press, 1996.

Penprase, Mike. "Religious Mission Expanding," *Springfield News-Leader* October 15, 1998.

Platt, Warren C. "The African Orthodox Church: An Analysis of its First Decade." *Church History* 58:4 (1989), 474-488.

Rushing, "A Note On the Origin of the African Orthodox Church," *The Journal of Negro History* 57: 1 (1972), 37-39.

Terry-Thompson, Arthur C. *The History of the African Orthodox Church.* New York, 1956.

Welbourn, F. B. *East African Rebels, A Study of Some Independent Churches* (London: SCM Press, 1961.

White, Gavin. "Patriarch McGuire and the Episcopal Church." *Historical Magazine of the Protestant Episcopal Church* 38:2 (1969), 109-141.

———. "Patriarch McGuire and the Episcopal Church." In *Black Apostles: Afro-American Clergy Confront the Twentieth Century* edited by Randall K. Burkett and Richard Newman, 151-180. Boston: G. K. Hall, 1978.

Williams, Juan. *This Far by Faith: Stories from the African American Religious Experience.* New York: HarperCollins, 2003.

Wintz, Cary D., ed. *African American Political Thought, 1890–1930.* New York and London: M. E. Sharpe, 1996.

Fr. Moses Berry

Unpublished Primary Sources

Berry, Moses. Interview by Dellas Oliver Herbel, August 13, 2006. Tape and notes available in Herbel's personal archives.

New Valaam Theological Academy. Certificate No. 330 Issued to Rev. Karl Berry. September 12/25, 1985. Archives of Fr. Moses Berry.

Podmoshensky, Herman. Abbot Herman to Fr. Moses Berry. September 11/24, 1988. Archives of Fr. Moses Berry.

———. Abbot Herman to Fr. Moses Berry. September 11/24, 1993. Archives of Fr. Moses Berry.

Swaiko, Herman. Metropolitan Herman to Archbishop Nathaniel of Detroit. June 16, 2006. Archives of Fr. Moses Berry.

Published Primary Sources and Secondary Sources

Altschul, Michaila. "31st and Troost: An Orthodox Mission Flowers in the Inner City," *AGAIN* 17:2 (1994), 24–25.

Altschul, Paisius, ed. *An Unbroken Circle: Linking Ancient African Christianity to the African-American Experience.* St. Louis: Brotherhood of St. Moses the Black, 1997.

———, ed. *Wade in the River: The Story of the African Christian Faith.* Kansas City: Crossbearers Publishing, 2001.

Anonymous. "Rediscovering Africa's Ancient Christian Heritage," *The Orthodox Church* 42:7/8 (2006), 16–17.

Athitakis, Mark. "Awkward Christian Soldiers," *San Francisco Weekly*, December 22, 1999.

Berry, Moses. "An Encounter with a Saint," *Again* 17:2 (1994), 26.

———. "Lost Heritage." *Epiphany* 15:4 (1996), 74–76.

———. "Full Circle: A Final Word from the Brotherhood of St. Moses the Black," In *An Unbroken Circle: Linking Ancient African Christianity to the African-American Experience*, 65–73. Edited by Father Paisius Altschul. St. Louis, Missouri: Brotherhood of St. Moses the Black, 1997.

———. "Lost Heritage of African-Americans." In *An Unbroken Circle: Linking Ancient African Christianity to the African-American Experience*, 65–73. Edited by Father Paisius Altschul. St. Louis: Brotherhood of St. Moses the Black, 1997.

Cone, James H. "America: A Dream or A Nightmare?" *Journal of the International Theological Center* 13:2 (1986), 263–278.

Goshay, Charita M. "Orthodox Church Drawing Converts from Other Branches of the Faith," *The Repository*, September 25, 2004.

Hieromonk Jonah (Paffhausen), "The Doors of Repentance: The Journey of the Holy Order of MANS/Christ the Saviour Brotherhood and the St. Herman of Alaska Brotherhood into the Canonical Orthodox Church," *AGAIN* 23:1 (2001), 23–26.

Kishkovsky, Leonid. "Orthodox reach out to African-Americans." *The Orthodox Church* 42:3/4 (2006), 28.

———. "Rediscovering Africa's Ancient Christian Heritage." *The Orthodox Church* 42:7/8 (2006), 16–17.

Lucas, Phillip Charles. *The Odyssey of a New Religion: The Holy Order of MANS from New Age to Orthodoxy*. Bloomington and Indianapolis: Indiana University Press, 1995.

Macaria. "The First African-American Orthodox Cemetery in America." *Epiphany* 15:4 (1996), 84–87.

Mathewes-Green, Frederica. "Men and Church." *Word* (December 2007). Available at http://www.antiochian.org/node/17069 (accessed December 12, 2012).

Nieuwsma, Virginia. *Our Hearts' True Home*. Ben Lomond, California: Conciliar Press, 1996.

Raboteau, Albert. Afterword to *An Unbroken Circle: Linking Ancient African Christianity to the African-American Experience*. Edited by Father Paisius Altschul, 161–163. St. Louis: Brotherhood of St. Moses the Black, 1997.

———. *Canaan Land: A Religious History of African Americans*. New York: Oxford University Press, 2001.

———. *A Sorrowful Joy*. New York and Mahwah, New Jersey: Paulist Press, 2002.

————. "American Salvation: The Place of Christianity in Public Life." *Boston Review* (April/May, 2005). Available at http://bostonreview.net/BR30.2/raboteau.html (accessed December 21, 2012).

Reeves, Derek Q. "Beyond the River Jordan: An Essay on the Continuity of the Black Prophetic Tradition," *The Journal of Religious Thought* 47:2 (1991), 42–54.

Sanderson, Jerome. *Saint Moses the Ethiopian*. Indianapolis: Christ the Saviour Brotherhood, 2001.

Sanderson, Jerome and Carla Thomas. *Saints of Africa*. Indianapolis: Christ the Saviour Brotherhood, 2006.

Thomas, Carla. "Holy Unmercenary Healers." In *An Unbroken Circle: Linking Ancient African Christianity to the African-American Experience*. Edited by Father Paisius Altschul, 133–139. St. Louis: Brotherhood of St. Moses the Black, 1997.

Peter Gillquist and the Evangelical Orthodox Church

Unpublished Primary Sources (in the author's possession)

Abud, Joseph. V. Rev. Joseph Abud to Metropolitan Philip, March 30, 1992.

Allen, Joseph. V. Rev. Joseph Allen to St. Anthony Orthodox Church, November 4, 1991.

Ballew, Richard. Richard Ballew, Kurt Speier, and John Sommer to Carol Barnett, May 11, 1979.

Bernstein, Arnold. Arnold Bernstein to Robert Guio. Undated, written prior to Guio's October 12, 1981, letter.

————. Arnold Bernstein to Rober Guio. Undated, written mid-October, after Guio's October 12, 1981, letter.

Clergy of Ss. Peter and Paul Orthodox Church. Presbytery to Ss. Peter and Paul Orthodox Church, August 28, 1997.

Former EOC Clergy. Former EOC Clergy to Metropolitan Philip, February 7, 1992.

Guio, Robert. Robert Guio to Arnold Bernstein, October 12, 1981.

Hardenbrook, John Weldon. Fr. John Weldon Hardenbrook to Metropolitan Philip, March 4, 1992.

Hopko, Thomas. "Reflections on the EVANGELICAL ORTHODOX CHURCH and its entry into full communion with the

Orthodox Church." Report Sent to Metropolitan Maximos, Metropolitan Philip, and Metropolitan Theodosius, February 1986. Available in the personal archives of Fr. Thomas Hopko.

Lazar, Theodosius.Metropolitan Theodosius to Metropolitan Philip, April 29, 1987.

———. Metropolitan Theodosius to Metropolitan Philip, April 29, 1987 [Letter 2].

———. Metropolitan Theodosius to Metropolitan Philip, January 30, 1987.

———. Metropolitan Theodosius to the OCA Synod, April 29, 1987.

Maloof, Gregory. Gregory Maloof to Metrpolitan Philip, April 6, 1992.

Meyendorff, John. V. Rev. John Meyendorff to Metropolitan Theodosius, April 15, 1987.

Rogers, Gregory. Fr. Gregory Rogers to Metropolitan Philip, March 16, 1992.

Saliba, Philip. Metropolitan Philip to Metropolitan Theodosius, October 12, 1986.

———. Metropolitan Philip to V. Rev. John Meyendorff, April 21, 1987.

———. Metropolitan Philip to Metropolitan Theodosius, February 2, 1987.

———. Metropolitan Philip to Metropolitan Theodosius, April 8, 1987.

———. Metropolitan Philip to Metropolitan Theodosius, June 2, 1987.

———. Metropolitan Philip to the Clergy of the Antiochian Archdiocese, April 9, 1992.

———. Metropolitan Philip to the Seventeen Former EOC Clergyman, February 24, 1992.

———. Metropolitan Philip. Archpastoral Directive, May 2, 2003.

———. Archpastoral Directive, August 7, 2008.

Sterzing, H. Keith Mephodie. "Orthodox Bishop Claims to Apply the Canons—Orthodox Question Application." Unpublished article, January 28, 1993.

Zell, Ronald L. Ronald L. Zell to Dr. Howard, February 7, 1984.

———. Ronald L. Zell to Bishop Maximos of Pittsburgh, February 18, 1984.

Additional Unpublished Collection Cited
National Association of Evangelicals Papers (SC-113). Wheaton College Special Collections. Wheaton, IL.

Published Primary Sources and Secondary Sources
Allen, Joseph. *Widowed Priest: A Crisis in Ministry*. Minneapolis: Light and Life, 1994.
Anonymous editor. "New church body formed." *Chicago Tribune*, March 11, 1979.
Bouma, Gary D. "The Real Reason One Conservative Church Grew," *Review of Religious Research* 50 (2008), 43–44.
Braun, Jon E. "Share the Vision." *AGAIN* 14 (1991), 28–29.
Counts, Bill. *The Evangelical Orthodox Church and the New Covenant Apostolic Order*. Berkeley: The Spiritual Counterfeits Project, 1979.
Fornoff, Robin. 'Ex-members call Glen Park church a cult." *Post-Tribune*, March 30, 1980.
———. "Healing by faith called extremist." March 30, 1980.
———. "Prophet' now calls church a cult." *Post-Tribune*, March 31, 1980.
———. "Members confirm some church extremes." April 2, 1980.
Francis, Matthew. "*The Orthodox Study Bible* and Orthodox Identity in North America," *Canadian Journal of Orthodox Christianity* 2:2 (2007), 37–55. Available at: http://www.cjoc.ca/pdf/Vol%202%20S1%20Francis.PDF (accessed February 5, 2013).
Gillquist, Peter. "Presiding Bishop's Corner." *AGAIN* 2:1 (January–March 1979), 2.
———. "Believing What is Right." *AGAIN* 2:1 (January–March 1979), 1, 7.
———. "Presiding Bishop's Corner." *AGAIN* 2:4 (October–December 1979), 2.
———. "Presiding Bishop's Corner." *AGAIN* 3:3 (July–September 1980), 2.
———. "Presiding Bishop's Corner." *AGAIN* (n.d., October–December 1980), 2.
———. "Editorial: Christless Church or Churchless Christ?" *AGAIN* 5:3 (1982), 2.
———. "Editorial." *Again* 8:3 (1985), 2.

———. "Editorial." *AGAIN* 11:1 (1988), 2.

———. "Editorial: Phase II," *AGAIN* 11:4 (December, 1988), 2.

———. *Becoming Orthodox: A Journey to the Ancient Christian Faith.* Brentwood, Tennessee: Wolgemuth and Hyatt, 1989.

———. *Metropolitan Philip: His Life and His Dreams.* Nashville: Thomas Nelson, 1991.

———. "Evangelicals Turned Orthodox." *Christian Century* 109:8 (1992), 242–245.

———. "Sealed: Five Years Later." *AGAIN* 15:1 (March 1992), 6.

Grove, Ron. "Authenticity and Discipline in Isla Vista: A Study of the Evangelical Orthodox Church." Paper delivered at the Southwest Anthropological Association in Santa Barbara, March 21, 1981.

———. "An Orthodox Perspective on the EOC." Unpublished paper for an anthropology class, intended as an extension of his conference paper. September 1983.

Guroian, Vigen. "Dancing alone—out of step with Orthodoxy," *Christian Century* 112:19 (1995), 608–610.

Hardenbrook, John Weldon. "Fr. John Weldon Hardenbrook's Defense." Transcript of his defense at a spiritual court. Available at: http://benlomond.wordpress.com/1998/05/26/fr-john-weldon-hardenbrooks-defense/ (accessed January 24, 2013).

Hardenbrook, Weldon and Terry Somerville. "Parachurch or Parasite?" *AGAIN* (4:21981), 2.

Hughes, Richard T. and C. Leonard Allen. *Illusions of Innocence: Protestant Primitivism in America, 1630–1875.* Chicago: University of Chicago Press, 1988.

Iannaccone, Lawrence R. "Why strict churches are strong." *American Journal of Sociology* 99 (1994), 1180–1211.

Jensen, Kenneth Samuel. "The Case for a Living Orthodoxy." *Touchstone* 3 (1989), 14–18.

Joseph (Al-Zehlaoui). Liturgical Directive, published as: "Bishop Joseph's Vision for Ben Lomond." *Grapevine* [Parish Newsletter] August 1997.

Kelley, Dean M. *Why Conservative Churches are Growing: A Study in Sociology of Religion.* New York: Harper and Row, 1972.

Keylock, Leslie R. "Evangelical Orthodox Church Seeks Official Recognition from Eastern Orthodoxy." *Christianity Today* 29:8 (1985), 69, 71–72.

Lash, Ephraim. "Report of reception into Holy Orthodox Church in North America of 27 of the original Evangelical converts to Antiochian Archdiocese." *True Vine* 3:4 (1992), 5–24.

———. Review of *The Orthodox Study Bible*, Peter E. Gillquist, project manager, Alan Wallerstedt, managing editor. *Sourozh* 54 (1995), 42–49.

Laycock, Joseph. "Where Do They Get These Ideas? Changing Ideas of Cults in the Mirror of Popular Culture." *Journal of the American Academy of Religion* 81:1 (2013), 80–106.

Lehmann, Daniel J. "Evangelizing the Evangelicals." *Christian Century* 105:30 (1988), 916–917.

Liacopulos, George Peter. "A Comparative Study of Selected Orthodox Missiological Approaches Emerging in Contemporary American Society." Doctoral dissertation, Princeton Theological Seminary, 1995.

Lucas, Charles Philip. "Enfants Terribles: The Challenge of Sectarian Converts to Ethnic Orthodox Churches in the United States." *Nova Religio* 7:2 (2003), 5–23.

Namee, Matthew. "The Myth of Past Unity." Paper delivered at St. Vladimir's Seminary. June 20, 2009. Available at http://www.orthodoxdetroit.com/stvladimirswebinar.htm (accessed January 25, 2013).

Nassif, Bradley. "Eastern Orthodoxy and Evangelicalism: The Status of an Emerging Global Dialogue." In *Eastern Orthodox Theology: A Contemporary Reader*, edited by Daniel B. Clendenin, 211–248. 2nd ed. Grand Rapids, Michigan: Baker Academic Press, 2003.

Neal, Lynn S. "They're Freaks! The Cult Sterotype in Fictional Television Shows, 1958–2008." *Nova Religio* 14:3 (2011), 81–107.

Parsons, Adam Scott. "Everyday Apocalyptic: Radical Politics and Evangelical Society, 1969–2000." Doctoral dissertation, Syracuse University, in progress.

Presbytery of Ss. Peter and Paul Orthodox Church Transfer Request. February 12, 1998. Available at http://benlomond.wordpress.com/1998/02/12/initial-request-of-clergy-for-release-to-the-oca/#more-7 (accessed January 24, 2013).

Reagan, Mike. "What Orderly Living Means to Me." *AGAIN* 1 (July–September1978), 11.

Saliba, Philip. Metropolitan Philip to the clergy of the Antiochian Orthodox Christian Archdiocese of North America, August 7, 2008. Available at http://www.antiochian.org/files/8-7-08%20 Re%20GOA%20Palestinian%20Vicariate.pdf (accessed February 15, 2009).

———. Metropolitan Philip to Petitioning Presbytery. February 14, 1998. Available at http://benlomond.wordpress.com/1998/ 02/14/archpastoral-directive-depositions/#more-29 (accessed January 24, 2013).

Stark, Rodney and Roger Finke. *Acts of faith*. Berkeley: University of California Press, 2000.

Tamney, Joseph B. "Does Strictness Explain the Appeal of Working-Class Conservative Protestant Congregations?" *Sociology of Religion* 66:3 (2005), 283–302.

Tamney, Joseph B. and Stephen D. Johnson, "The Popularity of Strict Churches," *Review of Religious Research* 39:3 (1998), 209–223.

The Opinion of the Superior Court of Santa Cruz for Metropolitan Philip v. Steiger (2000) 82 Cal. App. 4th 923 [98 Cal. Rptr. 2d 605]. Available at: http://law.justia.com/cases/california/ caapp4th/82/923.html (accessed January 22, 2013).

The Orthodox Study Bible: New Testament and Psalms, New King James Version. Peter E. Gillquist, Project Director; Alan Wallerstedt, Managing editor. Nashville: Thomas Nelson Publishers, 1993.

Turner, John G. *Bill Bright and Campus Crusade for Christ.* Chapel Hill: University of North Carolina Press, 2008.

Vecsey, George. "New Group Combines Evangelism and Orthodoxy: Ritual and Tradition 'A Spiritual Super Race.'" *New York Times*, March 11, 1979.

Wacker, Grant. "Playing for Keeps: The Primitivist Impulse in Early Pentecostalism." In *The American Quest for the Primitive Church*, edited by Richard T. Hughes, 196–219. Urbana, Illinois: University of Illinois Press, 1988.

Webber, Robert E. "Are Evangelicals Becoming Sacramental?" *Ecumenical Trends* 14:3 (1985), 36–38.

Webber, Timothy P. "Looking for Home: Evangelical Orthodoxy and the Search for the Original Church." In *New Perspectives in*

Historical Theology: Essays in Honor of John Meyendorff, edited by Bradley Nassif, 95–121. Grand Rapids: Eerdmans, 1996.

Webber, Timothy P. "Looking for Home: Evangelical Orthodoxy and the Search for the Original Church." In *Eastern Orthodox Theology: A Contemporary Reader*, edited by Daniel B. Clendenin, 249–272. Rev. ed. Grand Rapids, Michigan: Baker Academic, 2003.

Wollenberg, Bruce. "The Evangelical Orthodox Church: a Preliminary Appraisal." *Christian Century* 97 (1980), 698–702.

Zell, Thomas. "Once AGAIN," *AGAIN Magazine* 21:1 (Winter, 1999), 1–2.

Conclusion (Primary and Secondary Sources Not Cited Previously)

Demacopoulos, George and Aristotle Papanikoloau. *Orthodox Constructions of the West*. New York: Fordham University Press, 2013.

Erickson, John H. "Slavophile Thought and Conceptions of Mission in the Russian North American Archdiocese, Late 19th–Early 20th Century," *St. Vladimir's Theological Quarterly* 56:3 (2012), 245–268.

Guroian, Vigen. "Dancing alone—out of step with Orthodoxy." *Christian Century* 112:19 (1995), 608–610.

Herbel, Dellas Oliver. "Turning to Tradition: Intra-Christian Converts and the Making of an American Orthodox Church." Doctoral dissertation, Saint Louis University, 2009.

Mathewes-Green, Federica. "In the Passenger's Seat." In *Our Hearts' True Home*, 11–24, edited by Virginia Nieuwsma. Ben Lomond, California: Conciliar Press, 1996.

———. Unpublished collection of Christmas letters and letters to Nancy Waggener.

McNight, Scot. "From Wheaton to Rome: Why Evangelicals Become Roman Catholic." *Journal of the Evangelical Theological Society* 45:3 (2002), 451–472.

North, Gary. "The Escalating Confrontation with Bureaucracy." In *Tactics of Christian Resistance*, 141–190. Edited by Gary North. Tyler, Texas: Geneva Divinity School Press, 1983.

Schaeffer, Francis. *A Christian Manifesto*. Rev. ed. Westchester, Illinois: Crossway, 1982.

Schaeffer, Frank. *Addicted to Mediocrity: Contemporary Christians and the Arts*. Westchester, Illinois: Crossway Books, 1981.

———. *Sham Pearls for Real Swine: Beyond the Cultural Dark Age— A Quest for Renaissance*. Brentwood, Tennessee: Wolgemuth and Hyatt, 1990.

———. *Dancing Alone: The Quest for Orthodox Faith in the Age of False Religion*. Brookline, Massachusetts: Holy Cross Orthodox Press, 1994.

Somerville, Frank P. "Episcopal Priest takes a new path." *The Sun*, February 1, 1993.

INDEX

242 | INDEX